EXACTLY WHAT I SAID

EXACTLY WHAT I SAID

Translating Words and Worlds

Elizabeth Yeoman

UNIVERSITY OF MANITOBA PRESS

26 25 24 23 22 1 2 3 4 5

University of Manitoba Press
Winnipeg, Manitoba, Canada
Treaty 1 Territory
uofmpress.ca

Cataloguing data available from Library and Archives Canada
ISBN 978-0-88755-273-1 (PAPER)
ISBN 978-0-88755-275-5 (PDF)
ISBN 978-0-88755-276-2 (EPUB)
ISBN 978-0-88755-278-6 (BOUND)

Cover design by David Drummond
Interior design by Jess Koroscil
Map design by Julie Witmer
Cover image by Ryan Wood (Instagram: @ryanwoodphoto)

Printed in Canada

This book has been published with the help of a grant from the Federation for the Humanities and Social Sciences, through the Awards to Scholarly Publications Program, using funds provided by the Social Sciences and Humanities Research Council of Canada.

The University of Manitoba Press acknowledges the financial support for its publication program provided by the Government of Canada through the Canada Book Fund, the Canada Council for the Arts, the Manitoba Department of Sport, Culture, and Heritage, the Manitoba Arts Council, and the Manitoba Book Publishing Tax Credit.

Funded by the Government of Canada | Canada

ArtsNL

Tshaukuesh: Tshi mishta nashkumitin numat, nuitsheuan.
To Tshaukuesh, with heartfelt thanks.

Contents

A Note on the Cover

When the snowshoe design was proposed, I asked Tshaukuesh how she felt about it. I said I wondered whether the use of the snowshoe image might be seen as a cultural appropriation. Her response (used here with her permission) was this: "Maybe people will think you used the snowshoe picture because you were proud and happy that you learned from Innu. You walked with us and heard our stories and now you understand a little bit more about us. Some Akaneshau don't know anything about Innu life. That's why I invite them to walk with me, so they can understand us better. You walked with me so now you know I walk to protect the land, the animals, everything. You respect me and my walk."

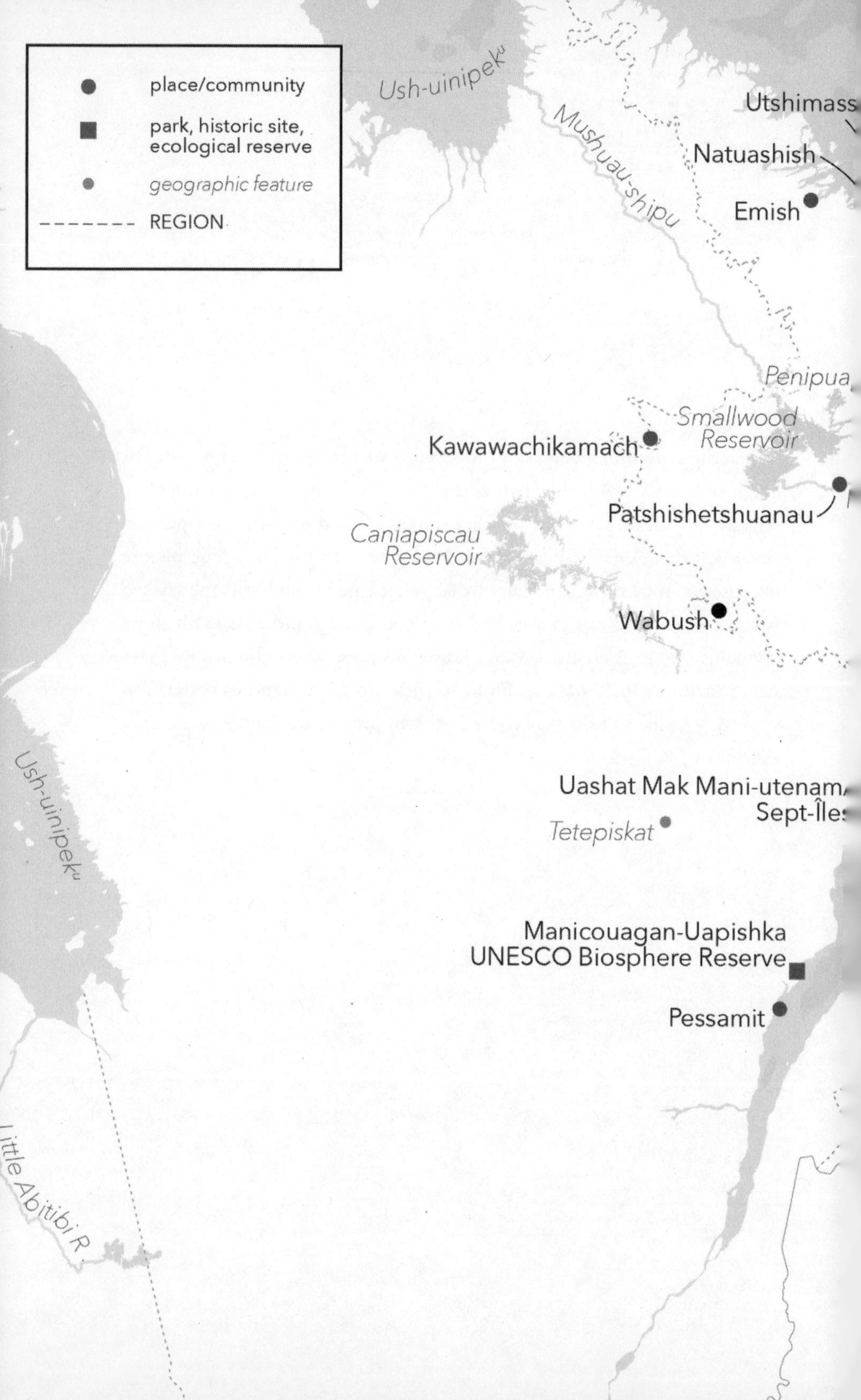
place/community
park, historic site, ecological reserve
geographic feature
REGION
Ush-uinipekᵘ
Mushuau-shipu
Natuashish
Emish
Penipua
Smallwood Reservoir
Kawawachikamach
Patshishetshuanau
Caniapiscau Reservoir
Wabush
Uashat Mak Mani-utenam
Tetepiskat
Manicouagan-Uapishka UNESCO Biosphere Reserve
Pessamit
Ush-uinipekᵘ
Little Abitibi R.

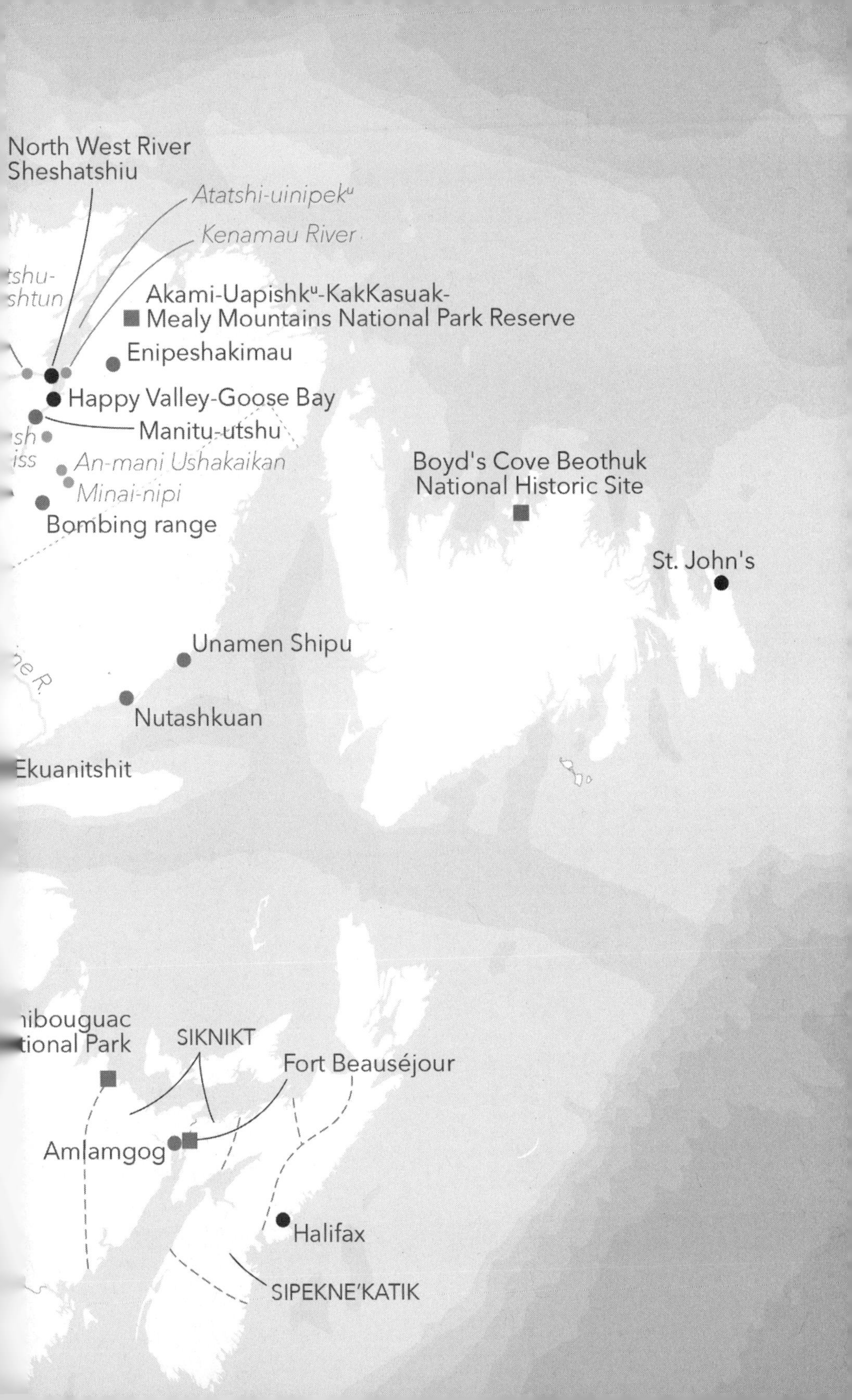

North West River
Sheshatshiu
Atatshi-uinipek^u
Kenamau River
tshu-
shtun
Akami-Uapishk^u-KakKasuak-
Mealy Mountains National Park Reserve
Enipeshakimau
Happy Valley-Goose Bay
Manitu-utshu
sh
iss
An-mani Ushakaikan
Minai-nipi
Bombing range
Boyd's Cove Beothuk
National Historic Site
St. John's
Unamen Shipu
ne R.
Nutashkuan
Ekuanitshit
nibouguac
tional Park
SIKNIKT
Fort Beauséjour
Amlamgog
Halifax
SIPEKNE'KATIK

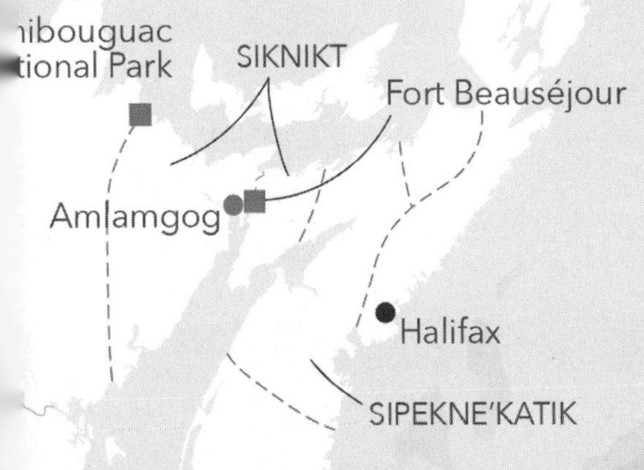

Introduction

"I remember my mom and my dad, always walking in the winter with the toboggan. Every time I walk, I walk everything protect. Sometimes evenings we sit down together, talk about why we walk: protect the land, Innu culture, animals . . . like a circle. I just couldn't wait next year to walk again. Be strong when we walk. So beautiful." Tshaukuesh's soft voice and hesitant English resonate in my headphones, her longing and determination palpable despite the geographical and cultural distance between us. She is at the CBC Radio station in Goose Bay and I am in a recording booth in St. John's. Her voice breaks as she continues: "Look, people, look, young children. I can see in their faces, so happy. I wish you'd be always like that. What's going to happen?"[1]

It was the first time Tshaukuesh and I had ever spoken to each other, but I knew her work and her reputation. Everyone in Newfoundland and Labrador does, and so do many more all over the world. She had been leading this annual weeks-long walk in Innusi—Innu territory—since the 1990s as a way of demonstrating that this is Innu land and the Innu are still here, still using it.

Tshaukuesh set out on her walk, or meshkanau, as a tiny child in the 1940s. Her first steps were taken in Innusi with her family when they were still living a nomadic life following the seasonal rhythms and bounty of the land. Her walk was disrupted by colonization in the 1960s, as she describes in her book, *Nitinikiau Innusi: I Keep the Land Alive* (2019). In the 1980s she began walking again, in protest, onto the NATO base in Goose Bay and into the vast areas of Innu territory where NATO was training fighter pilots and testing weapons. She had never spoken publicly before that and was not comfortable in English, but gradually she became a spokesperson for the Innu—in the courts, at hearings and inquiries, and to the media. Her anger at the invasion of Innusi

Looking towards Akami-uapishk^u (White Mountain Across). Photo by Camille Fouillard.

by the military gave her courage and, as her book documents, she has never faltered in her campaign to protect the land she loves so much.

I met Tshaukuesh in person a couple of years later when she came to St. John's to accept an honorary doctorate from Memorial University. We talked about the walk and, to my surprise, she invited me to accompany her and her family and friends as they travelled on snowshoes from Sheshatshiu to Enipeshakimau.[2] I said I thought it was only for Innu but she replied that anyone who wanted to come was welcome. In the early spring of 2008 I joined them. People ask me how far we walked, but I have no idea of the distance in miles or kilometres. We took our time, trudging wide-legged on bear-paw snowshoes and hauling all our belongings on toboggans across frozen marshes, through snow-covered boreal forest, and up into the mountains of Akami-Uapishk^{u}, sleeping on fir boughs and caribou skins in the big Innu tent at night. We might not have covered a huge distance by the standards of a society dependent on cars and airplanes, but each day revealed a new world, one where life was hard but where there was also extraordinary beauty, warmth, and comfort in the company of Tshaukuesh and her friends and family. I kept a diary during the days I walked with them, and I include it here because I think it conveys something of the world I briefly became part of.

Carl Mika and colleagues make an ontological distinction between "wording" and "worlding."[3] We constitute our understanding of the world not only through language and discursive practice but also through being in it. Although the walk can only be conveyed here through language, or wording, the immediacy of the diary (lightly edited for clarity) seems to be a way of conveying something of the worlding that was necessary for me to work with Tshaukuesh on her book and also to write this book. It was my first experience of Tshaukuesh's world, of living on Innu land on her terms. Excerpts from notes and recordings as well as narrative vignettes throughout the book are included for the same reason. Another reason for presenting the diary here is that Tshaukuesh wanted me to include some of its stories in my book—specifically the stories about the times we laughed and had fun together. Those stories didn't seem to fit anywhere else in this book, but a reminder of our shared laughter seems a good thing to include in the introduction.

Nutshimit Diary (2008)

March 11

We set out from Sheshatshiu walking, around 11:00 a.m. in bright sunshine, about twenty below zero. Tshaukuesh; three young Innu men: Pun, Mashan, and her grandson Kaputshet; Ming, a social worker from Singapore who is going to work in the other Labrador Innu community, Natuashish; Kari, an Akaneshau friend and longtime supporter of Tshaukuesh; Jerry, a photographer from Alberta; Tshaukuesh's five-year-old grandson, Manteu; three dogs (I only know the names of two: Ukauiak and Blackie); and me. We're hauling wooden toboggans piled with our possessions, covered in tarps and bound with rope, except for Jerry, who has two boat-like plastic sleds with an elaborate harness.

We walked for about three hours across a frozen bay of Lake Melville (which is not really a lake but more like a tidal inlet, though far inland),[4] then set up a tent. It was in place incredibly quickly. It's like a small canvas house, with a stove warming it up and a chimney to the outside. A supper of chicken and muffins Kari had made before we left. Chaos of making up beds of fir branches (which we first had to cut), caribou skins, Therm-a-Rests, sleeping bags and quilts, and then a cold and sleepless night as the fire burned down and no one rebuilt it. Tshaukuesh had offered me a caribou skin to lie on but I told her I was fine with my Therm-a-Rest, then regretted it later as it didn't seem to give much insulation.

In the night I heard wolves howling. After several hours lying there awake and frozen, wondering how I would get through a week of this, I needed to pee. But the wolves . . . . After a while I needed to go so badly I thought I would brave the wolves—assuming they wouldn't come near. I went outside into the cold and dark, and saw them in the shadows creeping toward me. At least, I thought they were wolves and leapt back into the tent to suffer it out until morning. Once it got light, I went out again and realized they were Tshaukuesh's dogs, now sleeping in a furry frost-rimed heap!

March 12

Some walkers struggling on the second day. Very difficult walking and an icy wind. Someone came by on a skidoo and told us we could stay at their cabin if we could get there. I asked Tshaukuesh if I could help pull her load. "No, go cook," she said shortly, so I walked ahead with Jerry and Ming.

I felt huge relief at reaching the cabin, a very simple wooden structure—if last night's accommodation was like a small canvas house, this cabin is like a large plywood tent. Nevertheless, I was exhausted and very thankful to be here, even more thankful we did not have to put up the tent. We made a fire and started melting snow for soup (Mr. Noodle) so it would be ready when the others arrived. When Tshaukuesh got in, she threw the side of smoked char I had brought into the noodle broth. I was taken aback at the sight of my beautiful fish boiling away in the pot and only learned later that many Innu won't eat food that isn't cooked and hot. We all grabbed whatever we could and ate ravenously—and how delicious it tasted after so much exertion! The cabin was warm too, in fact so hot at one point that I was sweating in my arctic sleeping bag. I did get at least a few hours' sleep after my restless ordeal the night before. Another thing that helped with that was that Jerry explained how the Therm-a-Rest actually worked—I hadn't realized it has to be inflated!

March 13

In the morning, I went out to chop ice from the lake with an axe. Strange formations rising up from the frozen surface, greenish blue and very clear. Ice is much preferred to snow for making water because it's purer—snow being full of spruce needles and other debris—and less trouble to melt. One large lump is enough. Snow has to be endlessly replenished in the pot and can taste burned if not watched closely. I hacked off a chunk of ice and took it back to the cabin, then leant over the stove to dump it in a pan. I smelled singeing and realized my new down jacket had brushed against the stovepipe. There were three gaping holes and feathers flying everywhere. I almost wept, though I managed to control myself. I thought the jacket wouldn't be wearable, and it was too cold outside to do without it. I came here with the idea that I would, above all, be unobtrusive and, if possible, helpful. Now, instead, I would cause trouble because I would have to be taken out by skidoo. When Tshaukuesh saw the blizzard of swirling feathers she burst into uproarious laughter, her eyes alight with mirth, until she saw my stricken face and then she clapped her hands over her mouth as if to shove the laughter back in. That made me smile a little. I collected my wits, Tshaukuesh got me some flowered cotton fabric, and I sat up in my sleeping bag sewing patches all morning.

Once I'd finished patching, ending up with much-admired floral splashes of purple and scarlet against the pale blue jacket, we started getting ready to leave. Lashing everything back onto the toboggans under tarps and heading out to walk across the main part of Lake Melville, hauling the toboggans. Very windy and bitterly cold. We walked and walked and walked and walked. After several hours we started seeing patches of open water and slushy areas, and we were still a very long way from shore. It occurred to me that the endless slog was nothing compared to the thought of plunging through the ice, and I worried even more about Francis, who goes back and forth on a skidoo to support the walk and who was now somewhere on the lake with little Manteu.

Francis and Manteu arrived a bit after we got there and Jerry told me that we weren't really in any danger on the ice. I just thought we were.

March 14

We spent the morning resting with the stove stoked up. Despite the physical hardship of the walk, it is stunningly beautiful: the expanse of the lake, the brilliant light, the snow and the tall thin trees of Labrador black against the sky.

I went outside for a walk and then realized how silly that was. I have such an ingrained habit of going for walks that even when resting from this monumental one, my instinct is to go for a short one, but I didn't go far. On the way back, I put my hand in my pocket and found two clementines that I had forgotten about, frozen solid. I took them back to the tent and shared them out in sections once they'd thawed a bit. After only three days with no fruit or vegetables, already the taste was exquisite.

We left in the afternoon to walk a relatively short distance, maybe three hours, but nevertheless arriving at our campsite a bit late and working frantically to set up the tent before dark—cutting trees for the frame, gathering boughs for the floor, getting it all assembled, stove and chimney set up, fire going, tarps and mattresses laid out, kettle on . . . an extraordinary amount of work. The first step is to tramp down all the snow, without snowshoes, to make a flat and solid site. We all do that. The rest of the work is divided by sex, the women gathering boughs and setting up inside, the men doing the construction work.

As we were madly trying to gather enough boughs before dark, a snowmobile arrived bringing Karlie, a doctoral student who is planning to make a film about the walk.

I was feeling desperately in need of a wash, itchy and uncomfortable. After the tent was set up, Karlie said to me, "I'm just going to have a little birdie bath." She took a small bowl of water from the kettle and retired into the inner tent, where Tshaukuesh, Francis, and Manteu sometimes sleep. It's just a small fabric tent to give a bit of privacy. Brilliant! When she was done, I did the same and felt so much better. These small gestures of cleaning are so simple, but mean so much.

Every day I learn something new about how to be comfortable in nutshimit. The first morning, after my sleepless night, I didn't brush my teeth because I didn't know how to get water to do it. Obviously, I could have taken it from the kettle but I felt I shouldn't because I could see that water was hard to come by. A lot of work to get it. But my mouth tasted terrible. I couldn't enjoy my food or even feel at ease. Strange how important such a small thing can be. By evening, though, I felt less shy and took a little water in a cup to brush my teeth. And now I also know how to take a bath!

March 15

One reason it's best to walk in early spring is that the marshes and lakes are still frozen and it's much easier to walk on their flat snow-covered surfaces than through the woods. Today we set out to cross a big marsh, Kamassekuakamat. I walked ahead by myself, thinking the others weren't far behind, but after an hour or so I realized I couldn't hear or see anyone—no one ahead or behind, just myself alone in the vast winter silence.

As I was getting toward the forest at the edge of the marsh, Francis caught up with me on the snowmobile and stopped briefly. "You walk fast," he said, a bit surprised. I guess those hours slogging in the gym and walking to work have paid off.

We set up camp, mad rush for boughs and scramble to get the stove and kettle going before dark. Freezing cold, in fact far below freezing as it has been every day, but for some reason it seems colder than before. Finally we settled in front of the stove to drink tea, eat fried eggs and bread, and warm our feet. In no time it was too hot! It's astonishing how warm you can be in an uninsulated canvas structure when it's thirty below or so outside.

March 16

Tshaukuesh made Innu doughnuts. I wrote down the recipe—so to speak—but, as she says, the Akaneshau use little cups but that's not the Innu way. "We just put some in until it looks right," she says. "Some people say I should put more raisins and molasses to make it sweeter, some say 'don't put any because I have diabetes.' I don't know what to do!" I think they're delicious either way. It's really just fried bannock (or pakueshikan, the Innu word) with a bit of extra sweetening. Somewhere I read a comment on an online recipe for bannock: "Considering the ingredients are pretty much the same as wallpaper paste, it tastes surprisingly delicious." Innu doughnuts are even more delicious, or differently delicious, because of the added sweetness.

Innu doughnuts
Flour
Baking powder
A little sugar
A handful of raisins
Add molasses mixed with hot water and stir. Shape into loops and pan fry in oil.

After we finished making the doughnuts Tshaukuesh was looking everywhere for the butter. Finally, we realized that I was kneeling on it! This led to much laughter as we devoured the doughnuts.

March 17

This morning there were people ice fishing nearby so we waited a couple of hours to use their hole when they were done. We didn't have any tools to make a hole ourselves. Any little thing is something extra to haul.

Each night after supper, dishes, and organizing for the morning, everybody gets into bed and we tell stories by candlelight, sometimes in Innu-aimun, sometimes in English. Sometimes Tshaukuesh will suggest a theme: "We're going to tell funny stories about a kiss!" You can talk or be silent. There's a lot of laughter. You can go to sleep when you like. Gradually the sound of snores and deep breathing takes over and the talking fades. I'm usually one of the last awake, partly because I'm a night owl, though less so in this environment where we live mostly by the rhythms imposed by the hours of daylight, and partly because I worry about the candle staying lit. It's a single fat candle, stuck on a pole in the middle of the tent. I don't know why I worry really. It's no more dangerous than the wood stove that burns all through the night, sparks flying up to the roof of the tent, beautiful to watch in the dark but perilous.

March 18
We made it to the Mealy Mountains. I was supposed to leave today, my flight tomorrow back to St. John's and work. I only had a week. Tshak was going to come by skidoo with the kids, drop them off, and take me back with him. By the time it was dark, it was clear he wasn't going to come. It was about thirty-five below zero. I resigned myself to missing my flight and being a day or more late back to work . . .

I could hear Francis and Tshaukuesh in the little inner tent talking back and forth, speaking Innu-aimun so I didn't understand, but I could get the gist from their tone of voice. Pretty sure she was asking him to take me back to Sheshatshiu so I can get my plane tomorrow, and he was protesting, very grumpy. Francis is a quiet man, taciturn, almost stern. He supports the walk any way he can: bringing supplies, giving rides to kids, helping set up the tent, hunting. This evening he's spending the night and was already asleep, snoring in the inside tent when Tshaukuesh found out on the satellite phone that Tshak definitely isn't coming because it's too cold for the kids. She and Francis talked for quite a while. I just waited quietly to see what would happen. Finally he emerged from the little tent, looking the way he sounded, grumpy, and told me shortly to dress warmly and get ready to go. Jerry added that I should put on every stitch of clothing I have. So I did. Layers of wool, fleece, and down. Extra leather mitts Tshaukuesh lent me. Scarf over my face. I put my stuff in the komatik, climbed on behind the still-grumpy Francis, and we set off. It was the first time I'd ever been on a snowmobile. I clung to the handles on either side of my seat, too shy to hang onto Francis. As we flew across the frozen terrain, I was more and more afraid my hands would get so cold I wouldn't be able to hang on any longer and I would fall off and, since I wasn't touching him, Francis wouldn't even notice. Terrified and frozen though I was, I couldn't help also being awestruck by the beauty of it all, the alabaster expanse of frozen lakes and marshes patterned with spiky black forests, the mountains in the distance, the ice and snow scintillating under the stars. I was also fascinated to see the land we had covered so painstakingly during the past week all laid out before me at once and rushing by. Somehow, I managed to hang on and we arrived in Sheshatshiu, where Francis dropped me unceremoniously here at Tshak's house, saying it would be more comfortable for me. Probably he felt as shy as I did, and Tshak's wife was at home whereas Francis was alone at his house. They offered me a hot shower and a bedroom which, even after only a week, seemed extraordinary luxuries.

March 19
Coffee in the morning is also an unheard-of treat. It's remarkable how quickly one can get used to a new reality: to think differently about dangers like the candle and sparks from the stove in the tent (yet we live daily without thinking much about the risks of driving a car); to worry only about the little band of people you are with and nothing else; to eat what you have or can hunt or gather (mostly hunt in the northern winter). When I finished breakfast and went back into my bedroom to pack up my stuff and prepare to leave for Goose Bay, I realized that everything I own smells of spruce, smoke, and frying oil, the smells of the tent!

Robin arrived to take me to the airport. As we were leaving, Tshak suggested I should offer Francis some money for gas for the snowmobile. I was mortified that I hadn't thought of this myself but glad he let me know. We stopped at Francis's house on our way to town and he came to the door, still looking cross. I gave him sixty dollars and thanked him for helping me yesterday. He cracked a small smile and said, "Give us a hug, girl," so I did.

After the Walk

A lot has happened in the thirteen years since I wrote that diary. Francis is no longer living in this world. He had Lou Gehrig's disease, ALS. The family arranged with hospital staff in Goose Bay for him to spend his last days in a tent outside the building. He was born in a tent and he would die in one, with the people he loved gathered around him. Tshaukuesh wrote about her grief in *Nitinikiau Innusi: I Keep the Land Alive*:

> *November 14, 2013*
> After my husband died I felt very depressed and lonely. I had no idea what I would do or how I would cope. My heart was broken. I was all alone in my house, crying and wondering what I should do. I prayed a lot and a lot of people prayed for my family. It comforted me when all my family was with me, my children, grandchildren, and great-grandchildren. I also felt that doing things the traditional Innu way would help me get through this hard time. I wanted to go walking in the woods, hunting and trapping marten, mink. Then I'd feel stronger. It comforted me to think about my parents, to remember my mother running to her traps when she caught a marten. When Innu people have good hunting, it makes them happy. We don't deal with tragedy the Akaneshau way—with treatment or counselling—but the Innu way—go into the woods, go hunting.[5]

Tshaukuesh is still going to the woods and hunting; still doing all the kinds of work she has always done to protect the land and Innu culture, which is so closely tied to the land and, as she says, to hunting. In the week in which I am writing this, early in 2021, she is preparing to testify in a case about illegal caribou hunting (illegal according to the government, the police, and the courts, but crucial for Innu culture, health, and way of life); planning a workshop for next week and her annual walk for next month. This morning she told me what she would say in court, how the caribou brings food, clothing, ceremony, and medicine, how it has almost everything you need to live well on the land. She also told me about the woman who invited her to do the workshop, a nurse and the daughter of the RCMP officer who had taken Tshaukuesh into the court hearing shown in the film *Hunters and Bombers* (1991) following one of the protests she had organized and led against NATO during its occupation of Innu land. She told the nurse that she remembered how kind this officer, the nurse's father, was to her, how he let her take her time and speak to people outside before going into the court. She is planning to meet him again now, after all these years. All of this tells a lot about Tshaukuesh: how hard she works, even now in her mid-seventies; the range of things she does in addition to making food and looking after children in her family and continuing to write; the way she makes friends so easily, including some unlikely ones, and how she never forgets them; her eloquence across huge social and cultural divides and ability to find commonalities. It is because of these gifts of hers that we were able to work together on Tshuakuesh's book, and that I am able to write this book about that experience and the questions and insights it generated for us.

Writing Together

Toward the end of the walk, Tshaukuesh asked me if I could help her turn the diaries she had been writing since the days of the anti-NATO campaign into a book. Like the Innu essayist An Antane Kapesh and poets Joséphine Bacon and Rita Mestokosho, she had felt compelled to document Innu history, language, and experience in Innu-aimun, to leave a record and to use writing as a form of activism. She had already published shorter pieces in journals and an anthology and had been interviewed by journalists and documentarists, but her dream was to have a book of her own.[6] At that time, there were few published works by Innu but today there is a vibrant Innu literary community, including influential young writers like poet Natasha Kanapé Fontaine, novelist Naomi Fontaine, and poet and critic Marie-Andrée Gill.

I spent the next ten years working with Tshaukuesh on what became *Nitinikiau Innusi: I Keep the Land Alive*. During those years, I travelled back and forth between St. John's, where I live, and Innusi/Nitassinan/Labrador,[7] where we worked on translating the diaries from Innu-aimun into English and editing them for publication. The fact that I suggest three different names for the place I travelled to indicates some of the complexities I explore in this book.

We did not have a strong common language. We sat together day after day, drinking endless pots of Red Rose tea—nipishapui—with tinned milk and demerara sugar, as Tshaukuesh explained what she had written, word by word, sentence by sentence, page by page. I tried, as she had asked me, to put her stories into standard English while still being as faithful as possible to what she had written. When we began working together, she gave me a note that she had asked her brother to write in English on her behalf. It said, "You don't have to write exactly what I said because my English is not that good. You can use different words but it has to mean exactly what I said." That note inspired the title of this book. How do you convey exactly what someone said across sometimes radically different languages, cultures, and histories? This was the challenge that started me thinking about all the questions of translation, representation, and collaborative writing addressed in this book.

I had to leave nutshimit before the walk was over to go back to work, and perhaps that was symbolic, since Canada has now officially begun a walk toward reconciliation that may never reach a final destination.[8] It is about the journey and the conversation. The book Tshaukuesh and I worked on together is done now, but the journey we began together is not. While reparations and remembrance are essential, reconciliation may always be a question of "how to live with what cannot be redeemed, what must remain a psychic and social wound that bleeds."[9] However, as Innu poet Joséphine Bacon wrote, "Menutakuaki aimun, apu nita nipumakak. Tshika petamuat nikan tshe takushiniht." "When a word is offered, it will never die. Those who come will hear it."[10]

As Tshaukuesh and I worked on her book, we also spent time together on the land and in Sheshatshiu: getting drinking water near Manitu-utshu, tidying up her tent on the North West River Road, checking her snares, visiting friends and family, going to funerals, yoga class at the Sheshatshiu school, the Christmas concert, the Truth and Reconciliation Commission (TRC) hearings in Goose Bay, fishing, and baking bread in the embers of a firepit on a beach at Kakatshu-utshishtun. Wherever we went, I was learning about the context of her book. I thought constantly about how to translate: from Innu-aimun to English, yes, but also how to convey not only words but worlds. This brings up questions of authorial voice, representation, illustration, mapping, language, listening, and learning. We talked a lot about language, when and where Innu-aimun is spoken, whether to use standardized language or Tshaukuesh's own dialect and spelling system, how much to use Innu-aimun words and names in the English version of the book, especially for words that could not easily be translated. Finally, the TRC completed its work and released its report while we were working on *Nitinikiau Innusi*, and I began to think about how collaborative writing and all the other work that goes with it could be a response to the TRC's Calls to Action. During those years, I wrote a few articles and chapters, gave conference presentations, and made endless notes. Although, at the request of the publisher, I did write footnotes and an introduction to help readers from outside Innusi understand the context of *Nitinikiau Innusi*, it was not the place for my ideas and experiences. I began writing *about* the work for very practical reasons, as a way of establishing myself as a scholar in the field so we could apply for research grants to fund Tshaukuesh's book. But the more I wrote and thought about it, the more I realized how little had been written about this kind of collaborative writing and translation. *Exactly What I Said* is the result of all that writing.

Translation theorist and teacher Carol Maier has suggested that both fictional and autobiographical explorations of the lives and work of translators could contribute to "an understanding of the complexities of the translator's task."[11] There is a movement in both literary studies and translation studies to recognize the role of the translator as much more noteworthy than was assumed in the past, and to teach translated works not as straightforward literary works but as ones that must be understood in terms of the context of the source and of how the translation was done. I want to clarify here that Tshaukuesh herself did the initial translation of about two-thirds of her book from Innu-aimun to English, and some sections of the other third had been translated into French and others into English by several other translators, most of whom were native speakers of Innu-aimun. I worked with her to transcribe her oral translations and to elaborate and edit the result in English. This made it a rather unusual translation project, which is one of the reasons I believe this account may add something to the literature called for by Maier and also provide some insight into writing collaborations between Indigenous authors and non-Indigenous editors.

One thing I want to do in this book is show the evolution of ideas and practices through autobiographical references to movies, conversations, and so on, as well as through traditional scholarly referencing. I have tried to keep in mind Sara Ahmed's point that the choices we make about whom to cite can render "certain bodies and thematics core to the discipline, and others not even part."[12] In particular, I have tried to cite Indigenous scholars and writers, following the reasoning and goals of the Citation Practices Challenge organized in 2015 by Eve Tuck, K. Wayne Yang, and Rubén Gaztambide-Fernández.[13] However, I have also used the work of other scholars who were very influential to me as well as ideas from people I talked to, films, radio documentaries, non-academic books, and media reports. Ideas circulate in complex and subtle ways. It is very possible that I have forgotten sources and unknowingly used concepts that others have spoken or written about, but I have tried to be honest and reflective about whose work I want to build on and which conversations I want to be part of. The topics of these conversations are organized into the following chapters:

Chapter 1, "Mapping," is an introduction to the physical terrain of Innusi. It opens with a transcript of a recording I made as Tshaukuesh and I talked about the large-scale maps we had laid out on the floor so she could tell me what we needed to include in the map for her book. This chapter discusses ways of representing Indigenous land visually and virtually, and the politics of doing so; the role of place names and map-making in how we think about places; and the idea of walking on the land as a form of mapping.

Walking says "we are here," especially in nomadic territories where others might say that no one lives there, as a NATO spokesperson did in justification of low-level flying over Innusi;[14] this is the focus of Chapter 2, "Walking." The chapter expands on the introduction of Innusi and the Innu in Chapter 1, and presents other Indigenous walks and ways of using and thinking about walking. Scholarly work on walking often focuses on urban and European settings, so this chapter adds to the emerging literature on walking in northern and Indigenous contexts.

Writing in Indigenous languages has often been overlooked because it does not fit the categories of literature in dominant languages or because many funders, course instructors, students, or reviewers cannot read it. Chapter 3, "Stories," introduces Tshaukuesh as a writer, situates her work in relation to other Innu writers, and lays out the literary terrain of writing in Innu-aimun and Innu writing more generally. The chapter also contextualizes this work more broadly with a review of selected works of literature and film in Indigenous languages and a discussion of challenges in funding, publishing, teaching, and translating them; code-switching; and the impact of Indigenous languages on writing in other languages.

Tshaukuesh has always emphasized that the pictures in her book are just as important as the written text. Chapter 4, "Looking," takes up issues that arose during the selection of images: the role of photographs in creating "structures of feeling,"[15] or shared emotions, perceptions, and values common to an era or cultural group; images of the North and the translation concepts of "foreignization" and "domestication"[16] applied to photography; and the idea of photos as "translations" and as media of political change.

Peter C. van Wyck writes that "the deep and intransigent Euro-Western cultural commitment to a particular idea of communication—that is, to a transmission model—frustrates attempts at understanding."[17] Chapter 5, "Signs," asks how that commitment can be shifted toward a model that recognizes how knowledge is intrinsically connected to the practices of daily life, and communication to the intricacies of languages and stories that are rooted in those practices.[18] The chapter considers the possibilities of words and structures in Indigenous languages that open up different understandings than those available in European languages. Communication gaps in translating and interpreting are seen as potentially productive and all acts of representation as provisional.[19]

Chapter 6, "Literacies," explores the benefits and potential drawbacks of written language standardization. The chapter also highlights connections between local literacies and community identity, including a discussion of the politics of written forms of Indigenous names.

Chapter 7, "Listening," considers research relationships as opening oneself up toward the other, and translation as listening. Thinking about research this way raises questions about standard procedures for ethics review and funding applications. The chapter also describes developing a method in one-to-one collaborations across social and cultural difference, drawing on the production of *Nitinikiau Innusi* as a story of writing together.

Chapter 8, "Songs," returns to the concept of structures of feeling to examine some much-loved songs and contrast the evocation of identity, land, and history in well-known Innu songs and poetry with works in English and French. The chapter focuses on Philippe McKenzie's "Tanite Mack Tshe Tiak," Kashtin's "Tshinanu," Georges Dor's "La Manic," Wendell Ferguson's "Rocks and Trees," Wade Hemsworth's "Blackfly Song," and Stan Rogers's "Northwest Passage." The sentiments expressed in these works contrast sharply in their evocations of Innusi: the English and French songs frame Innu territory as a harsh and alienating place while the Innu songs are full of love, longing, and connection to that same land.

The Innu word "nutshimit" was one of the hardest words to translate. It is often translated as "wilderness" or "bush," but Chapter 9, "Wilderness," investigates other ways of conceptualizing and translating the term. In the introduction to *Nitinikiau Innusi*, I wrote: "In any good story or any meaningful piece of research, something is at stake. Nutshimit is what is at stake in this book: nutshimit; Nitassinan—the land of the Innu; and Innu-aitun—Innu life and understanding of the world."[20] The concept of wilderness underlies much of southern colonizers' understanding of the North and enables us to act in certain ways, based on the idea that the North is empty and needs to be tamed and exploited. This final chapter also links key ideas expressed throughout the book with human responses to climate change and the COVID-19 pandemic, showing how wilderness, wildness, and the inappellable are themes for our time.

Where I Come From

Returning to the idea of worlding, I want to say something about where I come from, because that too is part of the conceptual and affective framework I draw on to make sense of this project. The project that led to this book was about Innu language and land, but I also use examples from other places, especially from the neighbouring territory of Mi'kma'ki. I want to acknowledge those lands and the relationships that enabled me to begin thinking about translating words and worlds.

I grew up near the border of Nova Scotia and New Brunswick, where the Wabanaki forest meets the wetlands and shores of Siknikt in Mi'kma'ki, the territory of the Mi'kmaq. According to Mi'kmaw historian Daniel Paul, the word "Siknikt" can be translated as "drainage area."[21] Referring to his translations of regional names, he adds that "because of the different perceptions of things by the two peoples, they are as close as one can come to conveying their true meaning in that language." We knew Siknikt in the anglicized form of Chignecto as the name for the isthmus between the two provinces and the innermost part of the Bay of Fundy.

There was an old French fort near where we lived, Fort Beauséjour—a windswept hilly place with long views out across the Tantramar marshes (the Tintamarre—an Acadian word for a lot of noise, a racket, perhaps because of all the shorebirds on the marsh) and Chignecto Bay, where the British troops had sailed in and won a decisive battle for control of the territory in 1755. As children we loved the old fort and were regularly taken there by our father, released to run wildly up and down the hills and in and out of the batteries and underground magazines. Once I said to him confidently, believing that loving a place makes it one's own somehow, "If we had lived back when it was a fort we would have been on their side, right?" "Well, actually," he responded, "we probably would have been on the other side." It was an early realization of the random senselessness of war. I still had not figured out that most of our friends might have been on the French side. There is also the thorny issue of the two sides, neither of which were the original inhabitants of the land, the Mi'kmaq. But until recently most history books said it was a war between the French and the British, as if the Mi'kmaq were not anywhere at all. Reassessment of these historical events is ongoing. Anne Marie Lane Jonah writes:

> The . . . erasure of Indigenous agency and political will from this history is the result of processes both at that time, and in later scholarship . . . As well as questioning the interpretation, we need to acknowledge the possible motives behind an interpretation

> that minimizes and dismisses Indigenous agency . . . That view of events, seeing European intentions and claims as more valid than Indigenous, still pervades North American history, and stands in the way of reconciliation. It is a daunting task, but necessary, to re-evaluate received narratives.
>
> . . . One effect of the commitment to Truth and Reconciliation is the recognition of the need to slow down and build relationships with communities. In this process, I am seeing one way that this commitment benefits us all, and I am grateful to be part of it.[22]

The descendants of all these people were still there in the village of my childhood, their children in the same classrooms, skating on the same pond, hanging out in the village square or the old hay barns on the marsh, swimming at the same muddy beach at high tide. The French-speaking Acadians made their long and arduous way back from Louisiana, where the British had deported them after the war, and the Mi'kmaq simply moved closer to the forest on the edge of the village and hung on. I know my childhood home so intimately, the cadences of people's voices, the patterns of the tides, the best places to buy fried clams or pick blackberries, the sites of my ancestors' graves. But in some ways I do not know it at all. I did not even know its name, Siknikt, until I looked it up to write this. Even more recently I learned that the First Nations people of the village where I grew up called their community Amlamgog.

I left Amlamgog a long time ago, although it still feels like home in many ways. I have lived in Newfoundland and Labrador for thirty years. The "and Labrador" part was added to the name of the province in 2001.[23] This name is often awkward in everyday conversation: really I live on the island of Newfoundland, not in Labrador. When this territory became a Canadian province in 1949, Labrador was not part of the official name. No treaties had been signed with its Innu and Inuit inhabitants or with the Newfoundland Mi'kmaq. The Canadian government argued that the Indigenous peoples of the new province would be better off unrecognized, since the Indian Act would extinguish their citizenship rights (for example, at that time they would not have had the right to vote or to own a boat).[24] Yet as Mi'kmaw scholar Bonita Lawrence cogently puts it, "Without recognition, making claims against the state for treaties, for redress for land theft, even to reclaim the bones of ancestors is impossible."[25] More than seventy years later, recognition is still in process in many ways, through land claims, environmental and cultural justice movements, and media and the arts.

Land acknowledgements have become very common as a form of recognition in certain settings such as political, arts, and sports events, and in academia. They are often inadequate in that they do not say anything about ongoing relationships or how those relationships might change. Anishinaabe writer and educator Hayden King has argued that territorial acknowledgements should be a way for non-Indigenous people to reflect on the obligation that comes with living there. Part of that obligation is "the hard work of learning about their neighbours and learning about the treaties of the territory and learning about those nations that should have jurisdiction."[26]

When Tshaukuesh asked me to help her publish her book, I felt daunted at the thought of how much work it would be and how ill-equipped I was to do it, but it also seemed like a chance to do better than I had in the past, to learn something and to help her share her profound knowledge of Innu land, history, culture, and language. The guiding principles of the TRC include engaging in public education and dialogue, paying attention to the perspectives of Indigenous elders, and "supporting Aboriginal peoples' cultural revitalization and integrating Indigenous knowledge systems, oral histories, laws, protocols, and connections to the land into the reconciliation process."[27] Working with Tshukuesh on translating and editing what became *Nitinikiau Innusi* was an opportunity to support those principles by helping her reach her goal of publishing her book, a contemporary history of the Innu from her perspective as an elder who has fought so bravely and so long to protect her culture and her land. *Exactly What I Said* is my account of our work together, for which we had no real models or pre-existing methodology, written in the hope that it will offer some insight (or at least some new questions) about listening, language, stories, and keeping the land alive.

One

Mapping

"We started the first walk just across from the North Mart. Uapush-shipiss—Traverspine River. We walked across the lake, a bit of woods, marsh, and then across the Mishta-shipu. After Anne Marie Lake before Minai-nipi there's a long lake where we used to stop for the night. The Innu call the place Fishing Camp."[1]

Tshaukuesh and I are crawling around on the floor of the cabin I rented across the river from Sheshatshiu, peering at the large-scale government maps I brought from St. John's and laid out flat on the linoleum, joining them up like pieces of a giant puzzle and taping them together. We have nearly finished her book, but it needs a map to show where the land is that she works so hard to keep alive and where she went on her walks and canoe trips.

"Where is Fishing Camp?" I ask her.

"Near where a small brook comes out. Here's Kamisekuakamat—a big marsh. We camped there too, sometimes at one end of it, sometimes the other.[2] We didn't walk all the way on the Uapush-shipiss. Francis said it would be too hard because it twists so much."[3] She draws a wavy line on the floor with her finger to show me. "We walked more straight and crossed the Uapush-shipiss a few times. If we saw the Kenamau River, we knew we were going the wrong way. Anne Marie Lake is almost the same size as Fishing Camp Lake."

"Is Fishing Camp Kukameu-nipi?" I suggest, trying to find it on the map somewhere south of Anne Marie Lake.

"Maybe," she replies, "we just call it Fishing Camp."

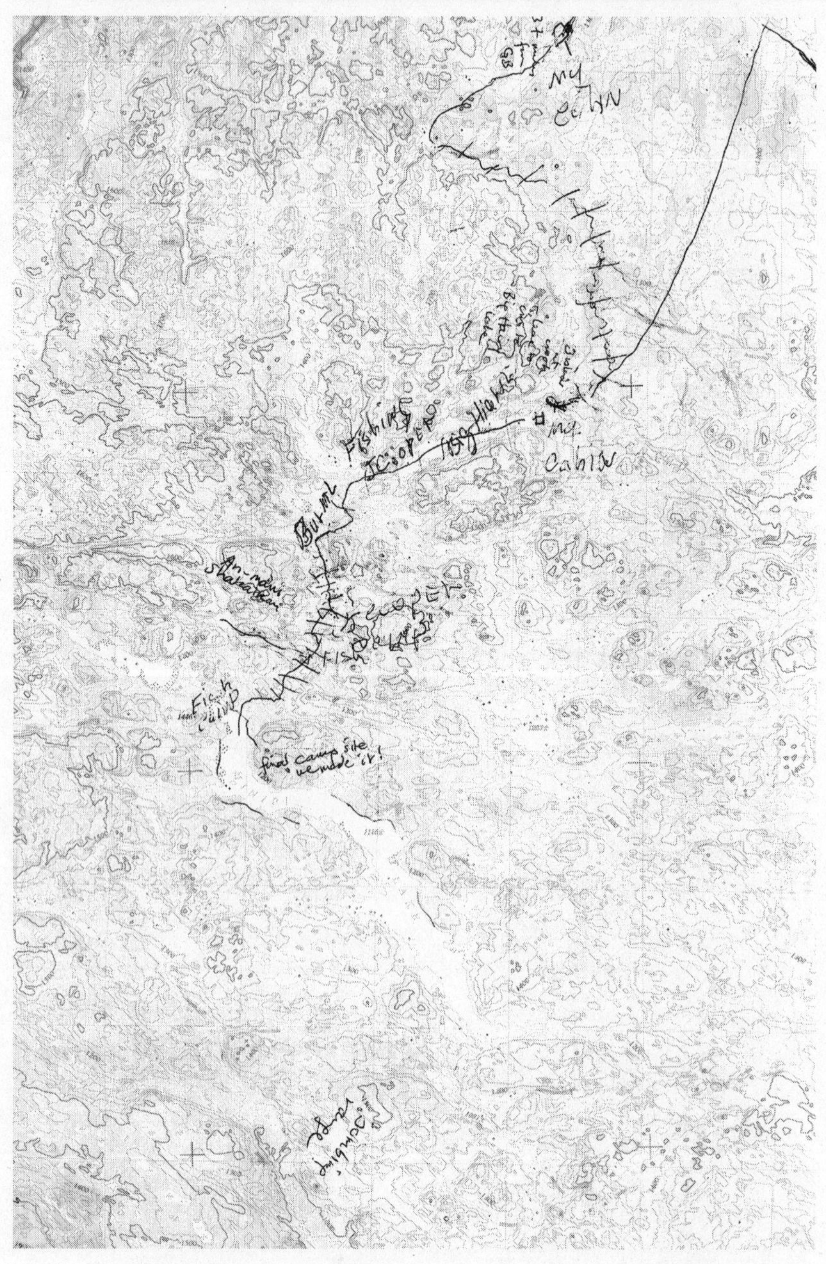

One of the source maps we used to make the map that appeared in *Nitinikiau Innusi*, with Henry Ike Rich's notes. Photo by Elizabeth Yeoman.

"How many days walk to Minai-nipi?"

"About three weeks. Maybe a month, with some breaks. Sometimes we'd stop for a day and somebody would go ahead to break a trail, then we'd wait overnight and the next day the trail would be nice and hard, easier for pulling heavy toboggans. Once a young woman asked me how I knew to do that and I said, 'I just know. My parents did it this way.'"

She traces the route with her finger as she talks. I ask her whether her family walked to Minai-nipi when she was a child.

"No, more on the Uapush side. Long walk! Sheshatshiu to Uapush! Kanikuanimau is where I was born, near Meshikamau Lake—a long long lake. Is this Uinikupau Lake? That's on the Churchill Falls canoe trip. And where's Sept-Îles? My parents came from Sept-Îles and one year they went to nutshimit, hunting, and they ran out of food, flour, everything. My dad had to decide if it was shorter to walk back to Sept-Îles or to Labrador to get food. He didn't know where Labrador was but somebody told him it was nearer. That's how we first came to Labrador, to get food. Maybe they thought they'd go back but they ended up staying here. It was too far to go back to Sept-Îles. I was very young. I don't really remember it but that's what my parents said. They walked all the way to come here, no skidoo, no plane. Then one of my sisters got married here and one of my brothers died and was buried here, so it was too hard for my parents to leave. My sister would cry and my dad and my mum wanted to go back to where they came from, but it was just too hard.

"But they always went to nutshimit still after they came here—not so much Pants Lake [Enipeshakimau, the destination of the rerouted walks Tshaukuesh led when the ice on the Uapush-shipiss was no longer reliably frozen because of climate change], always this way"—she sketches a route to the northwest of Grand Lake—"up the Naskapi River, hunting, and the Red Wine River—there are big mountains, Red Wine Mountains—Penipuapishk^u—there was good hunting there, lots of caribou. They'd stay there a couple of months to make pashteu-uiash—dried meat, make makushan,[4] clean caribou skins, make moccasins, snowshoes. When we went up the river we'd leave some food: baking powder, flour, sugar, salt . . . in a metal bucket up in a tree so animals couldn't get it. On the way back we'd have to find the stuff again because we'd be out of flour, even though we'd have lots of meat, but we needed to make bread. Remember I told you this in my story? When we'd come home in the spring we could hunt at Grand Lake too—fish, goose, ducks, good hunting here—sometimes the men would go to Sheshatshiu to get more flour and the old people and little kids would stay in the camp. They'd be gone just one night. The Hudson's Bay Company manager knew the people had beaver, muskrat, otter worth lots of money, so he'd let them stay for the night in a cabin and go home the next day. Once the ice was gone, we'd go canoeing along the shore."

"So they'd stay a couple of months in the spring on Grand Lake? Up near the mouth of the Naskapi?"

"Yes. The women would stay there while the men went out with toboggans, or by canoe once the ice was gone. The women would hunt for small animals. Where the reservoir is now there were burial grounds, and people used to hunt there. When they left, they would leave their equipment behind knowing they'd be back the next year—traps, canoes, tents, stoves—because it was heavy and they could only take a little with them, as much as they could pull on toboggans. When the government made the Churchill Falls dam it was all lost under the water. My dad talked about that many times. They never thought anyone would touch their things, or that someday all that beautiful land would just be gone. I feel so sad when I think about that."

Tshaukuesh peers at the smaller-scale map that I brought to help us visualize the whole region as well as the details. "Grand Lake is very important. I wish we had a better map."

I show her where it is on one of the larger-scale maps and she points to a spot at the northwest end of the lake.

"My parents used to camp here. Innu people call it Shatshit. There's a big mountain near Caribou, at the top somebody found a raven's nest, that's why they called the lake Kakatshu-utshishtun. It means Raven's Nest. We used to go fishing here at the Caribou River—fishing for salmon, trout, and white fish. My parents would canoe along the shore, or if there was going to be wind on this side they'd cross quickly to the other side and paddle along the shore there.

"Did I tell you one time we stopped to have a cup of tea on this little lake—at Shatshit—and afterwards we walked into the woods and found an old cache of food: molasses, tinned milk . . . I wish I could find some of those old supplies now so I could set them up for a photo for my book—the old bags of sugar, baking powder, salt, and flour, put them in a metal bucket like we used to do.

"Naskapi River—Pekissiu-shipiss. Sometimes we call it Naskapi-shipiss too but the elders called it Pekissiu—I don't know what it means.[5] When I walk there I see lots of old camps, just near Shatshit, along the shore there. When the Naskapi and the Kamikuakamiu Rivers froze we would walk along them from Shatshit to get to the mountains to hunt caribou. Elizabeth, I wish you could have seen these places before—those places meant so much to us! Now you hear Innu people saying they don't know what to do, but in the old days they always knew what to do.

"When I was little we'd get to the Red Wine Mountains and camp where there were trees for protection from the wind. We usually saw lots of caribou tracks and droppings when we got there. That meant that there were plenty of caribou around, and we looked forward to having meat. My sister and I would be so happy because the snow is hard in the mountains and you don't need to wear snowshoes—I could feel the happiness with my whole body—to be able to walk without snowshoes and to know we'd have a feast of caribou.

"I'm so happy you brought the maps! Now I can see the places I know and show them to you. This is the Mishta-shipu, these are the places I went to when I was young. Even though I don't know how to read maps, I can recognize the places I'm talking about. When I'm gone, my grandchildren can say, 'My grandmother didn't know how to read maps or to read or write English, but look what she accomplished, she tried so hard, she organized the walks and the canoe trips to try to save the land.' I never asked myself whether anybody would come with me and I never hesitated or thought it would be too hard. Where did I get that? I got it from my parents, from my ancestors, back through the generations. They taught me everything I know and then I taught it to the children."

We take a break and sit on chairs, resting our old bones after all that time on the floor, drinking steaming mugs of nipishapui. Tshaukuesh muses about the traditional ways she was reminded of as she travelled in her imagination across the land the map represents.

"See how smart people were in the old days? They didn't have any maps—they just knew where to go, where to set up their camps, where the trees were, how many and what kind to look for to know which way to go. They never got lost."

After we've relaxed for a bit, I ask her to show me the route of the walk to Enipeshakimau so we can put it on the map for the book.

"We went across to the point and then skidoos took us across the lake. We set up camp there at Kakusanut and the next day we walked and didn't use any more skidoos, just walking every day. After two days' walk I felt that I was getting stronger and I stopped worrying about whether I could make it. We walked across the marshes: Kapikuakunesekat, and camped there the next day, then Kaminusekast, and finally the third marsh, Miste Misek. After that we got to a small lake, Eskuamitinat, close to the mountains. We stayed there two days because of bad weather and then went to Takutaut, the top of the Mealy Mountains. We got to a place that we call Cree Kaikutet Umisin—Cree's Shoes under the Tree—because one year Rena put Cree's shoes to dry under the stove and they burned. Instead of throwing them away we put them in the branches of a tree so we would see them in years to come and remember that time. Next stop was Petshish Utisinim—Petshish's Rock.[6] We stayed there for a couple of days because of bad weather, then we went on to Atukupitin Peshish, the lake with two streams . . ."

On our next tea break, we talk about whether we have enough detail to show the routes of the walks. Tshaukuesh is worried she might not have them exactly right because of her lack of experience with maps. Given my own lack of the kind of knowledge that comes from walking on the land year after year, the sum of our cartographic skills is not what it should be. She is thinking maybe we could visit her friend Henry Ike Rich. "He's a very nice man. Maybe he can help us." Henry is a retired trapper whom Tshaukuesh encountered many times on the walks. Sometimes he gave them food when they were walking to Enipeshakimau.

Two days later, we are at Henry's house, repeating the process of organizing the maps on the floor and then crawling around on them, telling stories as places are recognized and adding our own notes, drawings, and diagrams. Henry and Tshaukuesh piece together the route of the first walk, and he shows me where the NATO bombing range was. Henry later sends me detailed digital files showing each stage of the walk.

The map for *Nitinikiau Innusi* was drawn by Peter Jackson, an architect and cartographer from St. John's. The place names and their spellings relied often, though by no means always, on the Innu places website *Pepamuteiati Nitassinat: As We Walk across Our Land*,[7] and *Natural Resources Canada*'s "Canadian Geographical Names Database."[8] But the map's source was Tshaukuesh, with help from her friend Henry Ike Rich, and all the years they spent walking on the land.

A few days later, on my way home in a small, low-flying plane, I saw the land we had mapped spread out below me and recognized the undulating Uapush-shipiss, which Akaneshau call the Traverspine. I knew some of its stories, how it is also known as the Manatueu-shipiss (Manatushipis in Tshaukuesh's orthography—so many names!), or Little Swearing River, because it was so rocky and miserable to navigate; how the walkers on Tshaukuesh's early walks used to cross it over and over as it twisted back and forth. I had not walked it, but I knew it when I saw it. The map-making and the storytelling had etched it into my memory.

Of course, my recognition was not like Tshaukuesh's. She too had written about recognizing places as she flew over them, but she had walked there countless times:

> I looked below us, trying to see where we walked last spring, to see our meshkanau. I could see Minai-nipi where we walked when it was frozen. Then I saw a tamarack forest that I call "My Father's Woods," because my dad once told me that a tamarack tree had talked to him and asked him if he had daughters. He said yes, lots of daughters, and the tree said to send them out to cut wood. That was his way of encouraging us not to be lazy.
>
> We saw more tamarack trees, and then I saw An-mani Ushakaikan and Tshaukuesh Minishtikuss and the place where we camped when we walked this way last month. I thought

> about how strong we were to walk all that way and I felt so proud that we made it.[9]

Tshaukuesh's memories are of a lifetime and a history of embodied and emotional knowledge of the places laid out like a map below her: her father's stories, her small self cutting wood, the smell of tamarack, the walk last spring with all its triumphs and frustrations, the names they gave to places. Like walking, working with maps can evoke memories and stories. I wonder sometimes why interviewing is so often a static process with two people sitting across from each other, when the experience and the result could be so much richer with movement and visual support—walking, mapping, storytelling, connecting to the land.[10] Historian Julian Brave NoiseCat of the Canim Lake Band Tsq'escen highlights connections between language, story, and the land: "In my Secwepemc language, which I had the privilege of learning with my kyé7e (my grandmother), the root suffix for people and place derive from the same ancient word: tmícw. But one need not study linguistics to recognize that the stories we tell flow from land and people—interdependent and inseparable."[11] Métis artist and cartographer Christi Belcourt sees maps as ways of depicting intimate knowledge of the places they represent and of reclaiming those places. She uses her art as a way of doing that and emphasizes that, unlike maps, the land itself is not abstract but full of life.[12] Yet abstractions, in the form of lines on a map, changed lives and the land itself forever.

An Imperial Enterprise

> *Cartography has long been an imperial enterprise used to claim territory and to imagine the geographic reach of empires.* In its imperial usage, map-making is an instrument of Indigenous erasure. It reconceptualizes the world in ways that ignore ongoing Indigenous presence, usage and governance.
>
> — MÉTIS SCHOLAR ADAM GAUDRY IN THE *INDIGENOUS PEOPLES ATLAS OF CANADA*

The impact of this kind of map-making on the Innu is vividly articulated in a 1984 exchange between two Innu men, Sylvestre Andrew and Pien Gregoire:

> Sylvestre: The government never told us in advance what it was planning. It drew a map and marked the places that supposedly belonged to it. It's not very long ago that the Government of Newfoundland first came here. I think it was in 1949 that it first arrived. That's when Newfoundland joined Canada and a line was drawn on the map to separate us from the French [Quebec]. Then the government of Newfoundland wrote on paper that they were responsible for us; for the Innu north of the line on that map. But it's all Innu land. . . . After they have drawn the lines on the map, dividing the land among them, they do whatever they want. They don't even stop to think that this is Innu land. All the land that has been divided up is land that has been stolen from us. And if the government had told us in advance of their plans, of the things they wanted to do, we could have stopped them little by little. If we remain unable to stop them, they will completely finish up on our land . . .
> Pien: And then we will be completely changed—we will be like French and English people. Before they had divided up our land they should have told us first. And they should have listened to us when we didn't approve of what they wanted to do. And today they still don't listen.[13]

There is a history of imperial map-making in my family, although it starts with a story that turned out not to be true. Until recently, many descendants of convicts transported to Australia had cover stories to hide their shame. (Now they are proud of the truth, but neither stance is really adequate when you think about what their arrival meant for the Indigenous peoples.) My family's story was that my great-great-great-great-grandfather Isaac Nelson had travelled from England to Australia to be surveyor general of New South Wales. In fact, he was transported as a convict after stealing some silver plate in 1789: the year the crops failed and people starved all over Europe, the year of the French Revolution, the year the prisons of England were so full of petty criminals—many of them guilty of thefts committed to gain some brief respite from cold and hunger—that they began to ship them to Australia. Isaac had committed this crime after his infant son starved to death, the famished mother, my twenty-two-year-old great-great-great-great-grandmother, Sarah, being unable to produce milk to feed him.[14]

Perhaps that grandiose story about his role as surveyor general was inspired by the fact that their granddaughter, my great-great-grandmother Caroline Orsmond, actually did marry a surveyor, Edward Jollie, sixty years later. The introduction to his memoir states that "as a pioneer surveyor and explorer of colonial New Zealand few names have been affixed to such a wide range of geographical features, and the streets of virtually every city and town of significance, as Jollie's."[15] He and Caroline became prosperous members of the colonial landed gentry. Perhaps she was the one who invented an even more prosperous past and the grand title of surveyor general for her desperate and destitute grandfather. I believed the story when I was growing up and only found out the truth years later when the internet enabled me to connect with distant cousins in Australia and New Zealand. Amongst us, pooling scraps of information, we worked out what really happened. Still, mapping was in my blood and my imagination, and so was colonizing. This story is one of many; there is a whole history of imperialism and colonization just in my own family. When I started working with Tshaukuesh, I thought the opportunity to help her with her book might be a gesture toward a different way forward, although I did not know how, or toward what exactly, but away from my family's imperial past in any case. And the work on the map was part of understanding and documenting what was at stake.

De-mapping and Re-mapping

But empires aren't the only ones who draw maps. Indigenous peoples also use maps to re-inscribe older ways of understanding

> geographic spaces, to replace the lines of nation-states, provinces and other boundaries with borderlines and edges of our own. Mapping our spaces, in both contemporary and historical practice, protects Indigenous peoples from imperial erasure. Map-making is therefore a deeply political process, as it is a process of world-creation. Whether it is creating a world that hides Indigenous conceptions of space, place and territory, or one that establishes a world of ongoing Indigenous nationhood, how we draw maps goes hand-in-hand with how we understand the world we live in.
>
> —ADAM GAUDRY IN THE *INDIGENOUS PEOPLES ATLAS OF CANADA*[16]

Gaudry suggests the terms de-mapping and re-mapping as ways of indicating the role of cartography in envisioning a different world, "a world built on Indigenous persistence and political rebirth."[17] If mapping has often been a colonizing practice, there have also always been Indigenous maps. And, of course, the power of maps and map-makers is limited. Carolina Tytelman points out that "maps of Labrador portray and arrange a space where another place 'Nitassinan' continues to be produced by the network of practices of the human and non-human persons that [dwell] there, and other actors with agency. Thus, while the maps of Labrador are a fundamental part of the colonial enterprise, they are not enough to erase the existence of Nitassinan."[18]

Today, with digital and geospatial technologies, maps can be created and shared across distance, and there is an extraordinary array of resources for making and using them. These technologies have also expanded the ways we think about what a map is, through interactive, multimedia, and multi-platform projects, satellite navigation and mapping. From Inuvik to Melbourne to the Amazon, people are de-mapping and re-mapping using digital and geospatial technologies to reclaim and protect territory. They are mapping culturally and environmentally significant places, traditional knowledge and land use, and oral histories; using the maps not only to navigate but also to educate themselves and others, tell their stories, support land claims, and slow climate change.

In Peru, for example, despite the Intergovernmental Panel on Climate Change (IPCC)'s affirmation of the critical need to protect forests and plant more trees to slow climate change, there was a 3.7 percent decrease in tree cover between 2001 and 2018, equalling 1.37 gigatonnes of CO_2 emissions.[19] Satellite mapping is being used both to document large-scale forest clearance by multinational companies and to educate local people on the impact of their subsistence farming practices, which also involve deforestation.[20] Indigenous people in Canada and Australia are learning how to use geospatial technologies to assess the potential impact of development projects on significant sites and on the environment, to make story maps to educate people about community life and issues, to document traditional land use and occupancy, to support land claims, for environmental monitoring, and for intergenerational knowledge transfer.[21] It is beyond the scope of this chapter to discuss these projects in detail, but I want to highlight one that is from and for Innusi and that illustrates some of what digital maps can and cannot do.

Pepamuteiati Nitassinat: As We Walk across Our Land was extremely useful for us in writing *Nitinikiau Innusi* and making the map that accompanies it.[22] The website began as a project to document Innu land use and occupancy for land claims. It uses Google Maps to enable viewers to explore Innusi virtually, to see photos and videoclips relating to sites on the map, and to hear the pronunciation of the Innu place names along with stories set in many of the locations. You can zoom in and out to see the names of lakes, rivers, mountains, and other geographic features. The website was launched in 2008 after over thirty years of research with Innu elders. Then Grand Chief, Mark Nui, explained that it was a gift from the elders to Innu young people. He said, "Place names are very important to our people because they are a gateway to our history on the land. Many younger Innu who have gone through the provincial educational system have never learned these names. We hope that the website will help them learn about their culture and history."[23] The project was also used later to seek official status for the names.[24]

At the St. John's launch of *Pepamuteiati Nitassinat*, there was a presentation followed by discussion. After several very positive and interested comments and questions, someone in the audience stood up and said, "If you really care about protecting Innu land and culture, this is the last thing you should be doing. You have to live on the land to know its place names and understand its stories." There was an uncomfortable silence and then protests that of course this was a valuable resource. I have already noted how Tshaukuesh and I used the website and how helpful it was. But this troubling comment stayed with me, echoed in a different—but I think related—context by Thomas King when he questioned the value of documenting and anthologizing Indigenous peoples' oral stories: "Nineteenth- and twentieth-century anthropologists and ethnographers . . . collect[ed] and translate[d] Native stories, thereby 'preserving' Native oral literature before it was lost. As a result of these efforts, an impressive body of oral stories is now stored in periodicals and books that one can find at any good research library. Not that anyone reads them. But they are safe and sound. As it were."[25]

The speaker's point and King's critique are haunting. They remind us of the loss of stories, languages, land. They are about the profound difference between wording and worlding.[26] Yet the official, public naming and documentation of places does matter. As critical cartographer and historian Brian Harley put it, "The steps in making a map—selection, omission, simplification, classification, the creation of hierarchies, and 'symbolization'—are all inherently rhetorical [in that] [a]ll maps strive to frame their message in the context of an audience. All maps state an argument about the world and they are propositional in nature."[27] In other words, maps are stories.

Nitinikiau Innusi was launched at the Labrador Research Forum in Innusi.[28] The keynote speaker was Unangax scholar Eve Tuck, co-author of "Decolonization Is Not a Metaphor."[29] She talked about the decolonization of stories, the need to move away from narratives of pain and despair that "document damage" as a colonial theory of change.[30] Instead, she said, we need abundance narratives. Later in her talk, she discussed the role of research in decolonization, prefacing that part of the talk with "sometimes you don't need research, you just need a billboard (or a blog, a YouTube video, an open house . . .)."[31] Some possible research projects that she did think were valuable included documenting "variety and complexity of ideas in a community; uncovering quiet thoughts and beliefs; finding ways to use Indigenous languages."[32] We had decided to use mainly Innu place names in *Nitinikiau Innusi*. Doing so made us think about the variety and complexity of ideas in the community, because Innu places, like Innu people, often have more than one name. We hoped using Innu names would also make

Innu-aimun more visible in the English version of the book and have the effect that Jordan Engel describes in relation to decolonial map-making: "It is amazing how a slight change of perspective can make the land we thought we knew unrecognizable. If we take away the political borders, turn the map so that North is no longer on top, and re-label every place in its original Indigenous language, we come to realize that not only has the land been colonized, but all the people living on it as well."[33]

When we made the map for *Nitinikiau Innusi*, we did not think of orientation as a possible way of re-mapping. Only after the book was published did I learn that Indigenous maps have been oriented to all of the compass points[34] and read Sherrill Grace's description of the effect of Scott Barham's disorienting map on the cover of Aritha van Herk's *Places Far from Ellesmere*—a map in which Ellesmere Island takes the form of a woman and is large, central, very near Calgary—and how it "decentres" Canadian geography and "jump-starts a dialogue."[35] I wish now that we had had that conversation and looked at possible ways of visually decentring Canadian geography with the map of Innusi. However, we did decide early in the process to use Innu place names. Documenting these names and mapping them is a way of responding to "colonial shatterings" and replacing them with "narratives of abundance."[36] So many places on a map, an abundance of Innu names—the Mishta-shipu, Kakatshu-utshishtun, Akami-uapishkᵘ, An-mani Ushakaikan, Atatshi-uinipekᵘ—and the process itself of making the map, the research, the conversations we did have, the stories. The *Pepamuteiati Nitassinat* website is not only a re-mapping but also a resource for other re-mappings. We used it to find translations or standardizations of names, and to locate places so we could put them on our map and in our index. Sometimes Tshaukuesh had a different name or we could not find a place she mentioned on the website, but that was also part of documenting the complexity of ideas, another part of the narrative of abundance.

There are also re-mapping projects that use older, more traditional technologies. Christi Belcourt's work, for example, includes paintings of maps that reinstate Indigenous place names and other motifs representing Indigenous world views, especially water as a sacred element. In one of her pieces from the series of paintings *Mapping Routes: Perspectives of Land*

and Water in Ontario, over 400 Anishinaabemowin and Mohawk names overlie the largely French and English names inscribed and made official by colonial map-makers. Belcourt describes the origin of the project in a drive she took across Canada in the 1990s with the intention of visiting Indigenous communities. She was shocked to discover that the names of many of these communities were not on the map. Instead, the name of a nearby white community often appeared, even if the Indigenous community was larger. When Indigenous place names, or corruptions of them, are used, as in Toronto, for example, she points out that their origins and meanings are largely forgotten and do not signify in most accounts of Canadian history. Belcourt suggests that "most Canadians are quite comfortable, and even comforted, by the names of the places they call home that are indigenous in origin—but only to a point. As long as they are in name only and don't come with the burden of acknowledging Canada's past colonialist history and the erasure of indigenous ownership of lands."[37] In contrast, Cynthia Sugars suggests that Canadians are haunted by these place names, longing for the words to reveal their history, but "the ghosts are steadfastly silent. The names are a mockery to the colonists' sense that they 'own' the past."[38] Belcourt's paintings make history visible but it is the history of erasure, not a comforting history that reinforces a sense of ownership for colonizers. The paintings are interconnected, some like the one mentioned above using European cartographic traditions to reclaim place names, others depicting or symbolizing waterways, paths and gifts of the land and water, or telling stories about relationships and spiritual connections in the natural world.

Grace discusses several maps that reinvent or call into question imperialist conventions of mapping. They range from "artistic subversions"[39] such as the Barham and van Herk map mentioned above, a north-centric (as opposed to north-oriented) map titled *Inuit View to the South* from Rudy Wiebe's *Playing Dead*, and Jack Warwick's *Map of Literary Regions of the 'North,'* to "radical re-mappings,"[40] including Stuart Daniel's 1989 map of the Northwest Territories from *The Modern North* by Ken Coates and Judith Powell, an 1866 map of the western coast of Hudson Bay by Inuk cartographer Ar-mou, a 1999 map of Nunavut by John David Hamilton, and Marlene Creates's memory maps installation, *The Distance between Two Points Is Measured in*

Memories, Labrador 1988. I have seen Marlene's installation more than once, most recently in 2019 at a retrospective of her life's work,[41] and been deeply moved and influenced by it. It is made up of eighteen hand-drawn maps by Labrador Innu, Inuit, and settlers, each map accompanied by photos of the person who drew it and the place it represents, a story, and something material from the place such as a rock or some earth. Grace suggests that memory maps may not be considered re-mappings but, whatever their intention, in their effect they are because they "add layers of meaning to what we find on official maps and remind us that we are all map-makers and that we map what matters most to us."[42]

On the Names of Places

Over the years we worked together, Tshaukuesh and I talked periodically about what to call her book. She knew she wanted something that reflected her dedication to the land. Finally, she narrowed it down to two possibilities, either "I Try to Keep the Land Alive" or simply "I Keep the Land Alive." The first choice was more modest and perhaps more realistic, but the second clearly had more power, so the decision on the English version was easy. Deciding on an Innu title was more complicated. Tshaukuesh had used the word "Innusi" to refer to the land, and this raised questions about language standardization and usage, technical meaning, and how it would be interpreted.

Innusi (or Innu-assi in standardized Innu-aimun) literally means "Innu land" or "Innu territory." In Quebec, where most Innu live, it has taken on an official meaning with the signing of an Agreement in Principle in 2004 between several Innu communities and the Quebec and Canadian governments. Innu-assi is the territory fully owned and controlled by the Innu. Within this legal framework, this represents less than 1 percent of Nitassinan, a vast territory under the jurisdiction of the Quebec government but where the Innu have certain rights.[43] Innu-assi is made up of the reserve itself along with some nearby lands and heritage sites.[44] In Labrador, Innu-assi might be understood to mean just Sheshatshiu or Natuashish, the villages. Nitassinan (literally meaning "our land," also sometimes spelled N'tesinan) is widely used in Labrador among Akaneshau as well as Innu to refer to all of Innu territory. But Tshaukuesh said that to her Innusi meant all of the land.

Defining Innusi seems to be another example of what Tuck might have meant by the "variety and complexity of ideas within a community." According to Jean-Paul Lacasse, the meaning has changed over time with Innuassi (his spelling, yet another instance of variety!) meaning "the whole of Innu territory" for elders, while for younger people it can mean just the village or the reserve.[45] However, Innu novelist and teacher Naomi Fontaine, who was born in 1987, makes a distinction between what Innu-assi currently means and what it *could* mean: "In my language, when we talk about the reserve, we call it Innu-assi, Innu land. Belonging is attached to the inside of those premises and the people who live there. The day the reserve no longer exists, and I believe that day will come, we will dream, we will make children, we will dance at the makushan, in freedom, in Innu-assi."[46]

For me, the widespread use of Nitassinan by non-Innu is troubling because it means "our land." I never feel comfortable saying it. Obviously, that wasn't a problem for the title of Tshaukuesh's book since it is her land, and for a while she considered using it to avoid anyone thinking she meant only the reserve, but in the end she decided to use the word that held more personal resonance for her and not to use the standardized spelling for the same reason. It wasn't the writing system she had learned. It didn't look right to her.

The title of the book *Nitinikiau Innusi* puts the older name on the map, both literally on Peter Jackson's map drawn for the book and figuratively by making the name visible, even perhaps to non-speakers of Innu-aimun who can still see the word "Innu" in it. Like a map, it "claims territory." Place names are part of the discursive frameworks and "imagined communities"[47] that shape our ways of understanding and acting in this world. Official Innu place names may assert an Innu presence and make the rest of us stop and think about the colonizing names we took for granted for so long.

Tshaukuesh tells a story about Patshishetshuanau—Clouds of Vapour Rising, how her parents on their travels could see the mist from far away, a joyful advance notice that they were approaching the giant and beautiful falls. The clouds of vapour are no longer since the dam was built and soon will not even be in living memory. Patshishetshuanau is known to English speakers as Churchill Falls, renamed along with the river itself by the colonizers to mark an alien history, to honour a wartime leader in a faraway country. The great river Mishta-shipu, which some Akaneshau call the Grand River, was also renamed for Churchill after having previously been designated the Hamilton River, after Charles Hamilton, the nineteenth-century governor who authorized John Peyton's expedition in 1818 in which a Beothuk woman, Demasduit, was kidnapped and her husband Nonosabasut and another man were murdered. Apart from the histories of oppression they transmit, these names tell us nothing about the places they were imposed on.

Inuk author and storyteller Michael Kusugak explains how the names of places are a form of cartography for many Indigenous peoples, since they so often describe geographic or natural features: "Rankin Inlet, in Nunavut, is Kangiq&iniq. It is in a kangiq&uk, an inlet. Baffin Island is Qikiqtaaluk, 'Big Island.' Baker Lake is Qamani'tuaq, 'Way in There.' It is way inland. Coral Harbour is Salliq, 'Farther Out to Sea.'. . The *Gazetteer of the Northwest Territories* (an extensive compilation of all official geographic place names in the Northwest Territories) lists places in their original languages. Dehcho is 'big river' in the South Slavey language. It is the traditional name of the Mackenzie River."[48]

While the clouds of vapour in the Innu name for the falls may no longer be seen, the name Patshishetshuanau still carries a whole history with it. Innu place names also carry geography and cartography, as they describe bodies of water or sites on the land, physical features, geology, flora and fauna. According to the makers of *Pepamuteiati Nitassinat*, the names "are used by travellers to find their way through the territory and to describe and remember places along travel routes. [They also] record Innu history and use of the land by giving names to places where people hunted, fished, and trapped, where they were born or buried, or even where humorous or romantic events took place."[49] Tshaukuesh's story of Cree's burned shoes is a good example. A look at the map and glossary in *Nitinikiau Innusi* reveals the cartographic aspect of Innu place names: as with Kusugak's example of Dehcho, Mishta-shipu also means Big River. (Mississippi, from the Ojibwe or Algonquin Misi-ziibi, is linguistically related to the Innu name and also has the same meaning.) Other names describing geographic features include Uinukupau (Willows Growing at the Mouth of Brooks), Unamen Shipu (Red Ochre River), Sheshatshiu (A Narrow Place in the River), Akami-uapishk^{u} (White Mountain Across) and Atatshi-uinipek^{u} (Cut-off Sea). The cartography is sometimes humorous, too: Nipississ means Little Small Lake, though the lake is actually very large, and my favourite is the already mentioned Manatueu-shipiss, or Little Swearing River, recalling navigational struggles.

We used Innu place names in the English version of *Nitinikiau Innusi*, even for sites like Patshishetshuanau that are widely known by colonial names. The translation scholar Lawrence Venuti describes translation as a process of looking for similarities while simultaneously confronting dissimilarities. He suggests that dissimilarities should be highlighted more to remind readers that they are exploring a different culture through their reading and to make that culture more visible in the text.[50] While this approach has been critiqued for oversimplifying the complexity of cultures, as I discuss in more detail in Chapter 4, purposely signalling cultural difference for non-Innu readers of the English version of the book was intended to remind them that European names have been superimposed onto others and ask them to do a little work: to use the map to figure out where the places are, to recognize the Innu names for sites they may have known by other names or may not have known at all, to stop and think about, as Grace puts it with reference to another map, "what it feels like to be written out of history."[51] For Innu readers, the use of Innu place names recognizes their history and experience and puts them literally and metaphorically on the map.

Until recently, there were only three officially recognized Innu place names in the entire province of Newfoundland and Labrador: Sheshatshiu, Natuashish, and Wabush (Uapush). However, in 2017 hundreds of Innu names were recognized officially.[52] This means the names can be used on maps and road signs, and will have legal status in land management and property transactions. Patshishetshuanau is now officially recognized as the name for the falls and Mishta-shipu for the river. This de-mapping and re-mapping process began with documenting places and their names for land claims, with elders walking around the school gym in Sheshatshiu and the parish hall in Utshimassit[53] and naming sites on giant maps spread out on the floor, and research projects to compile a database, verify meanings and spellings, and produce the *Pepamuteiati Nitassinat* website.

Grace suggests that the frames of reference for northern places might be transformed by renaming, along with the settlement of land claims and cartographic changes such as redrawn borders. She notes specifically the name of Frobisher Bay as a "prime sign of external colonization imposed through internal and unconscious colonization," which became Iqaluit with the creation of Nunavut.[54] Peter C. van Wyck, while expressing his sympathy for this view, which he describes as "a plea to understanding that strikes me . . . as similar to my own suspicions about the collusion of world and language,"[55] reminds us that "toponyms . . . are not just names—they are forms of knowledge that pertain to a way of life; they have their own stories, histories and practices."[56] Like the troublesome interlocutor at the *Pepamuteiati Nitassinat* website launch, van Wyck thought that the names had to have an emotional and narrative connection to experience on the land to be meaningful. When he asked the elders around Port Radium about Indigenous place names—of which he knew there were many—no one seemed to want to talk about them, even when prompted with a map. Instead, the elders wanted to talk about their sorrow that their children and grandchildren were not interested in their knowledge of the land, the language—including place names—and traditional ways of life. Perhaps this is what the critic at the website launch (who appeared to be Indigenous, although perhaps "from away," as we say in Newfoundland) was trying to express. He was wrong that recording, mapping, and digitizing place names was unimportant, but he was right about names as forms of embodied knowledge. The information on the Innu place names website is useful for land claims, for reference, and perhaps for scaffolding stories in the way Tshaukuesh used the large-scale government maps as she recognized places on the map and wanted to talk about them—unlike the elders van Wyck met with—including the history of their names. But if she had not lived on the land, she would not have been able to tell the stories.

Troublesome Re-mapping

Anthropologist Peter Armitage and linguist Marguerite MacKenzie, who worked on the Innu place names project, expressed their hope that people would use the names and not "feel the need to rename geographic features that are already named."[57] Over a century earlier, in 1905, Mina Hubbard travelled in Innusi doing just that. Her husband, Leonidas, had died in an earlier expedition as he and his partners unsuccessfully sought the source of the Naskaupi River. Determined to complete the expedition on his behalf, Hubbard travelled the George and Naskaupi Rivers by canoe to Ungava Bay.[58] She documented her trip with photography, a map, a diary, and detailed notes on topography, including names she gave to many features, sometimes naming them for friends (Bridgman Mountains and Helen Falls), sometimes for European stories or sites (Santa Claus Mountain and Mount Pisa). She also used Innu names when she knew them (Lake Meshikamau) and invented at least one Innu name (Wapustan River, named for the abundant marten—uapishtan—in the area). On the one hand, she colonized with her mapping and naming, engaging profoundly with "cartography's complicity with imperialism," as Wendy Roy puts it. On the other hand, it is rather sad to problematize her work and that of her Cree guide, George Elson, and their companions, when they were simultaneously "tackling what Sandra Gilbert and Susan Gubar call the problem of 'woman's patronymically defined identity.'"[59]

Roy continues:

> Women often disappeared from historical records because they were known only by their husband's or father's names. Hubbard lists herself on the title page of her book as "Mrs Leonidas Hubbard, Junior"; she never provides Mrs. Ford's first name, although she stayed with her for almost two months; and even in her diary she refers to friends as Mrs. Krafft, Mrs. Bartlett, and Mrs. Bridgman. On her map, though, she inscribes matrilineage by using given names to distinguish the women and girls she is honouring—including herself—from their husbands or fathers . . . By giving public geographic features names that,

> at least initially, had only private meaning, Hubbard's map takes the public and the outside, and turns it into the private and the inside.[60]

Roy illustrates the connection between name changes and colonization with the example of Patshishetshuanau, the Churchill Falls dam and Smallwood Reservoir, where the "maps literally changed overnight."[61] This happens with any dam, of course, and there are thousands of them across the North, over 15,000 to be more exact, including some of the largest in the world.[62] The flooding of the Caniapiscau Reservoir, part of the massive James Bay hydroelectric project in Cree territory, was followed by a particularly troubling re-mapping. In a move that was apparently intended as a counter-narrative to historic practices of naming places for imperialist leaders, Quebec's Commission de toponymie officially named the islands created by the flooding after post-war and contemporary francophone writers and works of literature.[63] The project was called "Le jardin au bout du monde" (The garden at the end of the world).

Spokespeople for the communities affected pointed out that while the islands might have been newly "created," they had been mountains, they already had names, and they were part of a landscape that their ancestors had lived on for millennia. Citing Albert Memmi on how colonial power asserts itself by erasing material traces of colonized peoples, Grand Chief Matthew Coon Come wrote, "Perhaps this is why, in Québec, perceived symbols of anglophone domination of the francophone majority are so well known."[64] This was the irony of this particular renaming: that it was imposed as part of a movement for the francophones of Quebec to promote their own culture against anglophone domination in the South.[65] Bill Namagoose of the Grand Council of Crees described the renaming as "a political move, an attempt to occupy our territory and rename it, rather than adopt local names," adding, "When you fight over territory or sovereignty, one of the important things is to have title to the names."[66]

There is a second irony in this project: with roots in critical geography and poetry, the geopoetics movement that inspired the renaming rejects colonization and exploitation. As one group of practitioners put it: "The reductionist's point of view from which we are trying to free ourselves is well known. On this view, the earth is said to be ours for the taking. It is described as a natural resource and as a source of economic wealth. As this kind of talk sustains and purports exploitation and abuse, the degree to which it is ingrained in our language is also exactly what makes the geopoetics political."[67] Thus, geopoetic writing is often seen by its practitioners as a form of anti-exploitative "worlding." Thinking back to Mika and colleagues' distinction between wording and worlding noted in the Introduction, this may seem like a contradiction in terms but the ways we use language are intrinsically related to the ways we live on the Earth. Geopoetics attempts to bring wording and worlding together through poetry's ability to influence human understanding of place, space, landscape, power, and the relationships of living beings with each other and with the Earth.[68]

In response to the controversy, the commissioners said they had acted in good faith, out of a belief that this was "completely virgin territory."[69] The Cree had been invited to submit lists of existing names for sites in the reservoir, and other projects were ongoing to document Cree place names in Quebec.[70] In 2003 the Commission published a 252-page document on this topic, *La toponymie des Cris*. Yet according to Kyle Carsten Wyatt, writing more recently in 2017, there is no intention to revisit the renaming project even though "the Commission remained open to 'enriching' other islands of the Caniapiscau archipelago with Indigenous names."[71]

Caroline Desbiens reminds us that for traditional Indigenous peoples, the land itself is the text—it must be read constantly in order to survive—whereas for cultures where written texts are fundamental to both knowing and doing, the text and the land are almost completely separate.[72] It is a sad irony that a geopoetic text based on some of the most beautiful literary works of francophone writers should have been written on land that was taken from Indigenous people as a source of economic wealth, erasing thousands of years of Indigenous life on that land, just as dams all over the North have changed and erased the landscape.

Big Science, Big Philosophy, and a Poetics of Land, Maps, and Place Names

Drawing on cultural geography and the ideas of Raymond Williams and the Birmingham School that social change is made through cultural production, Desbiens suggests that we need a shift from big science to big philosophy as a basis for policy decisions in the North. Big science refers to large-scale scientific projects from the Second World War onwards that had the goal of expanding industrial, economic, or military power, as opposed to "science as a pure quest for knowledge."[73] In Desbiens's view, research and policy relating to such developments should be informed not only by science but also by a better understanding of connections between nature and culture and a "critical reflection about the relationship between science and society in the North"[74]—thus "big philosophy." A similar view is expressed by Julie Cruikshank, who quotes anthropologist Stuart Kirsch on the inadequacy of science alone for analyzing "problems that are hybrid in composition, combining persons, things, and ideas into a single set of relationships," agreeing with him that Indigenous modes of analysis offer a hopeful alternative.[75]

Desbiens suggests that a new collective sense of place might be produced through a "transition to diversity as a mode of thought"[76] and a nation-to-nation "dialogic re-writing of the landscape and thus a poetics of creolized space."[77] I wonder whether the ideas of "dialogic re-writing" and "creolized space" would be well received by many Indigenous northerners, as they are so often trying to protect their cultures against a continuous onslaught from outside. However, Innu poet Natasha Kanapé Fontaine has also expressed her desire for "un Québec d'échange, un Québec de partage des valeurs . . . un Québec métis" (a Quebec of exchange, a Quebec of shared values, a creolized Québec).[78] Desbiens rightly notes that there have been métissage and cultural hybridity in the North for a very long time but that in many conversations, "Western culture is uncritically identified as the centre of knowledge."[79] A focus on Indigenous modes of analysis, as Kirsch proposes, seems to offer a way of ensuring Western culture is not at the centre of the conversation. Dialogue really is all we have, and some kind of shared poetics centring Indigenous modes could play a role in the long, hard conversations and analyses that still need to take place. Such a poetics could be developed through the arts, at least in part; the arts can also facilitate dialogue in ways that science, law, or politics cannot.

Cynthia Hammond, who has also written about the renaming of the landscape of Caniapiscau, suggests that "art-making is not only a form of knowledge and inquiry, it can also be a powerful means to mobilize communities around shared pasts and collective heritage."[80] Her early project, "The Gathering of Earth—101 Mountains, 1998," is reminiscent in some ways of Marlene Creates's work from the same time period. In response to the controversy around Le jardin au bout du monde and what she called "cartological recolonization,"[81] Hammond asked 101 people to bring her small amounts of earth from places they felt they belonged to or descriptions of those places. She wanted the collection to be a "metaphorical support for the Cree . . . in their struggle to retain their names for the mountains."[82] The arts also have the potential to mobilize people across communities and to bridge cultural, linguistic, historic, and geographic divides. They can enable listening, looking, and translation across all these kinds of difference in ways that might perhaps be both more open-hearted and open-ended than many other approaches.

I will discuss aesthetic and visual approaches in more detail in Chapter 4, but I want to end this chapter with one more illustration of how places and the ways they are documented and inhabited can be understood differently through the arts. Paolo Pietropaolo is an audio documentary producer, writer, and composer. His piece *Ode to the Salish Sea* presents voices and perspectives in ways that, while diverse and suggesting a "creolized space," highlight Indigenous perspectives. I cannot help thinking that if the Caniapiscau geopoetics project had been based on a dialogue around such works or even around the kinds of conversations that took place in the less overtly artistic *Pepamuteiati Nitassinat* place names project (a project that was nevertheless based on stories, listening, and the embodied experience of Indigenous elders), it might have ended very differently and more in line with the philosophy of the geopoetics movement.

When Pietropaolo created his piece in 2009, the Salish Sea was a proposed name for a large area of water off the south coast of British Columbia, including what were and still are known as Puget Sound, the Juan de Fuca Strait, and the Strait of Georgia. The name "Salish" honours the original inhabitants of the area, the Coast Salish nations, and is now official in both the United States and Canada. Composed of field recordings of voices and sounds of the region, the piece opens with George Harris of the Stz'uminus First Nation speaking about the name in Hul'qumi'num. Although the documentary is presented without comment from its creator, this sets up a politics of support for the new name, both by placing Harris first and by the powerful statement made by opening with a full minute of untranslated Hul'qumi'num. The rest of the *Ode* moves back and forth between Harris, monarchist Keith Roy, who opposes the name, and geographer and environmental activist Briony Penn, who supports it. The voices of the speakers are underscored by a rich soundscape of water, waves, boats, and local wildlife, along with a faint and haunting rendition of "God Save the King," reminding listeners that the Strait of Georgia, like the Mushuau-shipu/George River in Innusi, was renamed in honour of King George III.

Pietropaolo says that his intention was to create "a lyrical tribute to the unique beauty of this coastal region by capturing and recomposing the sounds and languages of the Salish Sea. [He] also wanted to explore the complexity of the relationship between the indigenous and non-indigenous cultures that call the Salish Sea home."[83]

The three speakers are superimposed over this soundscape, with the name "the Salish Sea" and certain other words and refrains repeated throughout the piece. I'm left with the soundscape echoing in my mind and the words of all three speakers:

> *"We've already named the body of water—let's stick with what we have."*
> —KEITH ROY

> *"That's the part that burdens my heart because we've lost so much.* I only have stories left to tell our children now. What we're proposing now is the idea that we have another layer and that layer be the Salish Sea . . . it completes our history."
> —GEORGE HARRIS

> *"This creek's named after my grandfather by my great-grandmother.* They lived on a village site called Wananich, so I call it Monteith Creek/Wananich. I still sit here and go, 'How *could* we have been so arrogant?'"
>
> —BRIONY PENN

There is so much more that could be said about the arts and the kind of dialogue that might contribute to decolonization. Some of this is addressed in subsequent chapters, especially with respect to public art, film, and literary work. The examples I have given here—the maps of Christi Belcourt and of the people who produced them for Marlene Creates, the stories and earth people brought to Cynthia Hammond, Scott Barham's map of Ellesmere Island and "environs," the *Pepamuteiati Nitassinat* place names website, and the audio cartographies of Paolo Pietropaolo and the people he spoke to—are just a few thoughts about the kinds of projects that could help us collectively reconnect to the land we live on and acknowledge its histories in ways that recognize their complexity. Such projects, through reaching for a more fitting geopoetics, can provoke thought, they can inspire, they can help us find fairer and more honest ways of living on this land.

Two

Walking

In the cold clear air of Uinashku-pishim[u], the month of the marmot, Tshaukuesh stands on the hard-packed snow outside her house pegging clothes out to dry in the sun. She is thinking about her ancestors, how at this time of year, early spring, they would have been heading out on the trail on snowshoes, pulling their belongings behind them on toboggans. She does not need a great leap of imagination, since she herself as a child lived that way; she just has to bring to mind the hard but beautiful life she knew then. Since their relocation to Sheshatshiu and Utshimassit in the 1960s, the Innu have been going to traditional hunting and camping areas by plane or helicopter, or by skidoo, but she wants to go the way her ancestors always went, on foot. She pegs up the last shirt and goes back inside. She makes a pot of tea, sits down at the big kitchen table with its colourful plastic tablecloth, and opens her tattered scribbler to write a diary entry:

> March 18, [1998]: . . . It's a lovely sunny day with a nice breeze. I went outside to get firewood and hang clothes on the line. While I was doing that, enjoying the good weather, a wonderful idea came to me. We could go to nutshimit this spring on foot instead of by helicopter or bush plane! That's how our people used to travel when they went to nutshimit. It would be so wonderful if we could do it and find people to help us. I want to ask my husband what he thinks about it when he comes home from work.[1]

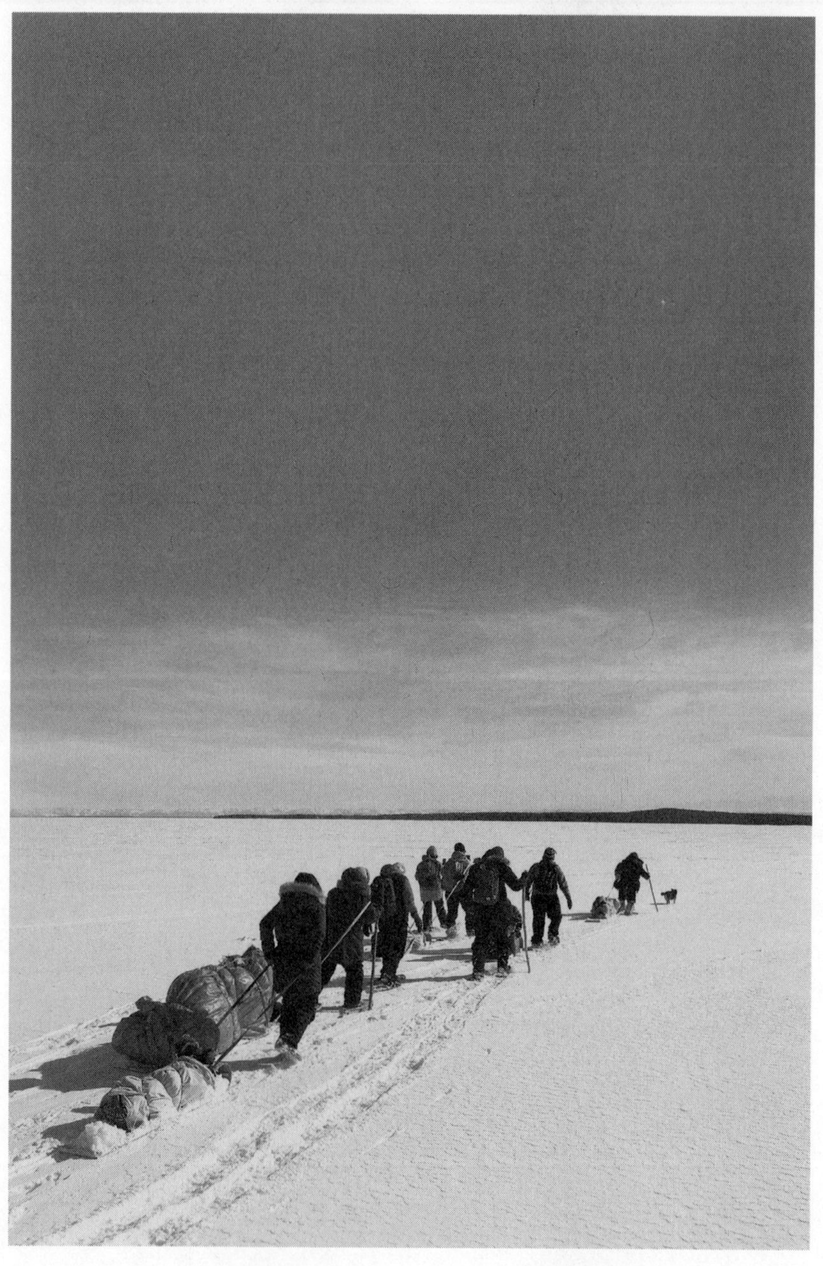

Tshaukuesh and companions on the walk to Enipeshakimau. Photo by Ryan Wood (Instagram: @ryanwoodphoto).

Tshaukuesh did not waste any time but set out with others within a week or two. She did not write about that first walk in her diary, except to note sadly that her companions decided to turn back and she could not go on alone. The second year, they almost made it to their destination at Minai-nipi but had many challenges. Sometimes they lost the trail and had to take time to find it again, and then bad weather led to them running out of food and Francis being unable to get through with supplies. Nevertheless, Tshaukuesh felt optimistic, and when she got home she wrote:

> The helicopter finally came and got us. While we were in the air I looked out the window to see where we had walked. I felt very proud we'd come so far—we almost made it this time. But I also cried because I wished that I was still walking down there, surrounded by lakes and rivers, trees, mountains, the animals. So beautiful.
>
> . . . We were hunters. I have so many memories of those years and I've wanted to walk again for so long, but there were too many challenges. Now I'm so glad I didn't give up on the idea.[2]

In a letter thanking her fellow walkers from Uashat and Mani-utenam for their support, she reflected: "This is my second walk, and now I know what we need to do to succeed next time. We need a guide, a leader to show us the best meshkanau. I don't know how to use a map, but once I've walked the route two or three times, especially if somebody can show me the way, then I'll know. I'm so happy that I know what to do next year now, so glad we didn't give up. One more trip and I'll never get lost again. Thank you."[3]

When they finally reached their destination the third year they walked, Tshaukuesh wrote jubilantly: "We made it to Minai-nipi! We made it, we made it! No skidoos, just walking on our own feet. I'm so glad we persevered—we never gave up, even when we were exhausted we kept on walking. I'll miss the walk."[4]

"You Can Feel the Earth with Your Whole Body"

Although Tshaukuesh doesn't use a map and says she doesn't know how to, she often writes about the Innu names of places as well as names she herself gives to sites that are significant to her and her family, and describes how she and her companions sometimes stop and write their names on boulders and cliffs or carve them into trees or on signs they leave behind. If, as Michael Kusugak argues, naming is a form of mapping, Tshaukuesh has mapped the land in loving detail by walking, naming, and marking it.[5] Walking itself is also a lived cartography in which one learns the land intimately, with all its contours, hazards, and affordances, by tracing routes across it.

Going to nutshimit on foot was a statement: it told the world that the Innu were strong, that their traditional ways were good and had not been lost, and most importantly, that the land was theirs. As Tshaukuesh put it, "When I walk in nutshimit with my people, I'm showing how much we respect Innu culture, the natural world, and all living things. I want people to know we won't give up our land. We won't allow the government to damage it with mines and dams and bombs."[6] Not only did the walkers communicate through their bodies by walking, however—their bodies also spoke to them as they walked across the land. And so did the land itself. Tshaukuesh's jubilation had many reasons behind it, but one that she talks about often is how much healthier and happier people are in nutshimit than in the sedentary villages. Innu surgeon Dr. Stanley Vollant agrees. Speaking to his fellow walkers on the Innu meshkanau he began in 2009, walking from one First Nations community to the next, day after day, he said, "I'm speaking as a physician. Right now we're feeling really good because of the endorphins we've generated. This sense of well-being can last for three or four weeks, but then you can fall into a deep depression."[7] He told them that when they got home, as soon as their blisters had healed, they had to keep on walking.

Tshaukuesh began walking partly to reclaim the sheer pleasure of moving across the land at a human pace. She writes regularly, almost like an invocation, of this pleasure. On the second year of the walk, even though they were often lost and hungry, she exulted: "Since we've been walking everything has gone well. No problems. We feel more confident each day: we're getting stronger and stronger. I've been wanting to do this for so long, and now it's all going well. I've seen so many beautiful things here in nutshimit.... Innut kapimutet! Innu walked here!"[8]

There is more to it than endorphins, though, much more. When the Nishiyuu walkers reached their destination at Parliament Hill in 2013 at the end of their 1,600-kilometre walk from Whapmagoostui First Nation in northern Quebec in support of Attawapiskat Chief Theresa Spence's hunger strike for Indigenous rights, one of the young walkers spoke on CBC Radio about his experiences. Asked what was the hardest part of the walk, he said simply, "When it ended." It reminded me of a Spanish man, Felipe, whom I met while making the same documentary on walking that introduced me to Tshaukuesh. He had wept when he reached the end of the ancient pilgrims' trail, the Camino de Santiago, in northern Spain. I asked his friend why he was so distraught and the friend responded, "Porque se acabó el camino." Because the camino has ended. Both the young Cree activist and the Spanish pilgrim should still have been high on endorphins on arrival, but instead they were sorrowful as they contemplated the loss of a single goal on which to focus all their energies, the end of moving steadily through challenging but often beautiful landscapes, and the return to the disjointed struggles of daily life.

The physical act of walking itself has been shown to make people happier, healthier, more creative, and more focused. Moving at what is literally a human pace enables us to see the world and appreciate it as we cannot when moving faster. Much has also been written recently about how walking among trees is especially life giving, and the Japanese concept of shinrin-yoku, or forest bathing, is becoming increasingly popular. Some research shows that people have lower levels of stress hormones after walking in the forest than after walking in urban or clinical settings. It can improve mood and ability to concentrate and sleep, reduce blood pressure and stress, and boost immune system functioning and energy levels.[9]

A Japanese study found that walking in the forest was especially helpful in reducing "depression-dejection" for people with high anxiety. British research has also indicated benefits from being outdoors, among trees, and in contact with nature, especially for people with vulnerable mental health.[10] The authors of the Japanese study suggest that "changes that have occurred over a very short period have been very drastic from an evolutionary perspective," with urban living associated with increased health risks, especially for mental health. They recommend that both health policy and urban planning consider the value of urban forests in increasing quality of life.[11] Yet another study, also from Japan, concludes that breathing in phytoncides, which are volatile antimicrobial substances released from trees, contributed to decreased production of stress hormones and might even have a preventive effect on cancer generation and development.[12] We are all connected to each other in the living world in so many ways that we are only beginning to understand.

Shinrin-yoku proponents emphasize spending time "under the green canopy" of a living forest, but Tshaukuesh believes that it is not only the canopy that matters but also what is under your feet.[13] When asked by a reporter in Amsterdam what she thought of life there, she responded, "It's so built up you can't see the trees and the land. You can't feel the earth under your feet, only pavement."[14] On a train trip to Uashat, she elaborates,

> I'd really prefer to walk so my feet could feel the earth, the marsh, the caribou moss. It doesn't feel the same in a vehicle; you go past things so fast, you can't touch them and you miss all the nice places. When Francis and I walk along the road, he walks on the pavement but I never do. When you walk in the woods you can see where to set your feet, and I love the physical feeling of putting my foot in just the right place. And you can decide for yourself where you want to stop and rest. Sometimes I don't just sit down, I lie right down on the ground. When you do that you can feel the earth with your whole body and you can think more clearly. I look up at the sky and sometimes I pray, surrounded by the animals who protect us. When I was born my parents laid me on the ground in the tent; no bed, just right on the ground.[15]

Research studies investigating planned environments, phytoncides, endorphins, blood pressure, and stress hormones offer one way of understanding how all living beings are connected.[16] Tshaukuesh explains it differently, adding connections to the animal spirits and to the earth itself. Speaking for anthropologists but perhaps by extension for all who spend little time on the land moving at a human pace or who focus solely on human interactions, Anna Tsing, Andrew Mathews, and Nils Bubandt add that "we have lost the habit of noticing through our own observations of the world in addition to conversations with human interlocutors. The Anthropocene is a wake-up call urging us to reinvent observational, analytical attention to intertwined human-and-nonhuman histories."[17] Travelling at human speed, feeling the ground beneath us and the growing things around us enables a kind of noticing and an awareness of connections we would otherwise miss.

Walking, Reading, Writing, Thinking

Walking is like reading in that it opens us to take in what the earth has to tell us, and it does so in a way that faster means of travel do not. The bodily engagement that Tshaukuesh describes is important, too: setting our feet on the ground, lying on the ground. And although this chapter is about walking, I am always aware that not everybody can walk, that someday I may not be able to walk, and so I think the broader idea of physical contact of any kind with the ground is important in that way too, that it can be accessible to almost anybody.[18]

Walking is also like reading in another way: people who live by hunting and gathering must read the terrain they walk over closely and constantly, as their survival depends on doing so. This means acquiring over a lifetime a literacy of the landscape[19] in which they live, of its plants, animals, weather patterns, routes, waterways, night skies, and so on. Tshaukuesh would often tell stories about places we visited or point things out to me that I had not noticed—chew marks on trees showing that a porcupine had been around, or a kind of moss that was good for insulation. To me it was just moss, and I had not noticed its details enough to recognize it as a specific kind of moss. Strangely, I know the names of many kinds of wildflowers, berries, and seaweeds but not of mosses or lichens, and the fact I do not know their names means I notice them less. Knowing the names is part of the habit of noticing and also part of the literacy of the land.

Walking is like writing too, again in two different ways. First, writing is a process that enables thinking. One of my professors used to say, "I'll have to write about that to see what I think." Walking can also enable us to discover what we think. I've known for many years that I often have new ideas and sort through problems while walking, and this is supported by research. One series of studies found that people thought more creatively and were better at problem solving both during and after walking than when sitting.[20] Another suggests that the ability to stand and walk, along with "rhythmic, purposeful movement" more generally, is intrinsically related to cognition and that they evolved interdependently.[21]

But walking itself can also be a way of saying something. As Tshaukuesh describes in her diary, the walks that she led were a statement to governments, the military, and developers that the land belonged to the Innu and that they were using it. The lines they traced across it were a powerful affirmation written with their bodies on a living place, a place where *they* lived. Tshaukuesh's son Peter also wrote about the statement they made when they walked openly instead of hiding, asserting that they had the right to hunt on their own land: "We kept walking with our guns, leading the RCMP on a chase. We were afraid, we'd never done anything like that before, actually provoking arrest. In the past we would have hidden, but not anymore, we're through hiding. It's time our rights are recognized on this land. So, when those Mounties finally caught up with us, you know, I felt they looked at us with some respect because they could see we were doing what we thought was right, and they could see we weren't afraid of them anymore."[22]

Caroline Desbiens suggests that the geopoetic Jardin au bout du monde, discussed in Chapter 1, is an extension of the writing on the land of the North that gained traction with hydroelectric development in James Bay from the 1970s onwards. It is a kind of cultural writing on the land, a text that will make francophone Québécois from the South "masters in their own house."[23] It is just one example. Every act of renaming or re-mapping, along with resource extraction, militarization, and industrial development does this. Meanwhile, Indigenous people like Tshaukuesh and Peter Penashue and their companions have written their culture onto the land for millennia, both through naming places cartographically and from their intimate knowledge of them and through walking. They continue to do so.

Walking to Change the World

When the Labrador Innu challenged NATO in the late 1980s that it did not have the right to use their land to test missiles and train fighter pilots, a NATO spokesperson responded that the land was uninhabited. The Innu stated that it was not, that they were living on it seasonally, that it was where they hunted and where their ancestors had always lived and travelled. NATO modified its statement to "there are no permanent dwellings on the land,"[24] a meaningless statement for a nomadic people yet extremely meaningful in practice, as it was used to justify the disruption of peaceful Innu life by the roar of supersonic fighter jets and the destruction of land where trees and ground were scorched, the mangled remains from weapons tests and fuel tanks left behind. After a helicopter pilot refused to take them to the bombing range, Tshaukuesh and other protesters walked in and set up camp, making their own embodied refutal of NATO's position.

Perhaps this was when Tshaukuesh first realized that the act of walking where her Innu ancestors had walked for millennia was, among other things, a powerful statement that the land was theirs. A few years later, after beginning her own annual walk in nutshimit, she wrote to fellow walkers from Mani-utenam: "This was a demonstration of our determination to protect our land and our culture for our children and future generations. This is Innu land. We showed the government and the people how much it means to us—Nitassinan, our homeland. When the elders are gone, our children and grandchildren will use it. The women were an example for others when we led the protests, and our walk will also inspire people. Sometimes people talk about what should be done, but they don't do it. We didn't just talk about it; we did it."[25]

That statement was made visible year after year, not only by the actual act of walking (though that was fundamental) but by marks Tshaukuesh and her companions left on the land they walked through, such as carved signs of Innu place names and painted names and dates on boulders. Their walking was also documented in media reports, documentary films, and testimonials of others who accompanied or visited them on the land, and iconic images by photographers and artists of the walkers, especially of Tshaukuesh herself. The image of her figure walking on snowshoes and pulling a toboggan in nutshimit is recognized by everyone in Innusi and has clearly inspired others such as Michel Andrew, who led a walk of young Innu north to Natuashish, then to the North Shore communities and to Schefferville/Kawawachikamach (about 3,400 kilometres return) after having walked with Tshaukuesh, and Stanley Vollant, the Innu surgeon who invited people to walk with him from Blanc-Sablon to Natashkuan. As more and more walks on traditional Indigenous territories take place, the significance of these models is obvious. Dr. Vollant stated, “If I can inspire one or two young people in each of the communities I visit over the next five years, I would say that would be mission accomplished.”[26]

The idea expressed so succinctly by the NATO spokesman—that permanent dwellings are crucial to establish ownership and to prove that the land matters—was and is key to colonization. The argument has been used over and over by church and government. Tshaukuesh described the process:

> When I was young, I thought the priests worked with God. I didn’t understand that, in fact, they worked with the government. They were always writing letters back and forth, and bit by bit they changed our way of life. Nobody realized it at the time. I remember the priest coming to our tent. My mother tidied everything up before he came and he said to her, “It’s very nice here. Your daughters must help you a lot.” Then he said to my father, “Why don’t you go hunting in nutshimit with the men but leave your family here so the children can go to school?” The government and the priests wanted us to stay in one place. They didn’t want us to go to nutshimit. After the priest left, I heard my parents arguing about it. My father wanted us all to go to nutshimit, but my mother thought we should respect the priest and do what he said.[27]

José Mailhot describes this process in more detail in *The People of Sheshatshit*, describing how the Innu were given the "incentives" (her quotation marks) of housing, school, medical care, and transfer payments but soon realized that there were also many disadvantages, including poverty-level incomes, problems with the law, and the erosion of their language and culture. She describes how many tried to revive their traditional way of life, going to live in nutshimit for at least part of the year, but notes that these people are no longer nomads in the traditional sense, despite maintaining their territorial system and individual mobility.[28] Michelle Lelièvre has analyzed the process in detail in relation to the Nova Scotia Mi'kmaq, showing how both church and Crown tried unsuccessfully to sedentize them.[29] She argues that to this day, common law and provincial and federal policy, as well as settlers in general, are biased toward sedentism, making moral judgements about Mi'kmaw ways of life and denying them title because of their mobility, yet oblivious to their own non-sedentism. However, as Lelièvre shows, the Mi'kmaq moved and continue to move for economic, spiritual, social, and political purposes, and these movements are central to their sovereignty.[30] Similarly, the Innu, while no longer traditional nomads, still move freely within their territories as well as far beyond.

Many Indigenous groups and individuals have used long-distance walks to protest unwanted development or exploration for oil, gas, and minerals; to assert their rights; to prepare for land claims and other legal processes; and to reactivate traditional cultural practices and knowledge. Lelièvre argues that walks such as the 2013 Nishiyuu Journey and the 2016 to 2019 Mi'kma'ki Water Walks show how borders created by colonizing governments are "historically contingent" and fragile, and also provide an opening for changing the sedentist ideology of these governments to one of movement and dynamism.[31] Research focusing on Indigenous sovereignty and First Nation–to–First Nation collaborations, and on the movement of peoples globally, rather than on territorial boundaries and concepts of ownership, might help us find a way beyond the Indigenous/settler dichotomy, which clearly is not always a simple one, and the very idea of a settler state.[32]

Hugh Brody's book *Maps and Dreams* (1982) highlights the extent to which Indigenous peoples have acquired their intimate knowledge of the land through walking. In her discussion of the book, Sophie McCall comments that if lines were drawn for all of the trajectories people have made across the land, the maps would be completely black.[33] In *Nitinikiau Innusi*, as we have seen, Tshaukuesh articulates the significance of the walking itself in relation to these other processes.

Some Indigenous projects are based not on walking as such but on knowledge and stories that are enabled by walking. One example is the Mapping Project,[34] coordinated by Phoebe Nahanni and other Dene in the 1970s to gather evidence for land claims and to try to stop construction of the MacKenzie Valley pipeline. The researchers (all of whom spoke fluent Dene) spent two years travelling to people's traplines and traversing hunting, fishing, and gathering areas with them. During the process, they interviewed them, collected stories, and made maps. The researchers later returned to verify the maps, thus ensuring a collaborative process from start to finish. Nahanni's work is an early example of a methodology that Brody called "map biographies,"[35] in which participants produce detailed maps of all the different ways they have used the land over the course of their lifetimes. McCall writes that "for participants in the mapping project, the politics of 'voice' and of 'land' were mutually constitutive and interdependent."[36] These maps and associated stories document approximately a century from the 1880s to the 1980s and are currently being updated and digitized for community-based environmental research and decision making.[37] As I noted above, the years of walking the land and the return to the land to prepare the maps were also constitutive of the knowledge that was organized and presented in the project. This was true also of the Innu mapping and naming project described in Chapter 1, in which Innu elders worked with outside researchers to map, document, and digitize place names and stories relating to them.[38] The elders' deep knowledge of places, names, and stories came from lifetimes of walking on the land they were mapping.

Notwithstanding Lelièvre's convincing argument that colonization has not succeeded in sedentizing the Mi'kmaq (or, by extension, other Indigenous groups), elders frequently express their dismay that younger people are losing their connections to the land.[39] Yet long-distance walking is being revived, often by young people, as a means not only of protest but also of reconnection to the land and to each other. Since the Innu walks from Windsor to Ottawa in 1990 to draw attention to the NATO occupation and from Mani-utenam to Montreal in 1993 to protest hydroelectric developments, there have been many shorter walks to demonstrate opposition to dams, logging, mining, and low-level flying, as well as to promote health, healing, and cultural strength. Many other Indigenous peoples have used walking as a way of speaking out about injustice. In 2008, after being imprisoned for peacefully protesting mining explorations on their land, six members of Kitchenuhmaykoosib Inninuwug walked from their community about 600 kilometres north of Thunder Bay to Ottawa to raise awareness of their long battle to stop Platinex from drilling for platinum on their land. In 2009, the Ontario government and Platinex reached an agreement in which Platinex would relinquish its mining claims in Kitchenuhmaykoosib Inninuwug territory in return for financial compensation.[40]

Just a year earlier, a group of Mi'kmaw women in Nova Scotia had begun walking in support of the sacred water walks of Ojibway elder Josephine Mandamin, who walked around all of the Great Lakes and along many other waterways to raise awareness of the need to protect water. The women walked along the Sipekne'katik (Shubenacadie) River to pray for the protection of the water and protest Alton Gas's project of flushing salt from naturally existing salt caverns into the river so it could use the caverns to store natural gas. The Water Walkers believed that doing so could destroy the watershed and, along with it, "all life that depends on the river to live." In 2019, the walk was extended to follow the coast of the Bay of Fundy into New Brunswick and Maine.[41] Meanwhile, the walkers also took direct action by building a treaty truck house[42] by the river to monitor the project, and embarking on court proceedings to ensure that their treaty and constitutional rights to consultation were upheld. In 2020, the Nova Scotia Supreme Court concluded that there had not been adequate consultations with Sipekne'katik First Nation and ordered the province to resume consultations with them.[43] In October 2021 AltaGas, the group of companies responsible for the Alton project, decided to decommission it, noting "mixed support, challenges and experienced delay."[44] The Water Walkers and their allies had saved the river.

I have also mentioned other walks earlier in this chapter. These include the Nishiyuu Journey, in which a group of young Cree and their guide were joined by hundreds more mostly First Nations young people who accompanied them on the walk from Whapmagoostui in northern Quebec to Ottawa to raise awareness of treaty rights, and the Innu walks of Michel Andrew and Dr. Stanley Vollant, both focusing on finding healthier ways of life through long-distance walking in Innusi. Lelièvre outlines motivations and discourses around these walks and others. They are about raising awareness of social and environmental crises; protesting government refusals to enforce laws, policies, and treaties; meeting with government representatives; deepening spirituality; and building solidarity and connecting with other Indigenous peoples. As Lelièvre puts it, the walks "reconfigure political alliances in settler colonies."[45]

Walking With

Juanita Sundberg proposes a strategy of "walking with," developed by the Zapatistas as they invited others to walk with them, as a way of contributing to the reconfiguration of alliances described by Lelièvre and decolonizing research. Sundberg highlights the importance of taking steps, both figurative—"moving, engaging, reflecting"—and literal. She emphasizes that decolonization is "something to be aspired to and enacted rather than a state of being that may be claimed,"[46] and that walking and talking together can enable a "dialogic politics" as we move toward social change. She builds on the Zapatistas' original invitation by suggesting three steps: first, following Gayatri Spivak, examining one's own epistemological and ontological assumptions; second, learning as a reciprocal engagement with the other, which, she explains, is distinct from learning *about* the other in that it is not possessive or dominating but humble and respectful; third, walking with as a form of mutual solidarity that will be different for each individual or group, depending on their circumstances. It may include learning from Indigenous knowledge systems, research, and theory, or developing methodologies for working against neoliberalism and toward justice. It also may take the form of working with Indigenous groups as allies toward shared goals, through research or activism. Sundberg points out, however, that walking with may mean postponing or abandoning one's own research goals if they diverge from community needs and interests.[47] It may also mean "putting our bodies on the line" if invited to do so. Camille Fouillard, an Akaneshau friend who has worked for many years with the Innu, added that "the meshkanu was also about my own relationship with the land, reconnecting, re-evaluating, relating differently, understanding differently, not only from what I was learning about the Innu but from a settler/colonizer and white/anthropocene perspective. I was constantly imagining walking with those that came before, and thus reimagining a whole world . . . all the while recognizing all the modern amenities of our particular meshkanu."[48]

Stephanie Springgay and Sarah E. Truman, guest editors of a special issue of the *Journal of Public Pedagogies* on walking,[49] note that walking is

> a research methodology that is attentive to place, situated knowledges, sensory experiences and movement . . . that is community-based, and that is attuned to more-than-human entanglements and encounters . . . In an era of complex social and political issues—such as climate change, capitalism, and forced migration, to name a few—there is an increasing demand for public and community action. Further, academics continue to grapple with ways to present research findings to non-academic audiences, while marginalized and oppressed people take up ways to transform and decolonize social and political space and institutions. To this end, walking has become more than a utilitarian or pedestrian mode of getting from place to place; walking is an ethical and political call to collective action.[50]

Critical walking methodologies are also anti-ableist, anti-racist, and anti-colonial.[51] They pay attention to connections with landscape and story. Drawing on Michel de Certeau's insight that places are made through everyday practices such as walking, Katrín Lund suggests that "the paths and routes that the wandering feet follow shape stories as they direct the walks, and are simultaneously shaped during the course of the walk."[52] Mary

Elizabeth Luka adds that in terms of methodology, structured group walks that include other activities such as singing, storytelling, image sharing, and ceremony can build community, enable us to revisit the past, and "imagine and mobilize" new cultures.[53]

First Story Toronto walking tours and a series of walks that retrace Indigenous songlines along the Nepean River in Australia are two projects that revisit the past to mobilize new cultures. First Story Toronto is an Indigenous-led organization that documents and shares stories and knowledge about Indigenous presence in Toronto. The walking tours follow old miikaans[54] that show historic, present, and future Indigenous relationships with the landscape. Karyn Recollet and Jon Johnson are researchers and guides with First Story. As they describe the work, the walks are "recuperative," and Indigenous pathways are understood as ephemeral glyphs inscribing "knowledge of territory into the land over millennia. In this sense, miikaans are like the petroglyphs inscribed in rock at sacred sites across Turtle Island."[55] Johnson notes that while there have been many studies of Indigenous knowledge in nutshimit, there has been much less research on such knowledge in urban settings.[56] Thus, their research and land-based stories contribute to an understanding of the large city of Toronto as a traditional Indigenous territory and reaffirm connections to Indigenous places in the city. The walking tours enable participants and guides to have conversations about Indigenous histories, knowledge, and landscapes. In the second example of mobilizing new culture for the future by revisiting the past, Australian researcher Margaret Somerville joins Darug artist and singer-songwriter Leanne Tobin and Darug language teacher, musician, and singer-songwriter Jacinta Tobin in an exploration of contemporary Darug songlines along the Hawkesbury Nepean riverlands. The walk is complemented by a public performance of art and spoken word at the Circular Quay International Passenger Terminal in Sydney, where colonization began and where many immigrants still arrive. Leanne Tobin and Jacinta Tobin are sisters who have deep family connections to the area, connections that had been almost lost but which they recreate through art, language, and music. The walk is a meditation on "the presences and absences of these river places,"[57] and the public pedagogy performance presents song, art, and spoken word about these histories.[58]

In another approach to critical walking methodologies and walking with, Maggie O'Neill and Brian Roberts suggest using walking as a biographical interview method to investigate participants' life experience as they move around areas that are significant to them.[59] O'Neill and Ismail Einashe provide an example in which they apply this method to the lives of migrants in Europe. Einashe is a journalist and a former migrant, and thus their partnership produces both critical public pedagogy and critical journalism. They argue that combining walking (which they see as an arts-based method in this context) with biographical methods and photography can help us understand connections between peoples' movements and their survival.[60]

The value of walking as a way of learning is demonstrated by the Tłı̨chǫ Dene. Anthropologist Allice Legat recounts how the Tłı̨chǫ are encouraged to walk the land as a way of coming to know it intimately and growing intellectually.[61] In one example, elders and harvesters were concerned that an environmental monitoring program was making recommendations based solely on data collected through airplane-based surveys and satellite tracking of animals. They believed this approach was limited and pointed out that some things could be observed only by walking. They were worried about a fine yellow powder they had noticed on plants, which could not be seen by plane or satellite and which they thought might have a connection to mining. They agreed to participate in the environmental monitoring process and developed a program based on walking and learning to which three generations could contribute. Elders would share their knowledge, young people would take photos and make notes, and the middle generation would prepare reports. As Legat explains, through walking, observing, and storytelling, the Tłı̨chǫ learn how to be flexible in a world in flux. They come to know how to think about new and unexpected situations and to pay attention to all beings on their land, animate and inanimate, as well as to stories of past, present, and future.[62]

All of these ways of walking with bring me back to walking with Tshaukuesh. When I joined her on the walk, I worried about burdening the group with my ignorance of how to live on the land and my lack of language skills. I am not alone in that worry. Hugh Brody expressed it in 1975, when he referred to "the awkwardness I so often felt in being an intruder."[63] Brody went back to England, but I am from Mi'kma'ki. I have nowhere else to go. More recently, Cynthia Chambers wrote, quoting Andy Blackwater, a Kainai elder: "The Blackfoot are not going anywhere; the newcomers are not going anywhere; now the same peg anchors the tipis of both." She continues: "It is not the grudge but the grief that matters, and what we are going to do about it. It is where we are that matters. By learning to do what is appropriate in this place, and doing it together, perhaps we can find the common ground necessary to survive."[64]

Tshaukuesh's hospitality was such that I never felt like an intruder in Innusi. But even after all these years living on the island of Newfoundland, I still feel that I belong to Siknikt in Mi'kma'ki, to the land of red mud rivers and tidal wetlands where I was born and grew up. One of the protesters at the treaty truck house on the Sipekne'katik River in Mi'kma'ki, a young man named Felix, spoke about what allies could do about the grief Chambers referred to, and the common ground: "Get involved with an action like this in your area; get informed about things that are going on; go to information sessions; maybe cause a little bit of havoc in a company; donate supplies to these camps; just go visit the people—it breaks up your day, makes things go by faster; keep those connections." Another protester, Kukuwes, commented, "The allies have been awesome here . . . we all work together building that trust and that love. It's amazing what we can do when we work together." And Felix concluded, "It's our job to make sure the earth stays green, to protect the sacred, protect the water."[65]

Akaneshau actor Elliot Page, who is originally from Nova Scotia, made a documentary film profiling Black and Indigenous women who are leaders in working to end environmental racism in the province. One of them, Michelle Paul, was also from Sipekne'katik First Nation. Like Tshaukuesh, and like Kukuwes and Felix, she emphasized connection, walking with. Speaking to Page in the film, she says: "Everybody who's living now, we have to be able to tell our grandchildren and those that are unborn, we did everything in our power to make a difference, to stop the destruction. We're just regular people . . . How we are connected to you is that you were born here, you're from here too. You have that connection to the land. When your feet touch on other territory, you're still from here, your spirit is from Mi'kma'ki."[66]

Three

Stories

It's an incredible honour to represent Tshaukuesh Elizabeth Penashue for NL Reads. *I Keep the Land Alive* is such a profound memoir . . . It's a book that alters perceptions in three ways:

1. It profoundly alters your perception of land . . .

2. There's a power shift that occurs with the use of Innu-aimun . . . It gives you a small measure of what the Innu faced in speaking truth to power when that power was not speaking their language.

3. This book also shifts what constitutes a memoir. This is an important and valuable contribution to an emerging form of writing, an anti-colonial, mid-reconciliation kind of writing . . .

I Keep the Land Alive is part of an incredibly rich wave of Indigenous writing that is altering our perception of genres and of Canadian writing. We are so privileged to have this insight into the Innu story and into the incredible life, determination and passion of Tshaukuesh. It is essential reading.[1]

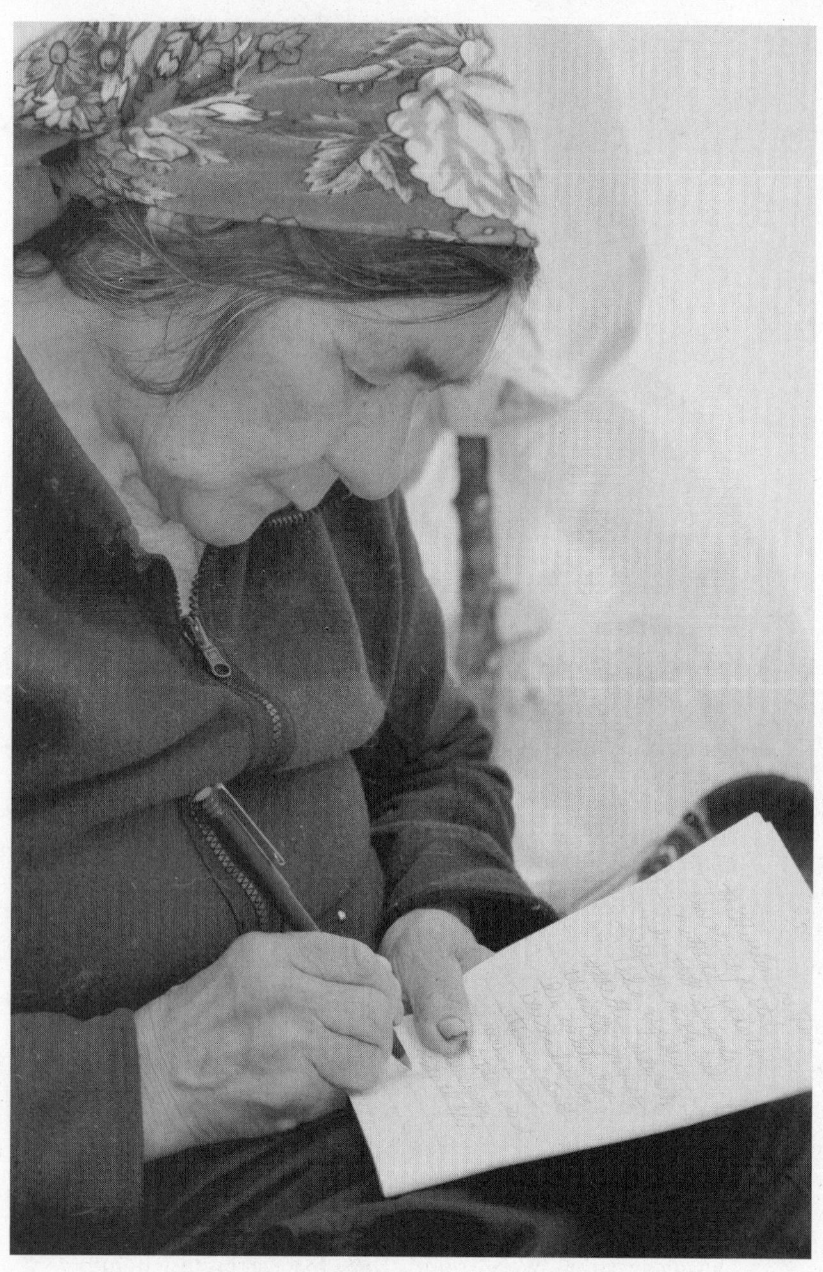

Tshaukuesh writing in her tent. Photo by Camille Fouillard.

This was the opening of Akaneshau writer and producer Angela Antle's defence of Tshaukuesh's book in the 2020 NL Reads competition. The book won the in-house vote following the defenders' speeches[2] and was also shortlisted for the Mary Scorer Award for Best Book by a Manitoba Publisher and for the BMO Winterset Award, which is "awarded to an outstanding literary work in any writing genre" by a Newfoundlander, Labradorian or resident of the province. Antle's defence clearly outlined why Tshaukuesh's story and the extraordinary gifts, knowledge, and perseverance behind it had been honoured in this way. Her point that it is an important contribution to anti-colonial literature is reminiscent of Innu poet and critic Marie-Andrée Gill's praise for the 2019 reissue of Innu essayist An Antane Kapesh's *Eukuan nin matshi-manitu innushkueu: Je suis une maudite sauvagesse* (*I Am a Damn Savage*), originally published in 1976:[3] "For me, choosing to reinscribe An Antane Kapesh's words in the literary history of Québec is a decolonial act and even a revolutionary one in Québec literature."[4] The same could be said of the recognition of Tshaukuesh's words. These were decolonial acts.

Both books were also in themselves decolonial acts. Both were originally written in Innu-aimun, and both tell stories of resistance. Kapesh's book begins: "When the White man decided to exploit and destroy our land, he didn't ask anybody's permission, he didn't ask the Innu if they agreed";[5] and Tshaukuesh's: "When the RCMP came in their helicopters we sat on the caribou our hunters had brought back so they couldn't take it—women, children, and elders."[6] The editor of the 2019 edition of Kapesh's book, Naomi Fontaine, describes it as a history, "one that I had never heard. My own. [Kapesh taught me] that I had a past to which I could attach the flame that consumed me. This desire to stand up straight, far from the prejudices, far from the lies, far, so very far, from self-hatred."[7] Kapesh concluded the dedication of her book with the following: "And it would make me happy to see other Innu writing, in their own language."[8] She was the first Innu to publish a book. Her recounting of history is angry and with such good reason that the book's translator, José Mailhot, recalls weeping as she worked on the chapter about relationships with the police, concluding, "This is colonialism in its most vicious form."[9] This book from a half century ago is still painfully relevant as I write this in 2021, after brutal acts of racism have prompted calls to defund the police.

Tshaukuesh's writing, published much more recently than Kapesh's, is also a history, one that in some ways updates the earlier text. It transcends genres as it ranges from heartbreaking firsthand accounts of the devastating changes in Innu life in the past fifty years and Tshaukuesh's ongoing campaign to keep the land alive, to political satire, prayers, and lists of people, places, and items that read like found poetry.[10] While the book, like Kapesh's, recounts the misery and chaos created by government policies implemented by police, courts, and the military, it also tells the story of how the Innu confronted NATO and the Canadian and Newfoundland governments to take control of their own land and future.

Eukuan nin matshi-manitu innushkueu and *Nitinikiau Innusi* are stories of extraordinary courage and perseverance by Innu women who lived the histories they recount. Both women wrote with no writing community, no written literary tradition, and little support, in hard-earned spare moments, out of sheer determination to tell their stories. In an interview after the reissue of *Eukuan nin matshi-manitu innushkueu*, Fontaine pointed to another kind of decolonial act: offering workshops and creating community for writers. She added that "we have to make our literature!"[11] Similarly, Abenaki filmmaker Kim O'Bomsawin, director of a documentary about Innu poet Joséphine Bacon, *Je m'appelle humain* (*Call Me Human*; 2020) also spoke of the importance of building community: "In Quebec, we're not in the same position as in the rest of Canada, where you have lots of filmmakers from First Nations and lots of actors. . . . There's so much to do [to tell Indigenous stories on film], and so few people that can do it. My obsession is to look everywhere and find youth that could become directors, producers, or whatever they want to do. . . . We have a list of young talent, and we offer them mentorships and real jobs so that they can learn."[12]

While Tshaukuesh and An Antane Kapesh chose essays and documentary writing to tell their stories, two other Innu women writers from this first generation of published Innu authors, Rita Mestokosho and Joséphine Bacon, are poets. They too understand their writing as activism. Acadian-Québécoise-Maliseet literary scholar Michèle Lacombe has noted that Mestokosho sees poetry as "more useful than political speeches for defending environmental causes closely allied to Innu people's traditional homelands."[13] Mestokosho campaigned against hydroelectric dams on the Romaine River through both her poetry and the justice system.[14] She is also a councillor for her community, Ekuanitshit, with responsibilities for women's policy, language and culture, and community radio, among other areas. Bacon began writing poetry to preserve Innu culture and language. When she realized that words relating to traditional Innu life on the land were being forgotten as the way of life itself changed, she decided "to save those words and to make poetry with them to keep them alive."[15]

When Natasha Kanapé Fontaine accompanied Joséphine Bacon to Paris, where Bacon would be the guest of Haitian-Canadian author Dany Laferrière at the ceremony admitting him to the Académie française, she wrote: "The moral of this story, and for all of History, the Haitian has opened the door for the Innu woman into this institution of dominant society, this historic site of the French language . . . an Innu woman who brought with her the fabulous heritage of our language, Innu-aimun. . . . Who else could represent the close relation between language, culture and the land? Who else could bring to the fore the importance of languages and cultures but this woman alone, Indigenous elder, native daughter of the territory of the Americas, totally open to the world?"[16]

Kanapé Fontaine describes a conversation with Bacon in which Bacon talks about her experiences at residential school in Mani-utenam, a school "less difficult than many others,"[17] but still she was required to be there, taught to read and write in French instead of learning to live in nutshimit. Like Tshaukuesh, she seized the gift of literacy and used it to tell her own stories of life on the land and the wisdom of the elders in her own language. She had brought her stories to France, "open to the world." And yet in Paris, too, she spoke to Kanapé Fontaine in Innu-aimun and taught her words she didn't know: "Nous parlions innu à Paris."[18]

Keeping the Language Alive: Literature and Film in Indigenous Languages

Daniel Heath Justice introduces his seminal book *Why Indigenous Literatures Matter* as "a book about stories, and some of the ways they matter. It's about the many kinds of stories Indigenous peoples tell, and the stories others tell about us. It's about how these diverse stories can strengthen, wound, or utterly erase our humanity and connections."[19] Until recently it seemed to be widely assumed, at least among non-Indigenous scholars, that there wasn't enough Indigenous writing for it to be considered a field in its own right, and that perhaps there was none at all in Indigenous languages. Heath Justice's book and his 2016 Twitter project were responses to that view. Each day of that year he tweeted the name of a work of Indigenous literature and its author, focusing on authors who were not so well known or on lesser-known works by celebrated authors. He explained: "The big names always get all the attention and so many amazing writers just don't get the public profile they deserve.... Some are working with various small, community-based publishers, or publishing works on their own. Some are trying to do as much in their language as they can because they're committed to keeping their languages alive."[20] The list of authors and texts from the Twitter project, which is reproduced in his book, includes around twenty-one works in Indigenous languages.[21] Much of this work is still not widely known. To make matters more complicated, it is difficult to do a search on the topic because one would also need to search for each individual language and to conduct the search itself in multiple languages, since searches in different languages yield different results.[22] This chapter does not attempt to present anything like a comprehensive survey but rather uses examples to discuss why such works matter; the challenges in funding, publishing, teaching, and translating them; adaptations; code-switching; and the impact of Indigenous languages on writing in other languages.

When we look closely, dividing lines and borders are seldom clear. Literatures in Indigenous languages and in colonial languages are not two entirely discrete categories, since many works mix languages to some extent. Some Indigenous writers refuse to translate words that have no exact equivalent or that have a more powerful affective meaning for them in their own language, such as Naomi Fontaine in *Kuessipan*: "There are two kinds of salmon: the utshashumeku which has returned to the sea and the pipunamu which has never left fresh water";[23] or Tshaukuesh's use of Innu words in the English version of her book. Other writers produce parallel texts in different languages in the same volume, for example Joséphine Bacon's and Rita

Mestokosho's bilingual editions of their poetry in Innu-aimun and French. Similarly, the dividing line between writing and oral literature is often blurred. As Cree-Métis literary scholar Deanna Reder notes, it is a false assumption that there is a hierarchy in which the oral and the written are opposites with written forms seen as superior to oral and representing "progress." Rather, she argues, both are "part of a multimodal communicative practice"[24] that includes various kinds of oral and written storytelling as well as audio, video, film and multimedia.

Indigenous writers in Canada, while often writing mainly for other Indigenous readers, are also influencing broader understandings of Canadian literature in terms of theme, form, and storylines. Writing that is entirely or partially in Indigenous languages, along with translations and collaborations, has arguably had less impact in this sense but could nevertheless offer new possibilities and insights. For one thing, as Sophie McCall has suggested, the collaborative editing, translating, and adapting that is often involved in bringing such writing to wider audiences calls into question the concept of the single author and oppositions such as oral/written and teller/recorder.[25] For another, original writing in Indigenous languages has often been discounted because it has been seen as ethnographic or linguistic material rather than literary writing, yet it could be understood and explored as opening up that category and taking it in new directions.

One example of a literary work that opens up the category is the Inuktitut novel *Sanaaq*, by Mitiarjuk Nappaaluk. It was written in the 1950s in response to the request of a missionary, Father Robert Lechat, for language learning materials. Nappaaluk began creating dialogues and scenarios that grew more complex as she went along, recounting events in the lives of Sanaaq and other family and community members. Collaboratively translated and edited with Father Lechat and later with French anthropologist Bernard Saladin d'Anglure, *Sanaaq* was first published in syllabic Inuktitut in 1984 and in Saladin d'Anglure's French translation in 2002.[26] The book was, until recently, almost entirely unknown in English-speaking Canada but is now available in English, translated by Peter Frost from the French version. Keavy Martin highlights Saladin d'Anglure's unusual choice as an anthropologist to work with the novel itself, thus giving its author interpretive authority instead of positioning her as an ethnographic "informant." Although some reviewers saw the value of the book as primarily anthropological or testimonial, Martin argues that it "is also a creative and critical intervention into the process of representing Inuit experience."[27] At the same time, she also points out that the novel has been taught in Inuit schools, and thus its ethnographic aspects are important, too, as it is a contribution to Inuit history as well as to storytelling.[28]

There is another early novel published in Inuktitut. Markoosie Patsauq's *Harpoon of the Hunter/Hunter with Harpoon* was written in Inuktitut and published in an English translation in 1974. The story of Kamik, a young man hunting a polar bear, it is told from several different perspectives, including that of the bear. Known as the first Inuit novel, the book was reissued in 2020 in Inuktitut along with new English and French translations by Valerie Henitiuk and Marc-Antoine Mahieu.[29] In fact, *Sanaaq* was written many years earlier but only published in the 1980s, decades after its original writing and more than a decade after the first publication of Markoosie's novel, so both are contenders for the "first Inuktitut novel" designation.

There are also numerous examples of diary keepers, life writers, filmmakers, and others working in Indigenous languages, particularly Inuktitut. Early works include the diary kept by Labrador Inuk Abraham Ulrikab, while he and his family were exhibited in European zoos in the 1880s; Peter Pitseolak's *People from Our Side*, which consists of his own manuscript and photographs along with a narrative by Dorothy Harley Eber; and the autobiographies of John Ayaruaq and Nuligak. Ayaruaq's was published in syllabics in 1968, and Nuligak's, edited by Maurice Metayer and published around the same period, was more recently made into an award-winning film: *I, Nuligak: An Inuvialuit History of First Contact*, produced by White Pine Pictures in 2005.[30]

Photography and film are forms of translation that retell stories for new audiences. As the Indigenous Australian writer Doris Pilkington Garimara pointed out in relation to *Rabbit-Proof Fence* (the film adaptation of her book *Follow the Rabbit-Proof Fence*), films in particular can reach people who might not respond to written text alone.[31] Inuk producer and director Zacharias Kunuk suggests that regular school attendance means young people are not learning their oral history from elders, so film offers a chance to tell that history.[32] Film also allows for subtitles, so that stories can be told simultaneously in more than one language (though the different language versions are not exact parallels, as we shall see). The Inuit production company Kingulliit (formerly Isuma) and the women's video collective Arnait Video Productions have made immeasurable contributions, producing major prize-winning feature-length films, most in Inuktitut, but also the Haida-language feature film *SGaawaay K'uuna* (Edge of the Knife), produced by Kingulliit through the newly created Niijang Xyaalas Productions. The film won six Leo Awards as well as Best Canadian Film at the 2018 Vancouver International Film Festival. The following year, another Kingulliit production, *One Day in the Life of Noah Piugattuk*, also won Best Canadian Film at the Vancouver festival. Both *Noah Piugattuk* and Arnait's *Before Tomorrow* focus on the impact of encounters between colonizers and Inuit—devastating, and yet the films also demonstrate and potentially enhance the resilience of Inuit life and culture.

The entire story of *Noah Piugattuk* takes the form of a conversation between the eponymous Inuk elder and Boss, a Qallunaaq who is trying to persuade him to move his people to a government-sponsored settlement. Based on an incident that took place in 1961, the film highlights the linguistic misapprehensions of Inuit-colonizer relationships: mistranslations and cultural misunderstandings, including untranslatable and untranslated jokes and social commentary. Director Kunuk sees it as an important historical contribution, stating, "It's part of our Canadian history, [what] happened up there nobody hardly knows because we were always focusing on St. John's to Vancouver."[33]

Before Tomorrow goes further back in history to one of the first encounters between Europeans and Inuit. It is based on the novel *Før Morgendagen* (1975), by Danish author Jørn Riel, in which Riel imagines what happened to an old woman and a young boy whose bones he found in a cave in Greenland in the 1960s. The film opens up ideas about cultural survival and the value of storytelling in ways that written versions arguably could not. Literary scholar Dianne Chisholm notes that in general, traditional storytelling allows for more creative adaptation than do life stories or written histories and that the screen adaptation of the fictionalized life story in *Before Tomorrow* by co-writers Susan Avingaq, Marie-Hélène Cousineau, and Madeline Ivalu "is more true to the spirit of Inuit history-telling than the original, novelistic script from which it was derived."[34]

Before Tomorrow opens with a scene of a group of people eating together, laughing, telling stories, and enjoying each other's company. The time is the mid-1800s, and some of the stories are about first encounters with white people. The film closes with a replay of the same event, but now we know that they are ghosts. Chisholm describes how, the first time she saw the film, she was "haunted by something [she] could not describe."[35] In her view, the spirits of the dead in this story are not frightening ghosts, zombies, or walking dead. Instead, they have come back to sustain the living and to ensure that traditions and culture are not lost. Thus "the spectral mode of Indigenous cinema [is] a potent form of cultural resistance."[36] *Before Tomorrow* is nevertheless harrowing and heartbreaking, both in the fate of the individual protagonists—a grandmother and her young grandson who have survived when the rest of their community is wiped out by smallpox, only to realize they cannot truly survive alone—and in the broader story of colonization. Yet despite this devastating storyline, Chisholm argues, the film is hopeful because it both begins and ends with the reanimation of the community, representing the survival of a culture and a people. It is also about cultural survival in another way, because it is based on the revival of traditional Inuit practices presented from an Inuit perspective in Inuktitut: "Under the auspices of elders, they set about learning and reviving a constellation of practices, including umiak and kayak building and handling, bow hunting, spearfishing, trap making, game playing, facial tattooing, fur and hide curing, and garment making. . . . Arnait's style of re-enactment should be understood as an activist practice that brings consultant elders together with younger cast and crew to cultivate collective memory and traditional life to resist the assimilative trends and forces of colonization, modernization, and globalization."[37]

Zacharias Kunuk also reflects on the idea of cultural survival in an interview about the making of *Atanarjuat: The Fast Runner*, which won the 2001 Cannes Caméra d'Or award:

> When I learned the story, when I was growing up, I imagined how it looked because they speak it in detail . . . we tried to get it right. But anything that wasn't in the story, we just made it up. And I have no problem with that. And I have no problem with people who know the story when they say "it's not like that." Because we've got seven different elders telling the same story. . . . It's been carried down for thousands of years and by the time it's our story, of course it's going to be different. When I say it's from an Inuit point of view, it's getting things right, getting the set right . . . the way the igloo is built, the way the bed is made, everything's right. That's my main argument. A lot of southern filmmakers or these actors, they don't even set their qulliq right. . . . I saw a qulliq in that movie *Honour and Glory*, where they were sleeping inside the igloo and they had a qulliq right in the middle, burning like the Olympic torch and that's not right. So a lot of times, when I say it's Inuit point of view, it's the way they had it.[38]

Kunuk also mentions in the interview that they used modern Inuktitut because, even though it might be less authentic, it would "get things rolling." Yet in other ways, as he describes, there was an enormous effort to tell the story in ways that were authentic. In the words of Paul Apak Angilirq, writer of the screenplay, "This movie will be based on an Inuit legend, and also it is all going to be in Inuktitut . . . all of the actors will have to be Inuit. No Japanese or whoever else who pretend to be Inuit. . . . It will be done the Inuit way. We want things presented in the movie the way they would have happened in real life."[39]

There is a tension between "just making it up," plurality of meanings, contemporary Inuktitut, and a quest for authenticity in which customs that are still remembered and practised must be done exactly the way "they would have happened in real life." The tension is also explored by an unnamed costume maker who worked on the film. She discusses how some of the clothing was traditional locally and familiar to the sewers, but other garments, especially the shaman's elaborate costume, were not but rather were based on drawings and instructions from the designers. Even the clothing that was familiar was no longer common: "We do not make such clothes out here anymore and it is important for me to know that we women can still get together and produce a lot like we did."[40] Continuity is expressed and maintained through this kind of sometimes paradoxical process—reviving ancient traditions but also imagining them otherwise at times—and through the medium of modern Inuktitut to "get things rolling."

A more recent and very different film, *Kuessipan,* based on a book by Naomi Fontaine, also explores linguistic and cultural survival but this time through a contemporary story. The book is described by the publishers as a novel but it is short, 111 pages in the original French (which tends to be lengthier than English), and most of the pages have a lot of white space highlighting what at first seem like prose poems more than a novel, telescopic vignettes of life in Uashat Mak Mani-utenam. But together the pieces weave a poignant story and the film develops the individual but interconnected episodes into a plot about the different quests and trajectories of two young Innu women, Shaniss and Mikuan, friends who feel more like sisters. Shaniss is slimmer, paler, shyer than Mikuan. She stays on the reserve, becomes a single mother, her life devoted to her children and to continuity. Mikuan is the narrator. She leaves the community to become a writer, to forge a different kind of continuity with her stories.

While a substantial part of the dialogue in the film version of *Kuessipan*, directed by Myriam Verreault, is in Innu-aimun, it would be more precise to say that the older generations—parents and grandparents—speak Innu and the younger generation—to which Shaniss and Mikuan belong—responds mostly in French. When Mikuan finds a non-Innu partner and plans to move to Quebec City with him to continue her studies, Shaniss says angrily, "It seems you have no pride anymore. . . . If everyone was like you, we wouldn't exist." But she says it in French. Yet language, like staying or moving away from home relationally and geographically, is part of who one is and how one tells one's stories.

Shaniss connects pride and distinctiveness, even the very existence of a people, with continuing to live in the same way and in the same communities, but continuity manifests itself in many ways, textual as well as geographic. The stories that we tell, the ways we tell them, and the languages we tell them in are fundamental to continuity. It takes only two generations for a language to be lost, and there are many Indigenous (and immigrant) communities where grandparents cannot talk to their own grandchildren. The film *Kuessipan* simultaneously supports the continuance of Innu-aimun by the very act of using it and shows how fragile it is.

The films discussed here exemplify very different ways of telling Indigenous stories through the medium of film: the Inuit films painstakingly reconstructed for historical accuracy (although with exceptions, such as the use of modern Inuktitut and the final moments of *Atanarjuat* when participants are shown in contemporary clothing, filming each other); the Haida film *sGaawaay K'uuna*, produced for and with the community to support people learning the Haida language; and *Kuessipan,* a contemporary story in which the characters switch more or less comfortably between Innu-aimun and French and live with both ancient and newer traditions. They play hockey, go to bars and writing workshops, and drive skidoos as well as hunt caribou and sleep in fir-bough-strewn tents. Yet all these films are Indigenous texts about cultural survival, produced through the medium of Indigenous languages.

Blurring Linguistic Boundaries

The linguistic term for the part Innu-aimun part French dialogue in *Kuessipan* is code-switching. Alternating between two or more languages or dialects in a single conversation is a very common practice in communities where more than one language is widely spoken. A different sort of language mixing is portrayed in Cherie Dimaline's *The Marrow Thieves*, a dystopian novel in which fugitive young Indigenous people in a world ravaged by climate change see language and story as their only hope for survival. More distanced from their ancestral languages than the characters of *Kuessipan*, most remember only fragments, but they do their best to reclaim them, with their council "piecing together the few words and images each of us carried.... They wrote what they could, drew pictures, and made the camp recite what was known for sure."[41] The elder Minerva teaches the young people some basic Cree. Dimaline said that she "purposely made the

Indigenous language in this book, when it is used, rudimentary to show that even when you use a word or a phrase as a beginner, as long as you are fighting for its survival, language is powerful, that it encompasses an ideology and life that is worth protecting at all costs."[42]

This theme in *The Marrow Thieves* resonates because language loss is one of the most haunting and painful legacies of colonization, of residential schools in particular but also a result of Canada's Official Languages Act and current schooling practices all over the country. Nevertheless, more than seventy Indigenous languages are spoken in Canada and, according to Statistics Canada, there was actually a 3.1 percent rise in Indigenous people who reported being "able to speak an Aboriginal language well enough to conduct a conversation" between 2006 and 2016. There are more speakers than people reporting an Aboriginal mother tongue, which suggests that people are successfully learning the languages later in life.[43] In Chapter 6, I discuss pros and cons of text-based literacy in an Indigenous language. Even if the advantages are not as straightforward as one might think, it seems likely that Indigenous language literature, cinema and multimedia stories will be vital resources for many new learners as they develop language skills and identities in the language.

Another aspect of boundary blurring between writing in Indigenous and colonial languages is that the former can have an impact on the latter. Renate Eigenbrod has suggested that "even if the Indigenous language is no longer known, an Indigenous author's awareness of the presence of an Indigenous language will influence the choice of language as a strategy."[44] Mareike Neuhaus puts it more strongly: "Reading Indigenous literatures in English amounts to nothing less than an exercise in reading the English language by thinking outside that very language."[45] Referring not so much to translations as to cultural influences on people's ways of expressing themselves, Neuhaus argues that contemporary Indigenous literatures in colonial languages are nonetheless continuations of traditional oral stories and performances. Thus intertextual references, figures of speech, even the structures of the language used may be influenced by Indigenous languages. "Indigenous concepts, rhythms, accents, and forms" can reinvigorate English.[46]

Lacombe also discusses the impact of Indigenous languages and traditions on contemporary literary works. She notes that "Indigenous poetics allows for a wide range of linguistic, formal and rhetorical strategies, realigning the contemporary poetic voice with older forms of storytelling."[47] Using the metaphor of walking, and drawing on the poetry of Rita Mestokosho and Joséphine Bacon, Lacombe examines movement between understandings rooted in Indigenous languages and cultures and European ones. This "walking" enables creative movement back and forth between a contemporary poetic voice and the rhythms, metaphors and cultural referents of traditional Indigenous storytelling. However, Lacombe also points out that, in French, there may be limits to how linguistically creative or experimental Indigenous writers may wish to be, citing constraints from modes of teaching in residential schools as well as Eurocentric prejudices against North American French combined with even stronger biases about Indigenous peoples generally. Because of these pressures, they risk being doubly marginalized by readers and critics if they use unconventional grammar, language or literary forms.[48]

Despite these constraints and prejudices, there is a movement toward reciprocity among francophone and Indigenous writers in Canada. One example is *Uashtessiu,* a volume of poetic exchanges between Innu poet Rita Mestokosho and Québécois poet Jean Désy.[49] Désy writes: "*Aimititau*[50] is becoming indispensable to our common literature. One way of reminding ourselves that we are equal and that we are capable of more than plain or fancy bargaining, much more than basic agreements or understanding. We are capable of love, let's admit it, and of dreaming together of a fundamental métisserie based on sharing and speaking together, despite the obvious differences between our communities."[51] While Mestokosho speaks more of protecting Innu land and language than of "métisserie" (a word Désy associates with a future when we will find inclusive words that describe all of us together, Indigenous and non-Indigenous[52]), she responds:

We'll go see that famous cave
where bears slumbered all winter long
where the bitter cold pierced our bones
where I fell into a sleep

that lasted a lifetime.
The route to the cave
is there somewhere
close to my breast,
on the left.
We'll go there together.[53]

In Chapter 1, I expressed some doubt about Caroline Desbiens's vision of a creolized poetics as a vital way forward for northern Quebec, and I still see a marked distinction between Désy's longing for métisserie and Mestokosho's "couleur de notre union, couleur de la solitude. Tshima Tshishe-Manitu nakutuenitak innu-aimunnu" (colour of our union, colour of our solitude. May the Great Spirit protect the Innu language). However, Lacombe points out that it is only in francophone contexts that there have been these particular kinds of exchanges and co-publications between Indigenous and non-Indigenous writers in Canada.[54] Despite the sometimes painful tensions in these encounters, something important is happening here, framed by Désy's "We are capable of love" and Mestokosho's response, "We'll go there together."

Re-imagining the Boundaries

Meanwhile, there are also some very practical challenges for poetic encounters and storytelling across languages—and particularly for work in Indigenous languages. In a Dilbert-esque exchange between Paul Apak Angilirq and anthropologist Nancy Wachowich, Angilirq explains the complicated linguistic contortions required to get funding for *Atanarjuat*.

NW: How many people did you interview?
PA: Maybe about eight to ten elders.
NW: So then you wrote a script from those interviews?
PA: Yes.
NW: Did you write it in English or Inuktitut?
PA: The story, I wrote it in English. And when I started writing the script, I wrote it in Inuktitut.

> NW: So let me get this straight, it was written out on paper from tapes of the elders speaking in Inuktitut, then turned into an English story, and then turned into an Inuktitut script, and then turned into an English script?
>
> PA: Yes, that is the system that we had to use in order to get money. Because, like, Canada Council and other places where we could apply for money, they don't read Inuktitut. They need to have something in writing in English. So that is why I wrote the story in English first, in order to get some funding to go ahead and continue with it.[55]

There were similar constraints in obtaining funding for *Nitinikiau Innusi*, as I discuss in Chapter 7. I also review the history and impact of the Official Languages Act on Indigenous languages in Chapter 5.

As literary translation specialist Nicole Nolette puts it, however, "both the process and the result of translation are telling manifestations of the power dynamics at play, dynamics that not only lead to language loss but also to a certain gain."[56] The losses are obvious: additional barriers to funding opportunities and recognition and the role such barriers play in the erosion of the language itself. Although Inuktitut, Innu-aimun, and other Indigenous languages are widely spoken in the North, and a number of them are officially recognized in two territories, speakers of these languages are forced to use cumbersome multi-layered translation processes in dealing with funding institutions. There are also constraints on the circulation of works in Indigenous languages. At some universities, Canadian literature can only be taught in its original language, not in translation. This means that nothing written or produced in an Indigenous language can be taught unless, of course, there is a whole class of students able to read that language. Even then, university structures might limit possibilities, since literature or modern language departments would not typically be offering courses in Indigenous languages, which are more often taught in departments of linguistics or Indigenous studies. As well, when literary works *are* studied in translation, as translator Carol Maier has observed, they are often "read in schools and universities as if they were written originally in English, thus erasing the very differences that make such texts valuable for instilling global awareness and sensitivity." Because of this, Maier has called for a pedagogy that "make[s] difference visible and in doing so . . . resist[s] the powerful homogenizing tendencies that accompany globalization."[57] This would mean drawing attention to the translation itself and to the strategies used to convey cultural differences in the original text. Martin proposes a more radical approach, using *Sanaaq* as an example:

> In asking, then, why a work like *Sanaaq* is not receiving the attention on a national scale that it undoubtedly deserves, we might imagine the solution to be the forthcoming English translation and its potential inclusion in anglophone classrooms in the South. But will that really solve the problem? Or will it merely perpetuate the categories that continue to limit us? Will there ever be a way in which discussions of Inuit literature in institutions can include that Inuktitut-language text in a prominent way? This is a radical idea, in that it suggests that the re-imagining of intellectual boundaries happens through a transformation on the part of the academy, rather than on the part of the literature. To what extent is the university-level Aboriginal literature curriculum perpetuating the nineteenth-century idea that the extinction of Indigenous languages is inevitable, and that the conversion to English- or French- language expression is a natural or even desirable process?[58]

Students studying other literatures are almost always required to learn the languages and to study them in the original. Why would literary work in Indigenous languages not be taught in the same way?

The gains of translation Nolette refers to may be less obvious. What value might there be in translating back and forth, in endless explaining, in trying to live simultaneously in two worlds? Perhaps doing so can help to synthesize what really matters about the work—why it is worth the effort, to reconceptualize, to encounter each other in conversation about the texts, and to find or create spaces where speakers of the dominant language are reminded that it is they who are deficient. After all, they are the ones who cannot read Inuktitut or Innu-aimun. The use of words like nutshimit and Akaneshau without translations or italics is a gesture toward making this gain visible. Perhaps the failure to translate certain words might remind us that they are not just words but part of a world that can never be perfectly translated. And perhaps when Tshaukuesh says she knows the animals don't talk (having just told us what they said to her), she is inviting the Akaneshau to try something that bilingual and bicultural people do constantly, to imagine two ways of thinking and to hold both in our minds at once.

After writing these thoughts on what might be an advantage of leaving some words untranslated, I read Valerie Henitiuk's discussion of translations of Markoosie's *Hunter with Harpoon*, in which she makes a similar point. Henitiuk is a specialist in translation studies and world literatures in translation, including Inuit literary texts. She compares Catherine Ego's 2011 French translation with Markoosie's own English adaptation (1970) and an earlier French rendition by Claire Martin (1971), noting one significant difference is that Ego retains the Inuktitut word "allou," which Markoosie gives as "seal holes" and Martin as "trous de phoque." The word refers to breathing holes that seals create in the ice and is used in the context of hunting, as both Inuit and polar bears wait at the holes to catch them. Henitiuk indicates the importance of this word in relation to the heavy negative impact the international boycott of the seal hunt has had on Inuit economies and indeed their whole way of life. She suggests that the use of "allou" instead of "breathing hole," combined with an in-text explanation in French the first time the word is used ("ces trous par lesquels les phoques remontent pour respirer à la surface des plans d'eau gêlés"), "disrupts the target-language text and its reader's experience, forcing him/her to recognize that the world unfolding on the page operates in another language entirely."[59]

Translation of Indigenous stories is vital, and so is an understanding of the challenges and limitations of this process, as I hope to have shown. Nevertheless, making the effort to learn an Indigenous language, to read and view Indigenous works in the original, even to understand words or concepts left untranslated, and to think differently about related issues such as funding and teaching would also be ways of "going there together," as Rita Mestokosho so eloquently put it.

Gathering Force

Storytelling in Indigenous languages demonstrates possibilities for "survivance," even in the most dire situations imaginable.[60] The term was first used in relation to Indigenous lives and cultures by Anishinaabe cultural theorist Gerald Vizenor to describe "an active sense of presence" and the renunciation of "dominance, tragedy and victimry" in Indigenous cultures and literatures.[61] The word, then, is not only distinct from survival but its opposite in the sense that contemporary Indigenous peoples are not just the survivors of land theft and genocide but peoples whose lives and cultures are resilient, dynamic, and creative. Eve Tuck calls survivance "a key component to a framework of desire" emphasizing that to her, Vizenor's term is about moving on and creating new ways of being, about resistance and sovereignty.[62]

As I worked on this chapter, I came to understand that it was not only about the continuation and renewal of Indigenous languages and storytelling in those languages, but also about the vitality of cultures, of nutshimit, the tenacity of life itself in all its variety, and thus about climate justice in the Capitalocene.[63] The impact of languages and literatures is potentially key to this, since the stories we tell are profoundly connected to the ways we live. Survivance is a key theme. As I thought about the poetics and storytelling discussed in this chapter, I realized that several of the most powerful and best-known works I have referred to deal directly or indirectly with the themes of endurance and renewal noted above. Perhaps this is not surprising, since Indigenous peoples have been facing the deaths of cultures, populations and environments for hundreds of years. As Nishnaabeg writer, performer, and theorist Leanne Betasamosake Simpson told Naomi Klein: "Indigenous peoples have lived through environmental collapse on local and regional levels since the beginning of colonialism—the construction of the St. Lawrence Seaway, the extermination of the buffalo in Cree and Blackfoot territories and the extinction of salmon in Lake Ontario—these were unnecessary and devastating. . . . I think that the impetus to act and to change and to transform, for me, exists whether or not this is the end of the world. If a river is threatened, it's the end of the world for those fish. It's been the end of the world for somebody all along."[64]

Language is an important aspect of the possibility of alliances that could help us respond to the "impetus to act," but so is geography. In *The Highway of the Atom*, which draws on Dene stories as well as other records of the uranium industry in Canada, Peter C. van Wyck writes: "[Stories from the North] are inaccessible, if we mean by that geographically remote from the south: a pious and ironic alibi. But, more than this . . . many from elsewhere have not had ears with which to hear them. It seems clear as well that voices from the North seldom gather sufficient force to rise above the colonial din of southern settler life."[65]

How can voices from the North "gather sufficient force"? And especially voices in Indigenous languages? Perhaps the examples I have given of Indigenous film productions, some of which are based on earlier writing and storytelling in Indigenous languages, suggest an answer. Henitiuk has written that in the context of the Truth and Reconciliation Commission (TRC), literature and translation studies might offer possibilities for restitution and productive debate.[66] She has also explored translations and adaptations of the eleventh-century Japanese classics, *The Tale of Genji* and *The Pillow Book*, works that are studied in high school in Japan and traditionally thought of as dry and difficult, if not completely incomprehensible.[67] Surprisingly, this work too may be relevant to enabling non-Indigenous southerners to hear voices from the North. Since the 1980s the Japanese classics have taken on new life in manga comic versions, films, and video games. According to Henitiuk, a main reason for this renewed interest is the fact that in English translation, these works became part of world literature, thus raising international interest that made its way back to Japan.[68] Henitiuk has noted elsewhere that the globalization of a given literary work through making it accessible to a broad international audience often "means forcing it into a new and unfamiliar mold for greater ease of consumption and assimilation, thereby eliding linguistic and other difference and harming the text and its unique contextual identity."[69] However, she also expresses hope for a different possibility—that readers themselves may be translated: "Receiving, transmitting, multiplying stories—one person sharing his or her tale with another, one culture with another—this beautiful, complex, and utterly human activity effectively translates readers to myriad, and inherently creative, interpretive spaces."[70]

This example from Japan suggests that translations and adaptations might play a role in enabling voices from the North to be heard, not only in the Canadian South but globally. Laurence Jay-Rayon has also noted the paradox that writing from the margins is often only recognized after having been translated into a globally dominant language.[71] Bringing "inaccessible" stories to national and international consciousness through translation potentially "introduces discourse shifts, destabilizes received meanings, creates alternate views of reality, establishes new representations, and makes possible new identities."[72] Can translation from Indigenous languages to ones that are widely spoken internationally, and adaptation—which can be thought of as another form of translation—into popular forms such as films or graphic novels, lead to further international interest in Indigenous writing in Indigenous languages? And, if so, what might be the effects of these forms of translation?

In academic contexts, wider reading of works in Indigenous languages or in translation and the study of translation itself could have a profound effect on literary studies more broadly and on how we conceptualize and categorize creative work. For one thing, writers in Indigenous languages, at least until recently, have been writing with few models and often without being parts of movements or communities of writers. This means they have often been extremely original, as demonstrated by the unusual form and content of *Sanaaq* and *Nitinikiau Innusi*, or the extraordinary cinematography and storytelling of Kingulliit/Isuma. Scholarly engagement with this kind of work requires rethinking all kinds of categories: departmental organization, intellectual traditions, literary genres, language hierarchies, and funding priorities, among others. Smaro Kamboureli has asked, with reference to how we think about areas of study, specifically Canadian studies, "why [do] we need a nation-centered study program at a time when the nation and the state have been radically questioned and reconfigured,"[73] when we study borders, peripheries, diasporas and liminality, feminist geographies,

Indigenous writing, and the challenges of translation and collaboration? When many, perhaps most, of us are not very interested in a homogeneous understanding of Canada? Lacombe points out that Indigenous writing "traverses and challenges geopolitical boundaries such as the 49th parallel."[74] This is especially the case with writing in Indigenous languages, since it is so obviously written from these communities of speakers. As Martin puts it:

> Traditional territories and languages draw different borders than the ones that appear on official maps, and thereby undermine the certainty of the boundaries that we have become used to navigating. Inuit territory, for instance, may now be divided up into new political units, but the common intellectual traditions of the Arctic can be seen as uniting these disparate pieces, and thereby suggest the possibility of cross-border dialogue. And this, no doubt, is something from which literary studies in Canada can benefit. Inuit literature, after all, does not always fall as easily into the separate French and English camps; rather, the ever increasing body of literature that is being produced in Inuktitut resists this polarization. Films like *Atanarjuat (The Fast Runner)*, not to mention Mitiarjuk's and Markoosie's original Inuktitut publications, to some extent, constitute their own solitude—a sovereign literary field.[75]

As a Canadian who has lived much of her life as an anglophone among francophones, then as a non-Newfoundlander in Newfoundland—a place with a passionate regional identity that is often defined in opposition to the Canadian nation—and doing collaborative work with an Innu writer in Innusi, I have never had any particular sense of Canada as a homogeneous place. And yet it may be that within this nation-state we could have crucial discussions that would reconfigure our understanding of who we are and what we are doing here, as well as whose writing counts, and for what. Linguistic, thematic, and disciplinary framings limit and shape the work we do or can even imagine doing. Kamboureli suggests that scholars develop new kinds of "research styles and networks that are more relevant to our times' disjunctive temporalities and mobility."[76] Perhaps doing so could also lead to new kinds of work that might become part of world literature and also find their way back home.

Four

Looking

At the launch of *Nitinikiau Innusi* in Goose Bay, people sit in the audience reading the book or looking at the pictures. A cheerful, ruddy-faced man shows me a photo in the book of children playing on a facsimile tank, designed as a target for testing missiles on the bombing range. "That's me!" he says, pointing to a round-faced, pink-cheeked boy.[1]

At the St. John's launch, Tshaukuesh speaks about the photos and how important they were, how much she appreciates the efforts of everyone who took them and sent them to her. "I can't read English," she says (though I've noticed she can puzzle it out slowly on the computer screen as we work together). "But I can read the pictures. People can look at pictures to understand the story." She goes on to describe a particular photo by Jerry Kobalenko of her little grandson Manteu, then aged five, walking away from the viewer on snowshoes into a vast snow-covered landscape.[2] She emphasizes its significance as a representation of young Innu facing the future.

Tshaukuesh often speaks about the value of documenting, of capturing things gone, or recreating scenes or events visually, just as she would with words. From the beginning of the protests in the 1980s, or perhaps even before that, she saved every photo she was given and made great efforts to take her own, despite all the challenges she faced to do so and all her other responsibilities. She also asked me to take photos of things she felt were important: tobogganing with her grandchildren; preparing symbolic plant arrangements for a funeral; an Innu tea doll.[3] And she sometimes expresses a desire to reconstruct events or objects from the past, for example when

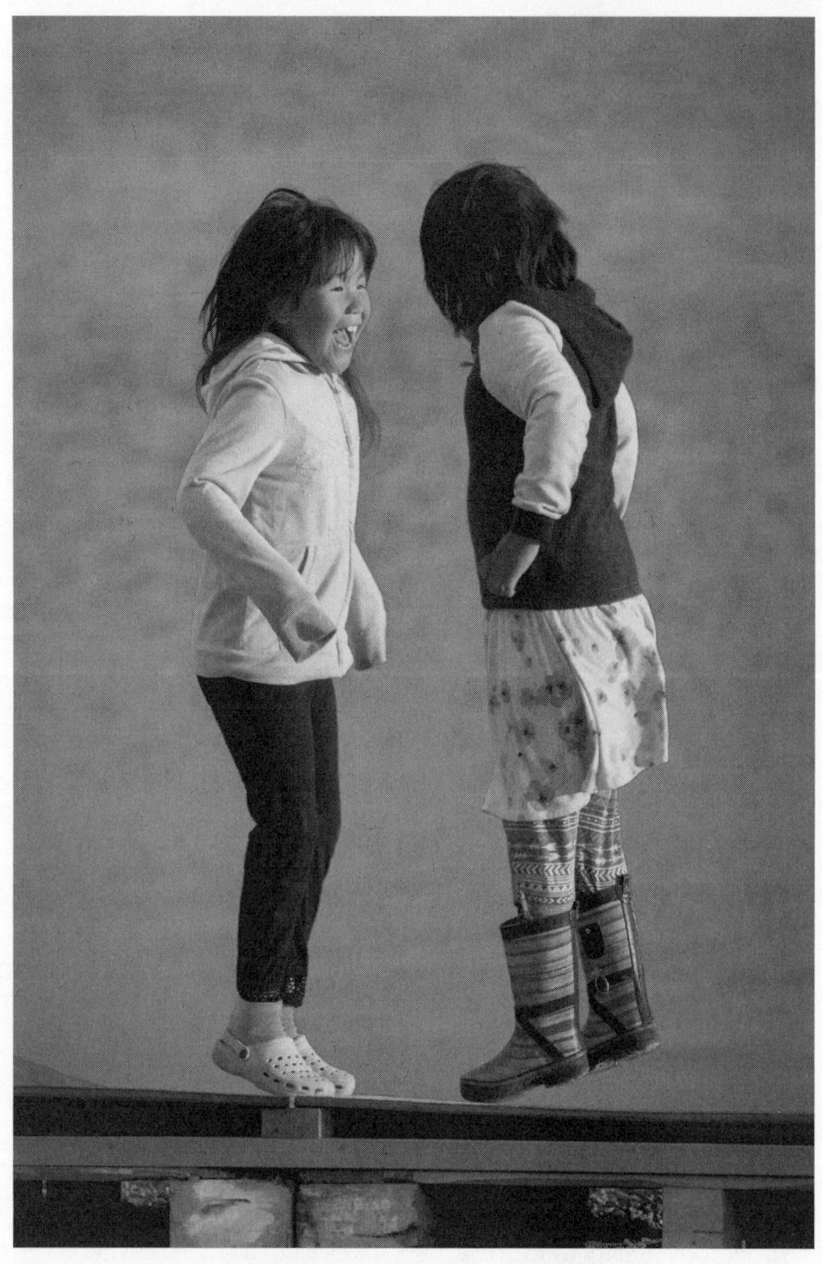

"Invoking wonder": Brittany smiles with delight as she and a friend play on the beach at Shango Lake, Natuashish. Photo by Lingxiao Yue.

she told me about the time they found an old cache of food in the woods and said she wished she could find the items again—tinned milk, molasses, flour, baking powder—so she could set them up in a metal bucket for a photo shoot.

I have always been surprised at how little attention is paid to pictures, other than diagrams, in so many kinds of academic work. Of course, there is work in the visual arts as a field as well as a focus on photography in cultural studies, visual ethnography, and arts-based research. Other fields such as biology, geography, and history use pictures to illustrate or prove specific points, but they are seldom considered as central as the written text. Yet photos are a form of translation, a version of the story. They are also more than that: they offer new insights and new ways of relating to each other as we look at them together. Anishinabekwe visual anthropologist Celeste Pedri-Spade notes that photos can play a key role as "technologies of memory" in reclaiming lost history and initiating discussions about decolonization, and as "technologies of the self" through which people can explore questions of identity and representation.[4] They can help restore a sense of cultural continuity; support people working through grief; expose the myths and stereotypes of dominant colonial discourse and bear witness to colonial violence by "implicat[ing] the viewer in a process of witnessing";[5] enhance or rebuild connections to people, culture, and place; and stimulate people's dreams and visions of the future.[6]

Using "repeat photography,"[7] a term put forward by researcher and artist Trudi Smith for a process in which an old photograph is recreated using the original as a reference point, Pedri-Spade reconstructed old photos by inviting descendants of the original subjects to pose at the same locations. The old and new photos were then juxtaposed in ways that highlighted family connections and could be used for "visiting with photos." This led to families and communities sharing memories and reclaiming stories and cultural teachings,[8] thus strengthening connections across generations and "reinscribing Anishinabeg presence"[9] on colonized lands.

Pedri-Spade sees at least four conceptual links between photography and decolonization: (1) both are relational processes that require us to "think, feel, look, listen and act"; (2) both are "about visioning and movement towards the unknown"; (3) photographs are historical documents that are key to reclaiming Indigenous knowledge; and (4) photographs help people remember.[10] As she worked with the collected photos, Pedri-Spade began to think of them as "sacred bundles," medicines for a healing journey.[11] She also found that discussion of photos can lead to conversations about topics beyond the representational significance of the pictures themselves, including stories that, while not directly related to the photos, were important in their own right. Finally, images that show strength and resilience can give courage to the people who see them. This is something Tshaukuesh has often mentioned: the importance of photos and film (as well as audio recordings) in inspiring and literally "en-couraging" the Innu to continue working for justice. These were often photos of Tshaukuesh and other Innu activists doing things they had never thought possible, walking long distances through difficult conditions, speaking publicly, confronting NATO soldiers or government representatives.

A significant aspect of Pedri-Spade's project was that the photos were all taken by Anishinabeg photographers, thus privileging Anishinabe views and countering colonizing versions of history. In *Nitinikiau Innusi*, roughly one-third of the photos were taken by Innu. It is difficult to be precise, since the photographers were not identified for many of the photos in Tshaukuesh's collection and she could not always remember who had taken them. After we began working together, we documented as many as we could and also contacted professional photographers to license their images for the book. She talked about the importance of showcasing photos of strong women and others connecting people to the land and the animals. She and her family also carefully documented military activities and destruction of land, as well as everyday practices such as hunting, fishing, berry picking, and the preparation of food. As we looked at the photos and talked about which ones to use, they helped me understand the background and context of the stories better, thus facilitating the translation of the diaries. In translation contexts where a translator with a high level of knowledge of both languages and cultures is not available, as often happens with languages spoken only by a small number of people, photographs can be enormously helpful for scaffolding, clarifying, and generating more detailed discussion and thus better translation.

Not long before *Nitinikiau Innusi* was published, I realized that Kari Reynolds, a longtime Akaneshau ally of Tshaukuesh and the Innu, had a treasure trove of photos from the 1980s and '90s that she had taken during the NATO occupation. One of them depicts a serious-looking Tshaukuesh walking toward the camera with a tent and an Innu flag behind her, framed by snow covered hills and a leaden sky.[12] The photo was taken when Tshaukuesh and others were camping on the NATO bombing range in Innu territory. When Tshaukuesh saw it, she remembered that they had not slept well because they knew the soldiers were just behind the hills and they expected them to arrive at any moment. In another of Kari's photos, Tshaukuesh is sitting under a tree.[13] To me, there was nothing especially significant about the photo, but she explained it was a very important one to include because the uishuaushkumuk, or yellow moss, depicted (which I had not even noticed) is very useful to insulate one's feet in winter. Thus the photo provides important cultural knowledge. Yet another photo shows a crowd of people walking toward a crane at work in the forest. Tshaukuesh told me that this photo illustrated an event she had written about, a protest at Anaktalak Bay near Emish, where a nickel mine was being developed. The event was particularly significant because it was the first time Innu and Inuit had come together to protest.[14] These are just three examples of how photos, in this case taken not by an Innu but by a close ally who had spent much time with the Innu during the occupation, helped enhance and deepen the translation and editing of the original diaries.

Environmental artist Marlene Creates has said that "photography has the power to form the images and ideas we have of places. But . . . what a photograph cannot reveal is the multitude of histories and experiences in a place because they are largely invisible and cannot be photographed."[15] Creates often combines written text with photography to address this, and her exhibitions and books juxtapose not only photos and written texts but also videos, hand-drawn maps, and objects, all of which reveal histories and experiences that the photograph alone cannot. She has also said, "It seems to me that the meaning of a place cannot be photographed . . . It's strange for a photographer, perhaps, but I am more and more taken by what I cannot see, by what is not visible—the flexible, elusive, and ever-changing layers of meaning in places."[16] Photographs have such extraordinary power, yet often that power needs to be articulated through writing, talking, and juxtaposition or illustration. Simultaneously, photos can bestow their power on writing, conversation, and testimonial. The very fact that there is so much they do not reveal is key to their role in eliciting more information in translation contexts.

Another way of generating richer and deeper discussions is to use photos that "break the frame."[17] This idea comes from visual anthropologist Douglas Harper, who found that when he used traditionally framed photos of typical farming scenes in interviews with farmers, the images did not evoke the kind of reflection on the personal meaning of farming that he had hoped for, perhaps because the photos had no element of surprise for the farmers. Harper argues that "breaking the frame" of peoples' everyday views can lead them to a new understanding of their lives and experiences and also provide bridges between worlds that are culturally distinct.[18] When he used aerial photos with the same farmers, much richer discussions emerged, which he suggests was because they were looking at their farms in a new way. In another study, Harper took photos from unusual angles and very close up to provide new ways of seeing familiar views. Reading about the ways farmers responded to the aerial photos reminded me of looking at the large-scale maps with Tshaukuesh and Henry Ike Rich, and Tshaukuesh's happiness that she could identify the places she was telling me about and show them to me. I remembered how she said that it can be hard to explain things but that visual support helped. It is possible that the scale of the maps also "broke the frame" by enabling a different vision of the land she had walked and paddled through so often.

Harper makes additional points about photo elicitation, or the use of photos to generate information and discussion. Photo elicitation produces different kinds of information than straightforward questioning, bringing feelings and memories to the surface. It does this, he suggests, because visual information is processed in different parts of the brain than verbal information and, when used in conjunction with words, draws on more of the brain's capacity than would words alone. Photo elicitation enables participants to connect themselves to society, culture, and history, sharpening and clarifying memories and prodding latent memory.[19] While breaking the frame is an important concept to be aware of in research and other uses of photography, many other kinds of photos can also elicit forgotten stories, information, and insights. As Harper puts it, "Photographs appear to capture the impossible: a person gone; an event past. That extraordinary sense of seeming to retrieve something that has disappeared belongs alone to the photograph, and it leads to deep and interesting talk."[20]

Often it is precisely what a photograph does not reveal that can lead to story and insight, as people recount what else happened at that site or to those people. However, this does not happen automatically. Breaking the frame by casting the photos or the sites and people they represent in a new light can help, as can approaches such as Pedri-Spade's use of significant juxtapositions to create sets of photos and visiting to create a context for a conversation; Smith's repeat photography; Creates's accompanying written texts and maps produced by project participants to elucidate the invisible. Versions of all of these approaches played a role in the collaborative translation of *Nitinikiau Innusi* and were most often suggested by Tshaukuesh herself.

Invoking Wonder

Jerry Kobalenko has his own food all packaged and prepared in advance, exactly calculated to match the calories he will burn during the walk. The rest of us eat together, but he is used to travelling alone or perhaps with just a single companion. One day he shares his coffee with me. I have not been craving coffee as much as I expected. I have adjusted and even come to love the ritual of tea in the tent and the companionship of it, the giant aluminum kettle and the battered mugs, the shared pleasure as we wrap our hands around their warmth, steam rising, after a long day on the trail—but the coffee, pre-mixed with powdered milk and sugar, is still a treat.

Jerry has found a way to make a living by doing what he loves, to get paid for his adventures in remote northern places. He sells his photos, he lectures, he tests gear, and he writes articles and coffee table books with spectacular glossy images along with informative and thought-provoking essays about the places and people he photographs. He has been doing all this for over thirty years, and he has thought a lot about what he does and why.

After the walk is over, I ask him to send me some photos that we might license for Tshaukuesh's book. I have just begun to realize that there are many beautiful and significant images that are part of the story. Jerry's are among the most striking I've seen yet. Most of them show a pristine northern environment, snow untouched by skidoo tracks or the mess that accumulates around a campsite: tarps awaiting use to wrap loads on toboggans; a chainsaw, because each time we make a new camp trees must be cut down to use as tent poles; the yellow of urine on snow at a little distance from the tent. He tells me he frames his photos to look pristine. I say I am interested in different ways of representing the landscape and people of the North and wonder about editing out things like modern equipment or dirty snow. I do it myself, too, and Tshaukuesh has also de-selected photos with chainsaws in them when choosing photos for her book, but I am wondering about the story these magnificent and flawless landscapes tell and to what end.

"I edit out visual elements like pee stains that are not an integral part of the image," he says. (I had asked him about pee stains specifically, because they are ubiquitous at winter campsites.) "I wouldn't call that ways of representing the landscape, just basic composition. I'd edit out modern equipment only if the image has advertising potential. Every photographer knows that an image of Inuit in caribou skins would sell better than one of them in snowmobile suits."

Jerry explains that one of the goals of his work is to inspire people to care about the beautiful northern places he loves so much and to protect them. In that sense he is an engaged "translator" of a world that few southerners see first-hand. Tshaukuesh has a similar perspective in some ways and often mentioned that she prefers photos that don't show modern equipment or untidy settings. Both Tshaukuesh and Jerry are committed to trying to show the beauty and challenges of the North. Someone asked me recently if I had any advice about how to teach young children about climate change. I said I thought it was best to start by teaching them to love the natural world and to appreciate its wonder. Perhaps that applies to adults, too, especially if they haven't thought about these things much in the past. Are photos that show spectacular sites unsullied by humans, yet including human interest, a way of doing that? What then should we make of Edward Burtynsky's hauntingly beautiful images of places devastated by humans? In a recent collaborative multimedia art project, *Anthropocene*, Burtynsky worked with filmmaker Jennifer Baichwal and cinematographer Nicholas de Pencier to produce stories and images of human-wrought destruction on a vast scale all over the world. He said of their goals: "We want to communicate out there with people. We want them to look at these things, to try to ask questions about these landscapes. And if you . . . make them ugly or . . . photograph them in an unsightly light or whatever, they don't resonate. They don't make us wonder about this place. So invoking that sense of wonder I think is one of the key tools we, as artists, can actually bring to the table. And once that wonder is invoked I think people begin to talk about it and begin to think about these places."[21]

Burtynsky and his colleagues are presenting a world that is in dramatic opposition to Jerry Kobalenko's in a way—the one cataclysmic, the other untouched, immaculate—yet it seems that their strategies and goals are remarkably similar. Both approaches could be seen as public pedagogies aiming to save the natural world, and both use aesthetic principles of beauty to reach their audiences. Baichwal explains what it meant to them to do this project: "It's . . . apocalyptic but it's also hopeful because there are all of these people working towards change." She also talked about photographing individuals at a human scale in the midst of these enormous factories, open pit mines, agro-industrial sites, wastelands: "We have to . . . find this balance between scale and detail to understand the complexity of the story, and also to bring people in to the witnessing in the right way. Because if witnessing opens up consciousness and opening up of consciousness is the beginning of a change in behaviour or understanding then we've done what we set out to do."[22]

As Tshaukuesh and I worked on *Nitinikiau Innusi* and as I write this book, I always have in the back of my mind the question of how to be a witness for the North, for the land and its inhabitants, to be one of those people working toward change in behaviour or understanding. Burtynsky's idea about invoking wonder and how it can be done better through beauty than through ugliness, and Baichwal's emphasis on finding a balance between scale and detail help to think this through and support Kobalenko's comments on the value of beauty and aesthetic composition in persuading viewers to care about the North and the natural world.

This discussion of beauty (whether the beauty of apocalypse or of the seemingly pristine) is timely in that during the twentieth century, as philosopher Alexander Nehamas puts it, critics, artists, and philosophers "gradually came to doubt beauty itself. The contrast between helping the suffering and painting them, between fighting for them and writing about them, became starker and deeper."[23] More recently, however, there has been a revived interest in beauty, but with a focus on communal experience and what Burtynsky might call "invocation." In this view, beauty is seen as an invitation and as "something we share, or something we want to share, and shared experiences of beauty are particularly intense forms of communication." Such experiences connect observers and observed in "communities of appreciation,"[24] and perhaps the intensity of the shared experience within that community can contribute to invoking wonder. One example is the work of Benjamin Von Wong, who notes in relation to his fantastical environmental art installations: "I've recently become very interested in the idea of community as a way to measure art. What if your art can convene people who then form tight bonds that last over the course of time? What if you create a spark that empowers a community and allows it to grow? Or you create a conversation piece that people can focus around? That might be worth a lot."[25]

Wonder can also be painful. Marlene Creates quotes Rilke: "Beauty is nothing but the Beginning of a terror we are just able to endure." She continues: "For Rilke, beauty was the beginning of a terror; for me, it is a loss—beauty is just the beginning of a loss that I know is inevitable and that I can hardly bear . . . The place I inhabit is both wondrous and constantly changing, which, I know, entails loss. My cosmology, I suspect, is basically elegiac."[26]

We watch the seasons change and with this, endless small losses: the blooming and waning of the wild rhododendrons in all their short-lived roseate splendour; the annual arrival and departure of icebergs, capelin, and whales; the dark acid soil of this island covered with berries in autumn; the beauty of the falling snow and the melt of spring. On an infinitely vaster scale, we are not just in a seasonal cycle of loss and renewal but in a terrifying decline, the ongoing devastation of species, of clean water supplies, of forests and land. There is only so much we can do, trapped in the system that has caused this loss. Elegiac documenting, invoking, and sharing wonder both at what remains and at the destruction itself are all ways of managing what is unmanageable and of telling stories that can help us live together and go forward in the best ways we can.

Counter-narratives and Aesthetics

Over the years we worked together, Tshaukuesh gave me thousands of photos, boxes of old prints to be scanned (and in some cases, repaired), CD-ROMs, and negatives. We had many conversations about which ones to use, but since we lived far apart from each other and were limited to telephone calls except when I travelled to Sheshatshiu or she came to St. John's, we had to find an efficient way to sort and organize the images. There was so much to do when we were together: the all-consuming process of translating the diaries and her efforts to teach me as much as she could about her culture and language left little time for poring over photos. After getting all of the images onto my computer, I first sorted them aesthetically, eliminating any that weren't clear and reasonably well composed, with a few exceptions for poorer-quality photos that were the only available illustrations of stories in the book. I then went through them for content, selecting those that related to the written text or could represent events described (for example, a photo of people canoeing, even if it wasn't the trip she had written about, could be used if we didn't have any from the actual event). This reduced the thousands to a few hundred. I then printed them out and sent them to her so she could choose the ones she liked best and eliminate any she definitely did not want in the book. I also made some of the best ones into an illustrated story book, using excerpts from the diary and a book creation software program, to give her an idea of what her eventual book might look like.

Tshaukuesh wanted readers to know how good life is in nutshimit, so we tried to select photos portraying purposeful activity and happiness, especially happy children. These images are a powerful counter-narrative to the ones that have been internationally circulated in the media of Innu children sniffing gas, and in films like *The Mushuau Innu: Surviving Canada* (2004) and *Being Innu* (2007), where the focus, especially in *Surviving Canada*, is on addiction, suicide, and the destruction of a culture. Camille Fouillard, another photographer and ally, and I also talked about this kind of portrayal. She argued that *Being Innu* was qualitatively different from *Surviving Canada* (which she had worked on but regretted) in that it focused on individuals and, she felt, depicted them with love and let them tell their story without an agenda about what that story should be. I think she is right. The individuals in *Being Innu* have stayed with me ever since I saw the film, and I have often wondered how they are doing. The film made me and many others care about them. I am still troubled by the fact that it is yet another film about Indigenous people and addictions, with the title *Being Innu*, but Camille has almost convinced me that it is more than that, showing "young people struggling for an identity and trying to find their way to adulthood, in a way that was very relatable, and . . . facing many of the same struggles that their counterparts in dominant society might be facing, the more resilient with all the additional layers of challenges. It allow[s] the viewer to really see the humanity, the people behind the stereotypes."[27]

The problem isn't always about the representation of individuals or groups but about which stories get told most and the need for counter-narratives that challenge stories of dysfunction and suffering as the dominant narrative about Indigenous peoples. Eve Tuck calls research that does this "documenting damage,"[28] and she points out that it is often done toward good ends and by well-meaning people. She and K. Wayne Yang write:

> Damage-centered researchers may operate, even benevolently, within a theory of change in which harm must be recorded or proven in order to convince an outside adjudicator that reparations are deserved. These reparations presumably take the form of additional resources, settlements, affirmative actions, and other material, political, and sovereign adjustments. [This theory] relies upon Western notions of power as scarce and concentrated, and . . . requires disenfranchised communities to position themselves as both singularly defective and powerless to

> make change. [As well], "won" reparations rarely become reality, and . . . in many cases, communities are left with a narrative that tells them that they are broken.[29]

Counter-images, like counter-narratives, can contribute to framing a different story. To quote Tuck once more, "A desire-based framework is an antidote to damage-centered research . . . desire-based research frameworks are concerned with understanding complexity, contradiction, and the self-determination of lived lives."[30]

While some of the photos in *Nitinikiau Innusi* document damage to the land and water in a very purposeful way, they also invite us into the lives of the people of Tshaukuesh's stories in all their "complexity, contradiction and self-determination" and portray them overcoming massive adversity. The photos by members of Tshaukuesh's family and friends are aesthetically composed but less formal than most of Jerry Kobalenko's or Edward Burtynsky's. They are often more intimate. They show the clutter and dynamism of lives lived to the full.

We had an extraordinary wealth of photos from the past twenty years or so to choose from. However, in the 1980s and '90s, when the Innu protests against government hunting bans, logging, mining, and NATO occupation of their land were at their height, there were few photographers documenting what was happening. Tshaukuesh, prescient as always, realized that photos would be key to documenting what was happening, along with her diary and audio recordings. Some of the photos from that historically significant period come from her personal collection, but with the costs, technologies, and preoccupations of the time, few Innu were taking photos, and she was only able to take a limited number herself. Nevertheless, despite her lack of any training in photography or archival practices, and extremely limited access to equipment and funds, she continued to take photographs whenever she could and to save photos that others took, believing profoundly in their value and importance.

Around the same time, three Akaneshau photographers, Camille Fouillard, Peter Sibbald, and Kari Reynolds, took many remarkable photos of protests, trials, walks, and daily life in nutshimit. Camille and Kari in particular had spent months and years working with the Innu against the occupation of their land. Kari had been arrested and gone to prison with them. They put their bodies on the line. Thanks to their commitment and their ability to document, we were able to use photos like Camille's lovingly composed black-and-white study of Tshaukuesh making one of her first speeches;[31] Kari's striking image of the first joint protest by Inuit and Innu, walking together to protect their land;[32] and other remarkable scenes and events such as Peter's unforgettable portrait of the province's then premier, Clyde Wells, elegant in suit and tie with classic cufflinks and highly polished shoes, sitting on an upturned salt beef bucket in a tent during discussions about logging.[33] The existence of these photos contributes so much to the book, and their significance is underscored when contrasted with the situation today, when so many Innu have almost unlimited power to photograph themselves and document their experiences and their world.

Indoor/Outdoor

If one critique of certain photos could be that they document damage, another type of image constructs what interdisciplinary philosopher Tobias Rees has described as "timeless others who have presumptively lived in the same way for hundreds, perhaps thousands, of years."[34] Interestingly, these "timeless others" are most often photographed outdoors. Perhaps that makes sense, as indoor photos date themselves through domestic details and thus can't be seen as timeless, but what is the effect of these outdoor settings? Marianne Hirsch, in her analysis of the famous 1950s photo exhibition *The Family of Man*,[35] observes that although displayed together, the photos of four extended farming families are markedly different in that the American and Italian families are shown indoors, while the Japanese and Batswana are posed outside. This, she suggests, highlights hierarchical differences rather than the similarities intended by the curator: "*the Bushmen have families like us they are farmers like us* [while simultaneously confirming] Western museum visitors in their own distinct identity: *we, unlike them, have our distinct domestic spaces . . . they can become like us but we don't have to become like them*."[36] Similarly, an African-American mother and two children are portrayed in an "external unspecified location," while a white mother and her children are shown in a location of "domesticity and specificity."[37]

The Family of Man was perhaps the most famous and well-travelled photography exhibition of the 1950s. Organized by photographer and curator Edward Steichen, it included 503 photos by 273 photographers of people in sixty-eight countries. The exhibition presented images of events and experiences assumed to be central to the lives of all humanity, such as love, childbirth, learning, laughter, work, play, grief, and death. Although the range of subjects of the photos was very international, the photographers were mainly white Europeans or North Americans.[38] The show was designed to demonstrate "the transcendence of the collective human family beyond the aspirations, trials and eventual death of individuals."[39] Yet it has been widely criticized ever since, precisely for not representing this transcendence. Roland Barthes was an early and highly influential critic, writing that "this myth of the human 'condition' rests on a very old mystification, which always consists in placing Nature at the bottom of History."[40] He goes on to argue that the exhibition demonstrated "the failure of photography"[41] to convey historic differences and injustices.

The indoor/outdoor distinction is just one of several aspects that can be seen as undermining the idea of human continuity and sameness, but it is the one I want to focus on here because I have often thought about it in my own work. I had realized when making a film about pedestrian rights[42] that interviews done outdoors are often much more dynamic on screen than the ones shot indoors. I felt the same was true of photos. Tshaukuesh wanted her book to be about life in nutshimit, so we agreed to use mostly photos that were taken there and thus either outdoors or in the tent, which has a beautiful light and dynamism of its own and is a sort of transitional space, domestic but impermanent.

Meanwhile, Newfoundland Mik'maw writer Maura Hanrahan also focuses on the indoor/outdoor distinction in her analysis of the location of Gerald Squires's commemorative statue of a Beothuk woman, *Spirit of the Beothuk*, at Boyd's Cove archeological site. She describes the statue as "permanently located deep in the quiet woods of Newfoundland, the only authentic setting for Indigenous people." She sees its external placement as decontextualized, "ineffective as well as disrespectful."[43] Hanrahan does not insist on the outdoor/indoor distinction; indeed, she states (and I agree) that a better approach would be a commemoration that focuses on an "entire cultural landscape" and is developed in consultation with the relevant Indigenous communities.[44] Yet the location of the statue "deep in the quiet woods," which troubles Hanrahan, was received very differently by Tshaukuesh, who did not see the site as decontextualized or disrespectful. She wrote, "It's a very beautiful statue and a beautiful spot where she was standing . . . you could see where they had their tents; it looked like nutshimit, surrounded by trees and green moss on the ground."[45] Perhaps in the context of nutshimit, the oppositions of outdoor/indoor or external/domestic are not useful. The forest itself is home.

Literary translation scholar Maria Tymoczko has pointed out that the binaries on which translation studies often rely, such as free/literal, are not necessarily useful in translations in postcolonial contexts, which are "complex, fragmentary, and even self-contradictory." In these contexts, translators are often allying themselves with the people whose words they are translating and thus "prioritizing particular aspects or elements of the source texts for specific activist effects and ends."[46] They may also be relying on a preliminary translation into a third language or on inadequate knowledge of the source language and culture, forced to improvise because no one else is available. One of the binaries Tymoczko is referring to came up over and over as Tshaukuesh and I worked with her story: foreignization/domestication. Foreignization is a translation strategy popularized by Lawrence Venuti as a way of drawing the reader's attention to the differences between the source and target cultures in the text to be translated.[47] The idea behind foreignization is that translators often domesticate a text by substituting words or concepts that are familiar to intended readers or by adding explanations or contextualization for words or passages in the original language that cannot easily be translated. This is usually done to make the text easier to understand and identify with. Such a text, as literary translator Michael Henry Heim argues, "lulls readers into the false security that 'they' of the source culture resemble 'us,' or, more insidious, that 'we' of the target culture are the measure of all things."[48] Instead, Venuti argues, translators should let the text remain strange or foreign in the translated version as a way of challenging readers to think harder about what they are reading and to be aware that cultures are not interchangeable. But is representing a pristine North and Indigenous people in traditional clothing domesticating or foreignizing? The assumed pristine-ness is perhaps likely to be seen as the opposite of the urbanized polluted South and therefore foreign to southern viewers but it, like domestication in translation, is the approach that would demand less reflection and would not be a counter-narrative. Is situating a statue of a Beothuk woman in the woods or photographing Tshaukuesh's grandson Manteu on snowshoes in a spotless white landscape foreignizing or domesticating? It depends on your perspective.

Structures of Feeling

"Structures of feeling," a concept originally theorized by Raymond Williams in the 1970s,[49] refers to shared perceptions and values common to an era or cultural group and circulated through aesthetic forms and conventions such as stories, songs, and cultural practices. Williams was convinced of what now is often taken for granted, that affective aspects of politics, culture, and daily life are as important as the social, economic, and material. Following Edward Said's suggestion that narratives can create "'structures of feeling' that support, elaborate and consolidate the practice of empire" or alternative structures of feeling and thus resistance,[50] Tymoczko argues that engaged translation can contribute to geopolitical change through raising awareness of and solidarity for people fighting oppression by translating their stories.[51] Emily Apter has developed similar arguments about translation as a medium of subject re-formation—a revising of one's view of oneself and one's role in the world—and political change.[52] I think there is also a parallel in the ways visual storytelling and "translating" a written story into images or film can contribute to political change. Some Innu and other Indigenous elders who may not be able to read written text in any language will read only the pictures in *Nitinikiau Innusi.* However, most of these readers will know much more of the cultural context than others, and perhaps will be looking more to see their own lives and histories reflected on the printed page—a fairly unusual occurrence for them—than to learn something new. The photos can reaffirm the value of what is most important to them already and give them strength. (Though, as we have seen, photos can also "break the frame" and enable new insights.) For other readers from outside these communities, the pictures can potentially raise awareness and promote solidarity.

The photos of beautiful scenery produced by photographers like Kobalenko are a striking contrast to some of Tshaukuesh's own, which often show all of the things professional landscape photographers might frame out. For example, I thought a lot about scenes of butchering animals, which may appear graphic or disturbing to viewers not from a hunting culture, and also very messy. Those viewers might be hard put to understand the enormous respect the Innu have for animals, the way their whole culture is built around a cosmology in which animals are at the centre of life and of spirituality. Author and art critic John Berger writes eloquently of the dual relationship of traditional small farmers and animals: the farmers love the animals and they kill and eat them (not "but" they kill them—"and" they kill them: that is the dualism).[53] This is obviously also true of hunters or others who live closely with animals. Potawatomi environmental biologist Robin Kimmerer broadens this point to include all of us: "Sadly, since we cannot photosynthesize, we humans must take other lives in order to live. We have no choice but to consume, but we can choose to consume a plant or animal in a way that honors the life that is given and the life that flourishes as a consequence. Instead of avoiding ethical jeopardy by creating distance, we can embrace and reconcile that tension."[54] Tshaukuesh had many photos of hunting and preparing animals to eat, photos that represented the happiest of memories. I wanted to show this tension in the book through some of the pictures but at the same time, wondered if such photos might seem harsh to some readers and thus lose potential allies. Berger concludes that the loss of this dualism in most of our lives today "to which zoos are a monument, is now irredeemable for the culture of capitalism."[55] Since Berger wrote that, one could add that the loss is also irredeemable (as everything is) with respect to climate change, destruction of habitat, and species extinction, the ultimate results of capitalism.

For readers beyond the world of the Innu or other northern hunting cultures, photos like Kobalenko's have enormous appeal. The fact that his images appear in national and international publications such as *Canadian Geographic* and *National Geographic Travel* suggests just how wide an appeal. Tshaukuesh is also a passionately engaged interpreter of her world who seeks to persuade both Innu and outsiders to protect it. What sorts of structures of feeling might each inspire, and for whom? The answer to this question is far from simple. The beauty and serenity of Kobalenko's photographs might challenge viewers to work to protect the places depicted or to develop solidarity with the people. Some of Tshaukuesh's images might invite the same viewers (or perhaps different ones) to leave their comfort zone and learn from a world beyond their current understanding; but others might also achieve a goal shared with Steichen: to show commonality of experience and shared humanity.

I am thinking of another example: the film, *Rabbit-Proof Fence* (2002), directed by Phillip Noyce and based on the book, *Follow the Rabbit-Proof Fence* (1996) by Indigenous Australian author Doris Pilkington Garimara. Both book and film tell the story of three children of Martu ancestry (one of them Doris's mother, Molly Kelly) who escaped from a residential school and walked across Australia to get home. Noyce described how, in his search for actors, he travelled all over Australia looking for children who were obviously Aboriginal but who could also "connect with a global audience."[56] It could be argued that the choice of children whose looks and body language would appeal to a non-Indigenous audience was a problematic domestication in the visual translation of this story for cinema. Yet the director made the film with the goal of telling an alternative history of Australia, a "counter-history," and it appears to have been successful in gaining widespread attention and support for the "stolen generations" and thus contributing to changing cultural assumptions and power structures, and to healing. I interviewed Doris Pilkington Garimara after the film was released and asked her about its impact. She responded:

> I work with the Stolen Generations people on the journey of healing—so that is part of my work, involving people in taking

> further steps on the journey. The first step many of them took was when they saw *Rabbit Proof Fence*, so that is amazing in itself. Men in their 70s and 80s in New South Wales have come up to me or invited me to go over there and meet them, and said to me, "Sis, by gee, we all hated that place where we were." And we're walking on that journey of healing together. It really fills me with pride that that thirteen-year-old girl and her sister and cousin walked all that way, and it gives me, I suppose, some peace, knowing that my mother didn't walk all that distance for nothing. The walk wasn't in vain.[57]

Tymoczko has argued that the translation strategy of foreignization, applied here to visual translations, is not always appropriate for peoples who are already overwhelmed by foreign cultural domination, and that it is also elitist and not suited to a broad readership.[58] Valerie Henitiuk has made a similar point, explaining that translations of minority literatures are often literal or heavily domesticated because more demanding translations could make them less accessible to many readers and thus have a negative impact on their circulation and potential influence.[59] In this sense, a strategy that could be read as domesticating, such as the choice of child actors to whom both Aboriginal and other audiences could relate visually, might have enabled the film to have a broader impact. Pilkington Garimara's response focused entirely on the film's significance for Aboriginal people and its role as a first step on the road to healing for the Stolen Generations. The film played a key role in producing a structure of feeling that enabled that first step. The fact that it was internationally successful and accessible to a wide audience was part of that; it meant that their stories mattered.

Five

Signs

On Hamilton River Road, the main road through Happy Valley-Goose Bay, there is a green and white federal government road sign near the military base. It reads: "Caution Possible Low Flying Aircraft Ahead" followed by the same information in French, Innu-aimun, and Inuktitut, in that order.

There is no more low-level flying but the sign is still there. I suppose the fact that it is in both of Labrador's Indigenous languages as well as the two official languages of Canada says something, but what exactly is a more complex question. The only other sign I have seen in all four languages is one beside the Mishta-shipu that states that lake trout and northern pike from the river should only be eaten once a week. Tshaukuesh wrote about this sign in her diary:

> Sometimes on our canoe trips the children find small fish dead and they ask what happened to them. At first, I didn't know what happened, why they died. In one of the places where we stop on the river, at the far end of Uinukupau, I was surprised to see a sign on the shore. It said in four languages—English, French, Innu-aimun, and Inuktitut—that we shouldn't take more than one fish per week because of mercury. Why? What are the dams doing to the fish? How many years do we have to live with their suffering? I think a lot about that and about how when I was a child we could eat anything. There was never a sign saying you can't touch this or eat it. There was so much freedom. Now it's not like that. When

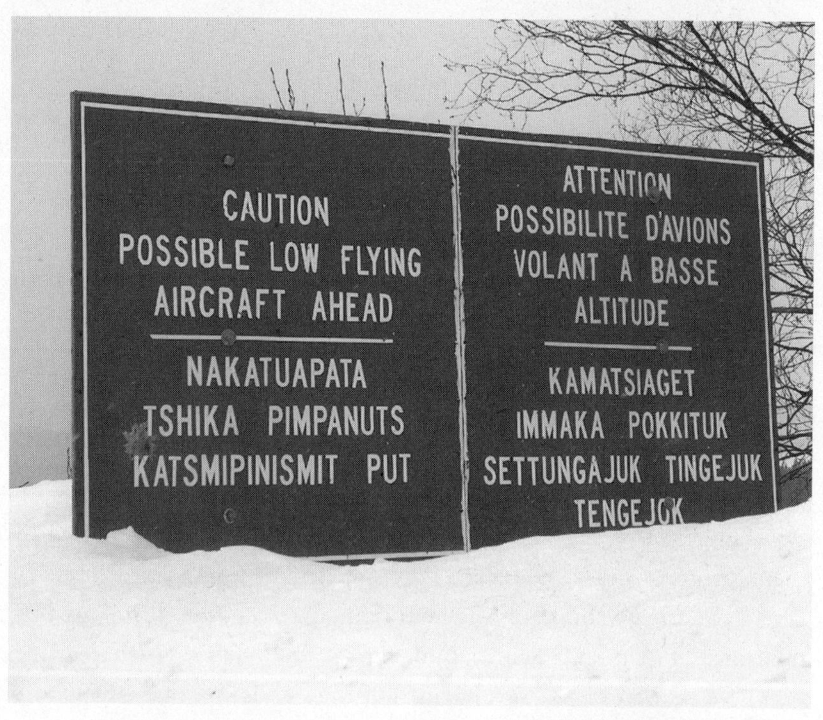

Federal government sign by the main road in Goose Bay. Photo by Elizabeth Yeoman.

> my husband, Francis, saw the sign about the fish he was very shocked that there's only one sign on the whole river. If they think they need to warn people, why not have signs all along the river? If somebody was camping in a different place they might not know that the fish weren't safe to eat.[1]

Both of these multilingual signs are warnings. Other signs were found in nutshimit on the edge of the bombing range during the NATO occupation.[2] They are also warnings, written only in Innu-aimun and Inuktitut, perhaps because, as Maura Hanrahan noted, these signs were "deep in the quiet woods . . . the only authentic setting for Indigenous people"[3] and therefore it was not considered necessary to post them in the official languages of the government. Translated, they read "Property of Land and Resources, Danger, target shooting area, if there is target shooting, do not enter," and "Property of Land and Resources, No Trespassing, Federal Land and Resources, Government." I wondered aloud what purpose the low-level flying sign could serve and my brother said, "It's so they don't poop their pants when they hear the sonic boom." Obviously, he was satirizing the government's perspective, but reactions to the boom could not be prevented by a warning. It frightened the animals and disrupted migration patterns; it terrified the children and made their parents worry that there might be accidents in nutshimit if people were startled by the blast while canoeing in tricky areas. A fish advisory that could easily be missed, telling people their food was contaminated; a no trespassing sign in the middle of the forest in Innusi; and a warning for something that no warning could prevent or mitigate. Signs. Language is powerfully symbolic and these signs are statements about who belongs and in what contexts, who has the right to know, who needs to be addressed and on what grounds. But signs could also do many other things. They could be a very practical way of making Indigenous languages more visible in daily life. TRC Call to Action 14 begins: "Aboriginal languages are a fundamental and valued element of Canadian culture and society, and there is an urgency to preserve them."[4] Like maps, signs are also a way of claiming territory and asserting power.

We have a history in Canada of a struggle for signs, not just semiotic signs but real physical road signs. A few years ago, I had an encounter that illustrated how much these signs can matter. Nancy Huston, the well-known Albertan-Parisian author of French- and English-language fiction and non-fiction, was presenting at a conference I attended in Montreal. Her topic was living in two languages. She spoke about how living as a foreigner, as she has been in Paris for much of her life, makes one humble in a way that she considers healthy. She recognized that she could not equate her cultural difference and disadvantage with that of, say, a Cambodian or a Senegalese in Paris, but nevertheless, she argued, having constantly to reflect on how to communicate, on whether the nuance is right, the syntax perfect, has a bracing effect and prevents one from becoming complacent. She emphasized the values of humility and openness to others. Then, toward the end of her talk, she told a story of being lost with her children in the mountains of Basque country, driving frantically on and on through remote countryside as night fell, unable to find her way because the Basques had painted out all the French directions (or Spanish—it was not clear which part of Basque country they were in), leaving only those in Basque. Huston's gentle tone changed to one of anger as she described Basque culture as sclérotique—intransigent, hidebound.[5] I was struck by the sudden change in tone and perspective and wondered why she described this experience so differently from everything else she had spoken about, as if it stood apart from her general analysis and her theme of humility. The exact same thing, the painting out of road signs, had been so common in Quebec when she and I were young. The roads of the region of New Brunswick—or Acadie, as it is called by its francophone inhabitants—where I grew up were also dotted with signs on which English was painted out and French added—often in dripping blood-red letters, though this and other symbolic acts were the extent of the violence in Acadie, unlike in Quebec, where there were kidnappings, bombings, and an assassination.

At the end of Huston's talk, the moderator called for questions, still speaking French but reassuring the audience that we could use either language. It was a bilingual conference. I longed to ask about the Basques, but I had heard that change in tone so I hesitated for a long time. Finally I went to the end of the queue at the microphone. When the moderator called me forward, she said it would be the last question and please keep it short. (A question about language and politics in Quebec—and please keep it short?)

"J'ai beaucoup aimé votre communication. C'était très émouvant . . ." I began by saying how moving I had found her talk, how insightful and inspiring. I spoke French. If my point, like hers, was about the salutary effect of living in a language not one's own, I thought I should. "On a vécu la même chose ici . . ." We had the same experience here. Our signs were painted out in exactly the same way; there were many parallels (I thought I heard a faint gasp from the audience—because I was comparing Quebec's "quiet revolution" to [Basque Euskadi Ta Askatasuna] ETA?[6]—or perhaps I imagined it) and I think you're right, it was good for us anglophones to learn a little humility, to struggle to express ourselves, to learn what it is like to be dépaysé—homesick and lost—in our own home. Your examples and your stories were fascinating. And I agreed with all of it. Except. What about the Basques? What is so different about them and their language struggles?"

"Madame! If you had experienced being lost in the mountains with your children . . . ! Ce n'est même pas une langue européene!" She was indignant, furious though controlled, hautaine. Not even a European language? Technically, Basque—the ancient indigenous language of the Pyrenees and the Bay of Biscay—is not an Indo-European language but surely it is, at the same time, one of the oldest European languages. And anyway, is that the point? Euskaria, the Basque country, is not a nation-state but neither (I would not have dared to say this aloud) is Quebec. It was through just such a struggle that French became the sole official language of Quebec, and New Brunswick became bilingual, through a campaign that included, among other things, painted-out signs. What about Indigenous languages here? I wanted to ask Huston these questions because I truly wanted to hear what she thought. However, given the vehemence of her response and the moderator's request to keep it short I thanked her and sat down, and she swept off the stage.[7]

Not a European language? What do we say in Canada about Indigenous languages and the histories and presences they mark, the knowledge they convey? What kinds of practices, what activisms, what teaching strategies, what creative acts can begin to address the ramifications of this question? Where do we end up if "not a European language," not a language of the "founding peoples," is where we start? If the only signs in Indigenous languages are warnings of war practices and poisoned food?

I am reminded again of Eve Tuck's counsel to move away from associating "decolonization" with narratives of pain and despair and toward narratives of "abundance."[8] So let me rephrase the paragraph above: We live in a land rich with languages. Each of them is a source of vast wealth of knowledge, insight, and experience. Languages carry with them immense bodies of wisdom and tradition: knowledge of potentially life-saving medicines; whole cosmologies and histories—including ancient history, which can be understood and analyzed through patterns of language and language shifts; poetry, songs, stories.[9] Learning something about even two or three languages can open up new and potentially better ways of being, of understanding and of doing things. Making those languages visible in things like road signs, maps, and place names can make them part of everyday life. For the native speakers of those languages as well as for the rest of us, doing so can say that their speech and their stories matter.

At the same time, it is important to remember that these ways of making a language visible, while potentially important both for their symbolic value and the access they can give to certain forms of knowledge, are extremely limited in other ways. Using the example of the Maori language, Te reo Maori, Mika and colleagues explain that "when Te reo Maori starts to be used as a simple translation of what people would say in English, Te reo Maori's capacity to present a different onto-metaphysics—a different sense and experience of the world—is gone. This translation (usually perceived as benevolent or 'revitalizing') could be interpreted as the last bastion of colonialism in the project of domestication of Indigenous thought."[10] This reminded me of Inuk curriculum developer Sophie Tuglavina's description of her work in the Labrador school system:

> [We have to follow] the provincial curriculum and we have to translate the curriculum materials . . . You can't just put it in Inuktitut; it doesn't work like that! You need to have the cultural context as well. If we're translating something about frogs, giraffes and elephants we can take that out and put polar

> bears and seals in. We try to put more Labrador kinds of things, or more northern content. Sometimes you have to change the content . . . but still get the message across and reach the outcome. Sometimes things that work in English don't work in Inuktitut. Snuffleupagus is not Inuk.[11]

Tuglavina goes on to reflect on more ineffable connections between language and culture: "I have heard a lot of people talk about how Indigenous cultures connect to nature and when it's disconnected people feel so lost. I do anyway. . . . All the things that I learned as I was growing up still mean so much to me and there are certain words and concepts that just don't translate. When I talk Inuktitut while I'm doing something, it has a lot more meaning to me than when I'm doing the same thing and I'm speaking English."[12]

Another example, from the final report of the TRC hearings, shows how even as Indigenous thought is often lost to colonizing language and wording when working across languages, struggling with translation can also help people who do not speak Indigenous languages to think differently about how we do things and how we understand and live in the world:

> Although Elders and Knowledge Keepers across the land have told us that there is no specific word for *reconciliation* in their own languages, there are many words, stories, and songs, as well as sacred objects such as wampum belts, peace pipes, eagle down, cedar boughs, drums, and regalia, that are used to establish relationships, repair conflicts, restore harmony, and make peace. . . . Elder Stephen Augustine explained the roles of silence and negotiation in Mi'kmaq law. . . . Reconciliation cannot occur without listening, contemplation, meditation, and deeper internal deliberation. Silence in the face of residential school harms is an appropriate response for many Indigenous peoples. We must enlarge the space for respectful silence in journeying towards reconciliation, particularly for Survivors who regard this as key to healing. There is also a place for discussion and

> negotiation for those who want to move beyond silence. Dialogue and mutual adjustment are significant components of Mi'kmaq law. Elder Augustine suggested that other dimensions of human experience—our relationships with the earth and all living beings—are also relevant in working towards reconciliation.[13]

Language and Belonging

I have read that language is to Canada what race is to the United States. Though the parallel falls down in all sorts of ways, there is truth to it, too. Our languages underscore histories of struggle and conquest, of power, loss, and passionate love. The ways we think about language, visible in public discourse and policy as well as in numerous aspects of our everyday lives, are central to how we understand who we are and where we are going as a nation. Language policy scholar Eve Haque asks, "How, in Canada, did language come to be the site for articulating exclusions which can no longer be stated in terms of race and ethnicity?"[14] Haque's question points to numerous others, such as how binary oppositions like English/French, settler/Indigenous, settled land/uninhabited land, Canada/unceded land shape our understanding of history and the present, who belongs and who does not, what is important and what is not. And how such things change over time and from place to place.

Indigenous peoples were intentionally and almost completely left out of the highly influential Royal Commission on Bilingualism and Biculturalism (B and B Commission) of 1963–70. Haque has shown how relations between the state and Indigenous peoples at the time were "transformed through the proposed elimination of the Indian Act"[15] and ensuing debates and challenges. The B and B Commission, through a related discourse of "two founding nations," enabled previously marginalized French-speaking Canadians to overturn, or at least join, the prevailing Anglo-Celtic hegemony of this settler nation, thus forcing a reorganization of the category "Other." According to Haque, the reorganization led to a more solidified exclusion of other settler groups and, even more thoroughly, of Indigenous nations.

The B and B Commission resulted in the 1969 Official Languages Act and the 1971 Multiculturalism Policy, the latter largely a result of effective challenges to the notion of biculturalism from multicultural groups. Royal commissions often play a key role in changing public opinion and discourse.[16] This particular commission, Haque suggests, generated a new mythology of belonging in Canada, one that was framed in terms of language and culture yet maintained a hierarchy of race and ethnicity.[17] The Commission, by its very terms (two founding races and a crisis between them which had urgently to be addressed) made it difficult for groups other than Anglo-Celtic or French to challenge the idea of official French-English bilingualism. Nevertheless, they did challenge it. Other settler groups, most notably Ukrainians, tried unsuccessfully to argue that their languages should also be made official. While they did not attain that goal, their arguments forced a rethinking of the notion of biculturalism and resulted in a key shift toward multiculturalism. Indigenous nations also brought forward challenges. Their arguments were in many ways harder to deny, particularly in terms of who the "founders" of the country were, and of treaty rights as opposed to privileges. Precisely because of the compelling grounds of their arguments, they had to be almost completely excluded from the Commission's discussion if it was to attain its goal of bilingualism in the two "founding" languages. Thus, they were denied recognition through being positioned as "pre-modern, pre-literate, and linguistically fragmented."[18] They were not included in the terms of reference of the Commission and then were reminded that unfortunately, they could not be heard because of the terms of reference.[19]

Haque argues convincingly that Canadian policies and practices in relation to multiculturalism do not represent a melting pot or a mosaic but rather a hierarchy. She shows how language became a proxy for race and ethnicity when it was no longer considered acceptable to exclude people on racial or ethnic grounds. She reveals contradictions in the development of the policies, such as the convoluted reasoning by which Indigenous peoples were excluded from the Commission. Another striking example is Prime Minister Pierre Trudeau's use of a definition of multiculturalism in which mother tongue did not matter while promoting an official bilingualism in which language was central to identity.

Despite this history, the results of the B and B Commission have been interpreted positively by some people. A Yup'ik teacher from Alaska once told me how inspired she was by a visit to Ottawa where bilingualism was the norm. Even two European official languages can have a symbolic value, can underscore the notion that there could be more than one way of doing things. This view was also expressed by Coast Salish actor and physician Evan Adams. He commented after the Quebec referendum of 1995, in which 49.42 percent supported sovereignty, that he felt devastated because he had always believed that if there was room for two peoples and their languages that meant that there could be room for others as well, but if French and English Canadians could not live together, there seemed to be little hope for Indigenous peoples.[20] This is one understanding of the symbolic value of Canada's bilingualism, and clearly it is shared by some Indigenous people, including Adams and the Yup'ik teacher. It is an argument that was also made during the Commission. Then New Democratic Party MP David Lewis, for example, stated in 1968 that Canada's official bilingualism provided "opportunity for the recognition of other languages and other cultures as well."[21] However, another perspective, put forward so clearly by Haque, is that on the contrary, Canada's official bilingualism explicitly and implicitly excludes Indigenous and other languages and cultures.

Translating Innu-aitun

At the St. John's launch for *Nitinikiau Innusi*, Tshaukuesh was on stage speaking in Innu-aimun to a large audience, few of whom understood the language. Her daughter Kanani was interpreting into English. At one point, Tshaukuesh told a sad story and Kanani, clearly deeply moved, joked, "This is why I hate translating for my mom!" Translation and interpretation can be cumbersome and expensive. As Kanani indicated, it can also be emotional work, painful. It can even be dangerous in certain contexts, since translators are often seen as inextricably linked to what they translate and that may at times be controversial or threatening.[22] But as with road signs and maps, translation can also make multiple realities visible and audible. It was the English version of the book that was being launched but the speech in Innu-aimun, its soft sibilant sounds echoing through the theatre at the Rooms, the provincial museum of Newfoundland and Labrador, was a statement. As Tshaukuesh had so often written in her diary: "We are here. This is our land."

As for the diaries on which the book is based, Tshaukuesh translated them herself, reiterating and explaining as she read aloud to me from the tattered notebooks she writes in whenever she has time: early in the morning in her tent before anyone else is awake, sitting in Tim Hortons waiting for a drive home from Goose Bay, on planes as she travels to speaking engagements. The translation was collaborative in the sense that I wrote what she said and edited the written English. But perhaps my most important role was to listen carefully, to create a space for the work to develop. This allowed Tshaukuesh not only to tell me what she had written but also to reflect on it, to add and edit as she went along, to take the time she didn't always have in the hurried moments of the original writing.

There are layers of translation in telling this story: the two-step translation from Innu to English (often, in fact, three or four steps because of checking back with Tshaukuesh or other Innu-aimun speakers, or the original diaries to make sure I have conveyed as much as possible "exactly what she said," as she asked me to do when we began working together); the representation of Tshaukuesh's story through selected images by multiple photographers (discussed in Chapter 4); and the standardizing of the Innu version (discussed in Chapter 6). As we worked together, we began to think about how difficult it is to translate certain key words such as "Innu," "Beothuk," "land," and "home." The English words do not map onto the Innu-aimun in any direct or transparent way. At times the photos helped convey the sense of land and home or of who the Innu are, Innu-aitun—Innu ways of thinking and doing things—but each version had limitations. English does not always have the capacity to convey what Mika and colleagues referred to as "a different onto-metaphysics—a different sense and experience of the world."[23]

Another challenge was representing the voice in English of an author who is a well-known and eloquent public speaker in English, but whose English vocabulary is nevertheless quite limited and who writes only in her own language. Before Tshaukuesh and I began working together, some of the diaries had been translated from Innu-aimun into French by Innu translator and poet Joséphine Bacon. Camille Fouillard and I translated these into English, after I discussed the French translations with Tshaukuesh. She thought that the French versions closely paralleled the original, so I felt very confident about this part of the translation. In one entry Bacon had used the word "élégante." The French word maps very closely onto the English one and I assumed that she chose a word that would also evoke what was written in Innu. But a local English speaker who knew Tshaukuesh saw the translation and said, "Tshaukuesh wouldn't use a word like elegant." It is true that in English she would not, but in Innu-aimun she presumably would and I believed she wanted me to convey the range of what she could say in her own language as best I could. Yet Fouillard speaks of the power of Innu elders speaking or writing in English, even though—or precisely because—the English is often pared down and stark.[24] And I can often hear Tshaukuesh's voice in my mind, even long after I have corrected and standardized her English, as she asked me to do. I can hear her telling stories: travelling by train to Uashat gazing out at the land and imagining her ancestors walking over it, the anguish of prison, the loneliness of a night spent meditating alone on a mountain, the triumph of reaching Minai-nipi on foot the first time. But I cannot reproduce the way she speaks in writing, and neither can she. Oral stories are not the same as written stories. "The good translation gets you far enough into the other world to begin to see what you are missing," writes James Clifford.[25] The oral stories are part of what the reader is missing and I think my job is to help them begin to see that, but how best to do it is not always obvious.

Tshaukuesh's lyrical description of waking up at dawn in her tent is an example:

> The birds woke me up this morning. It's wonderful to hear them singing so I stayed still and listened for a while, thinking about how I was hearing the same bird calls I heard as a child. I got up and made the fire and then lay down again, but I had the impression that the birds were trying to persuade me to get up. Then after a while they moved away, as if one of them had

> said, "Okay, Tshaukuesh is awake now." Then I thought about another kind of bird, the kautauassikunishkueunishit, which Innu people used to say had a call that said, "Tante nipatshi nita kutshikutshin?"— "How can I dive down and come back up?" I hadn't heard that bird for a long time. I wonder where they've all gone. Then I got up in a nice warm tent.[26]

This short passage raises many questions. In an earlier translation I had written, "I stayed in bed and listened for a while" but this was a domestication. It was a bed but not what an Akaneshau reader might visualize—it was a caribou hide spread over spruce branches. To make that explicit in the text might be to foreignize, to make non-Innu readers more aware of the translation. It might also lovingly evoke the scent of spruce and the warmth of fur, the smells and sensations of the tent. The kautauassikunishkueunishit is called that because it looks as though it is wearing an Innu baby bonnet, and this leads us to think it is a white-crowned sparrow in English.[27] But we aren't certain and perhaps a failure of translation is the best strategy here anyway. The verb "kutshikutshin" refers to diving repeatedly, but it is also an onomatopoeia that mimics the bird's call. Is an explanatory note called for? Or not? I had wanted to compare with English and French onomatopoeia for calls of a similar bird, the white-throated sparrow (and we really were not completely sure which bird we were talking about since the white-throated sparrow has a striped cap that looks perhaps even more like a traditional Innu bonnet than the white-crowned sparrow's cap does). Perhaps I could have replicated the onomatopoeia better with "How can I dive, and dive, and dive?" I wanted to use a domesticating strategy by identifying with Tshaukuesh through my own delight at the bird supposedly calling "Old Sam Peabody, Peabody" in the United States, "Oh Sweet Canada, Canada" in English Canada, and "Où es-tu, Frédéric, Frédéric?" in French. I listened to recordings of the calls of both birds. Each had several and none seemed to replicate exactly the beat of "Tante nipatshi nita kutshikutshin?" or of the English and French versions. Listening so carefully to them did make me feel close to the birds, however, and to think of them as kin who deserved respectful attention and from whom I could learn.

Carol Maier has written about the risks of identification: "identification is a function of recuperating the unfamiliar 'other' in terms of the familiar; reading this way relies on the stereotypes one culture utilized to understand, and domesticate, (an)other. [However], an uncritical assumption of difference, which presumes that (an)other is never accessible, allows readers to abandon, indeed exonerates them from, the task of ever reading cross-cultural texts. Deployed solely, each category produces an impasse."[28]

The bird in Tshaukuesh's diary entry is just one brief example. While it does not seem to me to be about a problematic identification relying on stereotypes, it does illustrate how complex even seemingly straightforward decisions can be. I wanted readers to "begin to see what they might be missing" and thought the appeal of the bird call might be part of that. But I also wanted to stay as close to what Tshaukuesh actually said and be as accurate as possible, while recognizing that neither she nor I could translate all the nuances precisely from the original, and we were not even certain which bird it was. Then, recently I read that the white-throated sparrow has changed its call. It used to have a three-note finale, as in "nita kutshikutshin" or "Sweet Canada, Canada," but has moved to a two-note finale. The birds too have different languages and, like ours, they evolve.

But what is the original?[29] Tomson Highway, for example, has written Cree versions of his well-known plays *The Rez Sisters* and *Dry Lips Oughta Move to Kapuskasing*. Highway told a CBC journalist that when he wrote the originals in English, he had often imagined the dialogue in Cree: "The Cree versions that are coming out tonight are actually the original versions. As it turns out, the original ones that came out 20 years ago were the translation."[30] The Cypriot-born poet and translator Stephanos Stephanides says, "It's difficult to know what the original actually is. . . . Borges asks how can we really know Homer from 3,000 years away?" One could bring that question much closer to home in time and space to ask how a non-Innu reader could really know Tshaukuesh or her world. Or what the original was. Of course, Tshaukuesh's handwritten diaries were in a sense the original, but they were also a first draft that she further developed and modified as we worked together. Stephanides reflects, "When my poetry is translated into other languages, I get new ideas. Sometimes I want to go back and change the original, because the translation seems to be more faithful to what I originally wanted to say . . . you always think through the gap, rather than in the centre of one or the other . . . and it gives the possibility of expanding the edges and the borders of possibility."[31] The original diaries were transformed, not only into English but through the editorial process, as Tshaukuesh considered what to keep, what to modify, add to, or delete. But anyone who writes does this. I do wonder about my own role in the process, though. I tried hard not to lead but to follow, to listen, but just my being there must have led to loss as well as gain.

A Gap Can Be a Creative Space

I worried a lot about not speaking Innu-aimun. I worked on it and learned enough for some basics like offering and asking for food and drink, giving directions, and talking about the weather. I made an Innu-aimun calendar, writing out the numbers for the dates in full as well as the days and months and referring to them regularly. I also gradually acquired enough knowledge of structure and lexicon to get the gist of what a diary entry was about and to think about specific translation challenges such as those discussed in this chapter. This enabled me to draw on both Innu and French versions in translating excerpts from Bacon and Kapesh and to refer back to the original Innu when editing Tshaukuesh's translations. But my knowledge never came remotely close to the kind of deep understanding of a language, culture, and cosmology that I really needed. Improvised translations are not uncommon in colonial, postcolonial, and human rights settings, and Henitiuk has noted that more than a few translators working with Indigenous languages feel a sense of inadequacy.[32] I still worried, but there did not appear to be anybody else available and Tshaukuesh had asked me to help her, so we carried on. When I saw Ann Marie Fleming's animated film *Window Horses* (2016), an exchange about translation in the film caught my attention. The main character, poet Rosie Ming, is struggling to translate a poem from Chinese to English. The author of the original poem, DiDi, tells her, "Don't be so stuck on the perfect translation. Make it your own. You know, Coleman Barks is the most well-known translator of Rumi and he doesn't read a word of Farsi . . . write what is inside you, write what you know." The idea was comforting, but I knew it couldn't be that simple; in fact, writing what I knew was the last thing I should do as a colonial occupier writing about an Indigenous elder's campaign against the occupation.

I had not heard of Coleman Barks, though I had often seen excerpts from poems that were probably "translated" by him. He is an American poet who has specialized in interpreting the poems of Muhammad Jalal al-Din Balkhi, or Jalal al-Din Rumi, better known in the English-speaking world simply as Rumi. Barks has been criticized for producing an English-language Rumi who is a "New Age poet, devoid of Islam,[33] the 13th century, or the themes and images of the golden age of classical Persian poetry,"[34] and for translating without knowledge of the original language and culture of the poems.[35] Barks himself wrote, "What I do is a homemade, amateurish, loose, many-stranded thing, without much attention to historical context, nor much literal faithfulness to the original."[36] This is fine in some senses, as long as it is clear to the reader, but books of Rumi's poetry are often marketed with Coleman Barks presented on the cover as either author or translator, not as a poet who creates "amateurish, loose" versions based on earlier scholarly translations. It has also been argued that Barks has a responsibility to be true to the original, and that in the current political climate, he misses an opportunity to show Muslims as multi-faceted and Islam as a rich cultural heritage, that keeping the Islam that permeates Rumi's poetry instead of effacing it "would help readers to recognize that a professor of Sharia could also write some of the world's mostly widely read love poetry."[37] Yet Barks himself suggests that "Rumi's transcending of religious boundaries [is] 'a powerful element in his appeal now,'"[38] and other scholars have also argued that Barks's versions "present a moderate image of Islam in the West."[39]

The film *Window Horses* further explores questions of what it means to translate a literary work and who owns the work. Rosie finishes her translation and performs her version of the poem at the poetry festival where she met DiDi, introducing it by saying, "It moved me so much, but I didn't know what it meant. But now, I think I do." Audience members protest that in translation it isn't the same poem, but DiDi responds, "That's her poem." The story in the film is told with a light touch and, of course, the context is very different from that of translating *Nitinikiau Innusi*, but I mention it as the genesis of my thinking about what it means to work on the translation of literary work originally written in a language one does not know. There are important issues here about who can own or convey something like a poem, or any literary work. Some of those issues are very practical and relate to earning a living from cultural production. Some are historical and political: for centuries, European colonizers have rewritten and taken credit for the cultural works of the peoples they colonized, and it is time, long past time, to make amends. But in yet another sense, to be truly moved by someone else's story and to take it into your heart through translating it is a way of thinking deeply about what they meant, about how to convey it—as Tshaukuesh put it, how to "use other words but mean exactly what I said." The act of translation can be an appropriation or it can be one of the most profound ways of listening to someone.

Edith Grossman, a translator of writers ranging from Cervantes to the Chilean antipoet Nicanor Parra, suggests that English-speaking regions of the world are not exposed nearly enough to writers in other languages because of a cultural antipathy toward translated works (although Rumi seems to be an exception, perhaps because Barks's versions have modernized and Westernized him). She argues that we lose not only the opportunity to read those works but the possibility of relationships beyond the English-speaking world.

> Translation not only plays its important traditional role as the means that allows us access to literature originally written in one of the countless languages we cannot read, but it also represents a concrete literary presence with the crucial capacity to ease and make more meaningful our relationships to those with whom we may not have had a connection before. Translation always helps us to know, to see from a different angle, to attribute new value to what once may have been unfamiliar. As nations and as individuals, we have a critical need for that kind of understanding and insight. The alternative is unthinkable.[40]

Translating in colonial or postcolonial contexts has particular challenges because of historic and actual power imbalances. Indigenous scholars have argued that North American Indigenous contexts are colonial rather than postcolonial in that Indigenous peoples are still colonized.[41] However, some postcolonial writers on translation understand the contexts in which they work in a similar way. For example, Maria Tymoczko defines postcolonialism in translation contexts as pertaining to situations where there is or has been conquest and dispossession; political, economic, cultural, and linguistic dominance; and a lack of self-determination.[42] She emphasizes that this is not a definitive list but rather suggestive, and that in these contexts we will gain more insight by examining cases individually than by placing them all together in a single category. Tymoczko also discusses the question of whether the translator must know the language of the source text: "Dominant models assume that a translator must 'know' the two languages and cultures involved. Postcolonial contexts challenge this view, showing that translation has a fundamental epistemological dimension: it does not merely reflect existing knowledge, it can also precede knowledge. It can be a mode of discovery used to create or amass knowledge [and thus a mode of resistance].... Postcolonial translations also indicate that a translation is not merely a text but an act, where the function is as important as the product itself."[43]

It is quite common in colonial, postcolonial, and human rights contexts for an author and a translator to work together despite neither having complete mastery of the other's language. It is also common for several people to be involved, as was the case with *Nitinikiau Innusi*, since we often consulted other speakers to verify difficult words or passages. This kind of process, known as "relay translation," is often used in translations from Indigenous languages, since frequently no one person has all the skills and knowledge required. Henitiuk emphasizes the need for careful listening and sensitivity in relay translation because of the power differential in colonial contexts.[44] Such collaborations often bring together two very different cultures and realities, with all the complications described by Tymoczko, and with author and translator simultaneously editing the text and relying on others with various agendas and understandings to clarify difficult points. For example, at one talk Tshaukuesh gave with an interpreter, she named a specific mining company but the interpreter softened it to "business interests." Translators and interpreters make endless decisions and, as with the example of Coleman Barks and Rumi, there is always a politics to the decisions and the translator always has a responsibility to the writer of the source text and the broader community, as well as to the reader. Others in the community may also have a role to play in the bringing over of stories and ideas. For example, Maier suggests that instructors of courses where translated works are read should make translations more visible by discussing not only the work and its context but also "the climate in which the translation was made, the translator, and the response to the translated work."[45] Making translation visible can be a way into new insights and understanding.

The role of the translator is clearly a controversial one. Theoretical understandings of translation range from "a field . . . defined by problems of linguistic and textual fidelity to the original,"[46] or what Grossman calls "the literalist fallacy,"[47] to Walter Benjamin's comment that "no translation would be possible if in its ultimate essence it strove for likeness to the original,"[48] from Lawrence Venuti's notion of the inherent violence of translation, in that it imposes the values of the "target" culture and its language onto those of the source[49] to the ethical stance that translation must be based on a deep responsibility toward the Other.[50] Henitiuk has also discussed several Inuktitut words relating to translation and concluded that the emphasis in Inuktitut is on listening, relationship, and aligning one's mind with another.[51] Indeed, one Inuktitut term for interpreter is tusaaji, meaning one who listens carefully. Finally, Maier proposes that translators must be open and vulnerable, recognizing that their efforts to convey meaning are merely "provisional reports of what [they] have learned from their travels with source authors, from observation and contemplation of other people and customs in the texts they have translated, and from their role as ambassadors or witnesses of that learning for receiving audiences. [They need] an appreciation of wonder, an open acknowledgment that translators do not fully master or possess what has been witnessed."[52] The recognition that translators (as well as editors, filmmakers, and other interpreters) are not experts but always learning must be fundamental to collaborations in colonial and postcolonial contexts.

Cross-cultural collaborative writing is often fraught with misunderstandings and mistakes. But it is also an extraordinary privilege and an opportunity: to learn, to give back, to build alliances. Working together can also help us think beyond binary oppositions such as teller and recorder or oral and written as we try to understand each other. Those binaries historically have given the advantage to the recorder and the written, so recorders and writers need to pay careful attention to listening and moving beyond such binaries.[53] Meanwhile, however, some binaries may be collapsing as broader ways of thinking about relationships change. Since the appropriation debates of the 1980s and early '90s, non-Indigenous recorders and editors of Indigenous stories have had to reconsider their roles in the production of collaborative texts as Indigenous authors and storytellers developed new forms of collaboration among themselves and with others, including not only written translations and edited books and stories but also public forums and commissions, ethnographic and autobiographical work, photography, films, fictions, and media reports.

Sophie McCall argues that the complicated and sometimes uneasy collaboration between Indigenous storytellers and non-Indigenous translators and interpreters may actually have strengths as well as weaknesses: "In every communicative act there is a gap—between teller and listener, between writer and reader, between signifier and signified. However, this gap can be a creative space in which new forms of agency and of voice may arise. . . . A diversity of forms of affiliation is possible and indeed necessary to recognize the struggle of writing and of telling a more just story of Indigenous presence in North America, through the mode of cross-cultural collaboration." This kind of work, done responsibly, can contribute to new ways of "honouring Indigenous sovereignty" and fostering "a sense of historical accountability" among non-Indigenous peoples.[54]

Some writers and scholars have expressed concern about translation from Indigenous languages into colonizing ones. For example, Sto:lo author and poet Lee Maracle emphasizes the relational and community-based quality of much Indigenous poetry and notes that these qualities cannot be translated, least of all by non-Indigenous people who may misunderstand and oversimplify.[55] Cree Métis poet and storyteller Duncan Mercredi gives the example of heartrending stories told during the TRC hearings and asks whether their emotions, rhythms, and cadence could be captured on the written page at all, and whether translations of Indigenous poetry could really convey the spirit and intention of the original.[56] Anishinaabe writer and teacher Niigaanwewidam James Sinclair draws attention to the incommensurability of terms but nonetheless adds that "there are cultural and ideological possibilities in English, regardless of . . . historical and discursive baggage."[57]

For many Indigenous writers, however, translation into and between colonizing languages is crucial, not because they are seeking connection within the literary canons of these languages but because they need to be able to read each other's work across nations, even if only in translation.[58] For Innu writers specifically, the problem is not just reading across nations but even within their own nation, since the Quebec-Labrador border means that while Labrador Innu speak English as a second language, Quebec Innu use French. As Natasha Kanapé Fontaine put it, "Where I come from, French is a second language. Very optional. English trails far behind."[59] This may be a reason that Innu-aimun is still widely spoken, since it is the only common language of the broader community, but some Innu authors write mainly in French. Literary scholar Isabelle St-Amand explains that Indigenous authors writing in French do so under a double set of constraints: first, for them colonization has created linguistic barriers to communication with their counterparts writing in English; and second, the market for literary works in French is smaller, which limits their chances of publication and critical reception.[60] Thus, translation is particularly important for Indigenous authors writing in French and also for nations like the Innu who are divided internally by the linguistic divide of colonization. Indeed, some critics have argued that translation is an important support for contesting colonial power structures, as it enables Indigenous writers and thinkers to communicate nation to nation across colonial jurisdictions and linguistic frontiers.[61] As well, even though writing in French may reach smaller readerships than writing in English, Joséphine Bacon has explained that she sometimes writes directly in French rather than Innu if she wants to reach a broader Indigenous readership or readers who are not Indigenous.[62] Rita Mestokosho, referring to poetry as activism and to her search for allies, said something similar in an interview with Christophe

Premat and Françoise Sule: "And when I wrote the poems, every word was thought in Innu before being transcribed in French. . . . I conceived them in my Innu soul . . . And to have the privilege of writing in French and be[ing] able to share it, I am all the more happy, because I find that poetry is a secret weapon, even if I do not like the word weapon."[63]

Apart from arguments for and against translation, there is also a literature on strategies for doing it. In the context of translating Indigenous works for non-Indigenous audiences, Nolette explores the idea of "countertranslation."[64] This could mean using "supplementary explanatory measures" such as pictures, definitions, and explanations, or simply leaving some things untranslated or partially translated so that the reader must recognize that there are things that cannot be carried over directly from one language to another and will perhaps be inspired to try to learn. Untranslated material hints that there is another, possibly better, way to live, if we could only understand.[65]

McCall suggests that one of anthropologist, filmmaker, and writer Hugh Brody's writing tactics "is the failure of cultural translation, which draws attention to the provisionality of all acts of representation."[66] Brody uses various strategies—such as juxtapositions of differing versions of a story, indirect rather than direct (but still mediated) quotation, or the highlighting of inaccurate translations in land claims consultations—to remind us that representations are not transparent. McCall makes a similar point about Inuk filmmaker Zacharias Kunuk's use of partial translations in *Atanarjuat*. Parts of the dialogue are presented in Inuktitut but not explained in the subtitles. Thus a non-Inuktitut speaking audience might realize they are excluded and can only follow the story on certain levels. The use of partial translation is a way of reminding the dominant group that they are missing something, something they might want to know, might even long to know. (Of course, I am referring mainly to people who feel some degree of sympathy or solidarity, the Akaneshau or Qallunaat who are likely to watch Kunuk's films or read Tshaukuesh's book in the first place. Mainly but not solely.) The non-translation in Tshaukuesh's book of Innu words that are either difficult to translate or have special importance or emotional intensity for Innu, such as nutshimit, Akaneshau, and Mishta-shipu, is an example of partial translation. McCall argues that this strategy enables "two parallel texts [to] interact and speak to each other in complex and imperfect ways"[67] and address different audiences. In the case of *Atanarjuat*, both versions are simultaneously available, as voiced and subtitled versions of the film.

In an example of a poet who both translates and refuses to translate, Lianne Moyes describes how Natasha Kanapé Fontaine uses Innu-aimun words and phrases in her poetry to "interrupt the French and open alternative spaces of knowledge."[68] Moyes sought ways of echoing these interruptions in her English rendition of one of Kanapé Fontaine's slams. She used a visual strategy of alternating lines of English and French, with Kanapé Fontaine's original French following the left margin and the English lines offset to the right to remind readers of the "movement—and disturbance—of colonization."[69] Following Kanapé Fontaine's lead, she also left some parts untranslated, for example invented words referencing territory such as terrimaterre and terripagaie. Refusing to provide an equivalent suggests "that translation has the potential to fail."[70] Kanapé Fontaine implies in the poetry itself that invoking Innu words and an Innu cosmology are decolonizing acts: "Nos fils et nos filles sortiront des réserves, ils invoqueront les esprits des légendes, ils prononceront 'Papakassik,' 'Tshiuetinishu,' 'Tshakapesh,' 'Tshishikushkueu.'"[71]

Opening Up New Ways of Seeing

Various writers, including social theorist Thomas Homer-Dixon[72] and linguists Tove Skutnabb-Kangas and Robert Phillipson,[73] suggest that we need a diversity of languages as much as we need biodiversity, because different languages can offer different insights that could help us cope with many kinds of challenges. For instance, Tomson Highway describes some of the ways that Cree offers "room—and plenty of it—for the notion of God as female *and* for more than just two genders." He concludes that "without speaking other languages . . . you would *never* know that such a vision of life, one so different from your own, existed."[74] In this section, I look at some examples of words and grammatical structures that we found difficult to translate as we worked on *Nitinikiau Innusi*. The difficulty itself suggests a different "vision of life" and alternative ways of thinking about our relationships with each other and the land.

As I wrote "the land" above, I was wishing I could use the Innu word, "nutshimit." It conveys a concept that has no English equivalent. It has been variously translated as "in the bush," "in the country," "on the land," "inland," and "in the wilderness." In French it has been interpreted as "à l'intérieur des terres," "en forêt" and "dans la nature." Tshaukuesh's annual weeks-long walk in nutshimit has been called the "wilderness walk" and in French, "une randonnée sauvage." In New Brunswick and Quebec until at least the 1970s, some French speakers still referred to Indigenous people as "les sauvages," or savages. This is also the referent for the French translation of the title of An Antane Kapesh's *Eukuan nin matshi-manitu innushkueu: Je suis une maudite Sauvagesse (I Am a Damn Savage)*. It should be noted, however, that the French word "sauvage" is not always pejorative and can also be translated as "wild" in a more neutral way, as in "fleur sauvage," or wildflower. There have also been moves to "take back" the word from its more negative connotations. For example, Kapesh herself wrote, "I feel proud when they call me a SAVAGE. When white people say that word, I know that what they mean is that I am a real Innu woman and that I was the first to live in the forest . . . May they always call me a SAVAGE."[75] More recently, Joséphine Bacon has said, "'Savage' means to be completely free."[76] Thus, freedom and life in the forest are also potentially aspects of what "nutshimit" means.

All of this gives a sense of the challenges of translating "nutshimit." Something fundamental is missing in all of the attempts to convey its meaning in English or French. Bacon describes nutshimit as the source of all that is needed for life: healthy food, medicines, shelter, and so on.[77] The late Innu leader Tanien Ashini explained it by saying "to reduce the meaning of the word 'nutshimit' to 'in the bush' does not describe what it means to us. It is a place where we are at home."[78] Jean-Paul Lacasse states that "nutshimit" used to be widely understood as the opposite of "uinipek^{u}" (the sea) but currently is more often used as the opposite of the reserve.[79] It seems to be in this sense that Tshaukuesh uses the word most often, and in her diaries she frequently contrasts life in Sheshatshiu with the peace and happiness of nutshimit. Recognizing the difficulty of translating the word, she often says in English "in-the-bush-in-the-country" as if it were all one word. But it is clear in the diaries that it also means home to her. This definition of "home" is particularly important, since settlers tend to think of the inland forests and tundra as "away from home" or "unhomelike," or even "unheimlich" in the Freudian sense of "frightening, repulsive and distressing."[80] We use the word "wilderness" metaphorically to describe a place or state where one is lost, perhaps frightened and disoriented. (There is so much to say about wilderness that it has its own chapter in this book.) It is also often thought of as a place that can be "developed," where we can extract resources for use elsewhere. Understanding nutshimit as someone's home, and home to all the living things it encompasses in Innu-aimun, enables different ways of thinking about what we can or can't do there.

Somewhat related to the word "nutshimit," although perhaps less extensive in its meaning, is the word "mushuau," which can be translated as "tundra," "barrens," "a treeless area," or "bare ground." Bacon has translated her poetry collection *Nipishapui nete mushuat* as *Un thé dans la toundra (Tea in the Tundra).* "Tundra" has a kind of romantic ring to it, a nordicity, evoking caribou, wild berries, starkly beautiful landscapes, and snow. Through the combination of tea and tundra, Bacon marvellously juxtaposes the comfort and coziness of a steaming mug and the dramatic contrast of the treeless, snow-swept northern landscape. Elsewhere, however, she renders the same word in French as "terre dénudée": "bare earth" or "barren ground." In Newfoundland and Labrador, "mushuau" is often translated this way, as "barrens" or "barren ground," which on the one hand may have a domesticating effect for settlers, since there are areas on the island of Newfoundland known as barrens, too, and the term is familiar; but on the other hand, barren means unproductive, empty of life, which is not true of either the Newfoundland or the Labrador barrens. Similarly, the Mushuau Innu of Natuashish have been known in English as Barren-Ground Innu, or people from the barrens.[81]

The words "Innu" and "Beothuk" are also difficult to translate. Tshaukuesh and I have written elsewhere about this, but I will summarize some of the discussion here.[82] I begin with a diary excerpt that was particularly difficult to translate but also revealing of how Innu might think differently about who the Beothuk were than settlers do, and how knowing this might help reframe understandings of Indigenous-settler relationships in Newfoundland and Labrador today. The following is a transcription of what Tshaukuesh wrote in Innu-aimun and a possible version of it in English:

> Shetan Pishum 7 2000
> Sitshanishit
> Eku uiapak masten tuskan eku tshietshishepaushit nitshitshipeitunan nete nuiashamikutan tshetshi eimiat nin mak Peter ekute nititutenan. Ne uet uishamukuiat nete pet shashish kanipanikuet innut ute Beothuks akinishaut espish uakashinuat innu ekunu uet nipanit kuet innut. Euakatanit. Kie miste mitshetinanu nete etuteiat kie mitshet uen eimut kie tshitatimut mishinikana. Eitenimanit nanat innut pise akinishaut miste ispitentakunu eisishuet. Kie Peter iat miste minekash eimu. Kie pise niuitamak nenu eitistet mishinikana Peter kie niminuetamuan nenu eshi uitamut. Eukun ume nistam eitinanut eku katshi tshistakit eku minuat tshatutanut pimutanu pitshashu etutanut nete shatshuatikinu. Nte tauakupin ntshet innut kie nte kauitshit. Nete mak tekushinanut ekute tshemishut ne innu iskueu tutuanisha unapiska uakinu. Miste minushishu kie miste minuashinu nte tshemishut ne unapiskauakinu innu iskueu. Miam nte nutshimit ekun eshinakunit tshemishut. Eku minuat tshatutanut iat pimutanu nete uste itutanu ekute uiatamat nte uatshuakuet nas nte nukunu nenu uitshuau. Kie miste minuashinu nte uatshuakuet. Eukun ume eitinanut. Kie ninan Sheshatshit innut ne katshi uatamat nimiste uauinanat nanat innut. Espish miste piuenimat nit innut espish uakatanit kie espish nenekatshianit innut nas tapue nipakanut.
>
> July 7, 2000, St. John's
> On Saturday morning Peter and I went to the place where we had been invited to speak. Long ago, white people killed the Beothuk because they hated the Indigenous people so much. They despised them so they murdered them. There were a lot of people there

> and many made speeches. Everybody was reading the storyboards that explained what happened and I was glad Peter could translate them for me. After that we walked to where they used to live, a lovely place. Then we walked around looking at everything and saw a statue somebody had made of an Innu woman. It's a very beautiful statue and a beautiful spot where she was standing. Then we walked further and found an old camp. You could see where they had their tents; it looked like nutshimit, surrounded by trees and green moss on the ground. That's what we did today. Afterwards we Innu from Sheshatshiu talked for a long time about those long ago Innu. They were the outcasts, the ones that were abused.

The Beothuk were an Indigenous group who lived on the island of Newfoundland until Shanawdithit, the last member of the group known to Europeans, died of tuberculosis in 1829. It is possible that there are still living Beothuk descendants, and recent DNA studies seem to confirm this,[83] but their distinct language and culture were almost certainly lost with this death and the deaths of Shanawdithit's relations in the years leading up to hers. We do not know how closely related the Beothuk were to other Indigenous groups in the region, but Tshaukuesh's diary entry above, about a visit to the Beothuk archaeological and commemorative site at Boyd's Cove, suggests deep connections. Tshaukuesh had been invited to speak at the unveiling of the statue she refers to of a Beothuk woman by Gerald Squires titled *Spirit of the Beothuk*.

In the original Innu-aimun text, Tshaukuesh refers to the woman as "innu iskueu" (an Innu woman) and to herself and Peter as "sheshatshit innut" (Innu, or people, from Sheshatshiu). She also uses the terms "nenekatshianit innut" (the ones who were abused) and "nanat innut" (the people of long ago) with reference to the Beothuk. The words "Innu" and "Innut" can refer to the people known in English as Innu, but also more generally to First Nations people, and even more broadly, to human beings, the people, the ones. Lacasse cites William-Mathieu Mark, an elder from Unamen Shipu, as saying "Innu is what we are called, and the name belongs to us . . . it's the name we've always had."[84] The word is often used as a suffix to indicate what region a person comes from, as in Uashunnu for someone from Uashat or nutshimiunnu for someone who lives on the land, or in nutshimit. Cree people are also referred to as Mishtashiniunnu (people from Mistissini), Ush-uinipekunnu (people from James Bay) and so on. Lacasse also points out that variations of the word, such as Ilnu, Eeyou, and Iriniu, are or have been used in many Algonquian languages.[85] The Mi'kmaq also use a version of the word, L'núk, meaning "the people" and referring to themselves. Tshaukuesh does use the word Beothuk in her text as well the first time she introduces them in the diary entry above, but the use of Innu(t) with reference to them in the rest of the entry suggests a sense of commonality that is absent in the English word Beothuk and its collocations: extinction and unknowability. She also emphasizes that she felt at home in their territory. This is not necessarily to argue that the Beothuk and the Innu have exactly the same heritage, genetic or cultural—though it does seem almost certain that the Beothuk were Algonquian-speaking hunter-gatherers, "simply one end of a continuum of peoples that extended from the island of Newfoundland to the northern portion of the Quebec-Labrador Peninsula."[86] Rather, I am suggesting that the Innu-aimun words describing identity and belonging categorize things differently than English does, and that this has implications for how we imagine the communities we are part of.

Translator Sherry Simon outlines the role of languages in establishing "tabula of relationships," arguing that translations can report on "areas of interchange between colonizer and colonized and reveal the nature of the interaction . . . languages are understood to participate in the process by which individual and collective selves are fashioned [and] brought to bear on the relations between self and other."[87] Thus translation can enable new ways of understanding who the inhabitants of Newfoundland and Labrador are and how we might relate to each other. It provides insights into how communities are shaped by the ways we think, talk, and write about ourselves and others.

Innu historian Aputet (Ben) Andrew says elders talk about how Innu used to canoe across the straits regularly, and that elders speak of the Beothuk as being Innu and the same people as themselves.[88] Discussing his interviews with Innu in Labrador in 2013 as part of his doctoral research, Christopher

Aylward notes: "All the Innu elders interviewed expressed [the] idea of referring to the Beothuk not as a separate people but rather as Innu living in Newfoundland. None could remember having heard the word 'Beothuk' used among members of their community."[89] The use of the word "Innu" with reference to the Beothuk may or may not have anything to do with shared DNA, language, or culture, but it clearly has something to do with a different mode of thinking than the one operating in dominant English-speaking contexts. Language constructs categories and enables or limits the ways we conceive of the world. In English, "they" (the discrete group, Beothuk) are all gone. "We" are still here. In Innu-aimun, the Beothuk are Innu, human beings, albeit human beings of long ago or "the ones who were abused." There is a sense of connection that is missing in English. For the Innu, the Beothuk (as settlers called them) were human beings who lived on the land, in a way of life similar to their own and a place that was familiar, beautiful and homelike. To take Tshaukuesh's text and its translation seriously we must understand the Beothuk as Innu—not because of new DNA, linguistic, or archeological evidence, but because the categories are different in Innu-aimun. An imagined community in which the Beothuk are part of a larger and still-living cultural group enables new ways of thinking about who we all are.[90]

Non-human inhabitants of the land might also be thought of differently if our language enabled it. While emphasizing that the relationship between grammar and behaviour is not causal, Robin Kimmerer argues that "grammar, especially our use of pronouns, is the way we chart relationships in language and, as it happens, how we relate to each other and to the natural world."[91] She elaborates that in English we use gendered pronouns, "a grammar of personhood," as a way of showing respect for our own species but generally use the grammatically neutral "it" for other living inhabitants of the earth. Kimmerer is studying her ancestral language, Potawatomi, which like Innu-aimun (both are Algonquian languages) has two forms for verbs and nouns, animate and inanimate. Every living thing, plant or animal, is animate, along with some other natural formations such as rocks, "imbued with spirit," Kimmerer writes. She suggests that this grammar "challenges the fundamental tenets of Western thinking—that humans alone are possessed of rights and all the rest of the living world exists for human use. Those whom my ancestors called relatives were renamed natural resources."[92] She argues that our minds are colonized by our use of English,[93] and that we need words and language structures that can help heal our relationship with nature. Kimmerer proposes borrowing from Potawatomi the word "ki" from "aaki" (land) and the English "kin" as a plural. Her students tell her that when they refer to plants and animals as kin, they think about them differently. She writes, "the grammar of animacy is an antidote to arrogance; it reminds us that we are not alone."[94]

Vanessa Andreotti, Cash Ahenakew, and Garrick Cooper argue that "scholars and educators working with Indigenous ways of knowing are called to translate these into the dominant language, logic and technologies in ways that are intelligible and coherent (and, very often, acceptable or palatable) to readers and interpreters in the dominant culture."[95] Tshaukuesh recognizes this dilemma when she speaks publicly. She often says the animals told her things and then follows such statements with "I know the animals don't really talk but . . ." She says she does this because her children told her the Akaneshau will not take her seriously if she says animals talk to her. How can we resist the language and logic of the dominant culture? How can stories and social practices become "spaces of resistance and hope?"[96] Refusing to translate the untranslatable and making translation visible in ways that offer new insights and modes of thinking are two possible ways of answering these questions.

Six

Literacies

One evening, Tshaukuesh and Francis were in the living room at Tshaukuesh's friend Robin's house, drinking tea and poring over the typescript of the original Innu version of Tshaukuesh's diary. Francis was correcting mistakes in the transcription with a stub of pencil while we waited for Robin's husband, John, to arrive home for supper. Tshaukuesh put her mug down, sighed deeply, and said, "Who will read my book in Innu-aimun? Maybe nobody!" Francis looked up from his work. "Maybe Akaneshau who want to learn to speak Innu?" he said dubiously.

It was a question I had not asked myself. I had simply assumed that it would be essential to publish the book in Innu-aimun as well as English (and French, since most Innu live in Quebec). It would be important for Innu literacy in their own language, for making a contribution to the vitality of the language, and as a record for posterity. Wouldn't it? This chapter is an attempt to answer that question.

Literacy, Standardization, and Language Revitalization

A few weeks later, I was working on the manuscript at a neighbourhood café, sitting by the window with my laptop and a steaming latte. Pausing to think about an edit, I peered through the condensation on the window at the piles of grimy late-winter snow on the sidewalk outside and savoured the contrasting coziness and bustle indoors. Then I caught the eye of a colleague at the next table. St. John's is a small world. We fell into conversation and,

Two girls, Maggie and Manian, use literacy skills to build paper skyscrapers at school in Natuashish. Photo by Lingxiao Yue.

somehow, into an argument about language standardization and the need for it in the Innu version of the book. There are two main dialects of Innu-aimun, several sub-dialects, and various versions of a writing system that uses the Roman alphabet and is based on French orthography. So, for example, there is no "w," despite that letter being widely used in related languages such as Cree. There is also the Kawawachikamach syllabic writing system, which is similar to but not the same as the system used for Cree. Historically, most writing was based on oral patterns and usage and many different spellings were accepted.[1] However, linguists and community members across Innusi worked for many years to develop a single system that everybody can use. It seems straightforward: it would enable everybody to communicate clearly in writing and would also make it easier for students to develop literacy in the language. Cree Métis writer Chelsea Vowel gives a good example of one advantage of standardization when she discusses correcting her daughter's name on her birth certificate after it had been misspelled as Sakiwayo: "Spelling [her name] correctly, in standardized Cree, was very important to me . . . sâkowêw means s/he makes a joyful sound, or war whoops—it depends on the context. sâkêwêw, on the other hand, means s/he comes into view! Now you tell me . . . if anyone could be sure which meaning the spelling Sakiwayo intended to evoke?"[2]

Clarity is important. Tshaukuesh's book would be easier for more people to read and understand if it was standardized. It would be a resource for literacy. That was what my colleague was arguing, anyway. I responded that her voice and dialect would be lost, and that many English "classics" are not written in standardized English—there is an entire dictionary of Shakespeare's non-standard English, for instance.[3] There is also one of Newfoundland English. Non-standard spelling, grammar, and vocabulary have been used in writing ranging from millions of tweets and Facebook comments to prize-winning fiction and non-fiction, from the dramas of Codco and Michel Tremblay to works of literature by Zora Neale Hurston, James Kelman, and Toni Morrison. Actually, I did not say all that. My voice trailed away before I got very far. It was obvious I had no persuasive power on this topic. I really just wanted to say that I thought Tshaukuesh's own way of expressing herself should be respected.

In the abstract, standardization makes perfect sense. It emphasizes similarities rather than differences between languages and, in the context of Indigenous languages, aims for a mutually intelligible written form for each group of related languages.[4] (Though this is not always what happens in practice, as examples later in this chapter will show.) But what about the aesthetics of Tshaukuesh's writing, the place and history it comes from? What happens to the nuance, cadence and rhythm, to her sense of story and poetry, and perhaps also to the way her writing in Innu-aimun captures the passionate haste, the rush of words and thoughts as she jots things down in quiet moments in the tent, in her husband's truck as she waits for him in Goose Bay, in the long hours in prison awaiting trial, and time spent on airplanes travelling to speaking engagements? James Costa, Haley De Korne and Pia Lane, following Kathryn Woolard, frame these questions succinctly in more academic terms when they suggest that "standards for minority languages may come to be perceived by social actors as lacking both the authority and anonymity of a national language as well as the authenticity or the capacity to index locality often ascribed to minority languages."[5]

The first time Tshaukuesh and I worked together on a piece for publication in English and Innu-aimun,[6] I thought it should be standardized and so I made sure that was done. I now feel that I was expressing my English-speaking culturalism, a term put forward by Mi'kmaw scholar Marie Battiste to refer to a theoretical perspective based on the assumption that colonial and Eurocentric understandings and practices are the global and universal norm from which Indigenous and local cultures and knowledges deviate.[7] People who speak languages that have a standard (or whose speakers believe there is a standard) tend to assume it is essential to have one and use it, especially in written form and grammar. However, this is far from being a universal view, and many speakers of less widely used languages are more concerned about whether the writing represents their particular way of speaking than whether it conforms to a uniform standard.[8] When the proofs came back, Tshaukuesh laboriously went through them, correcting everything back to the way she had written it. The way she saw it, it was full of mistakes. It didn't represent her way of speaking. Standardization is a kind of translation, and as with any translation, something important is lost, even though something might be gained as well.

A standardized writing system is often seen as a way of revitalizing Indigenous languages by making it easier to teach them systematically and develop and share resources.[9] Some specialists also believe that languages that do not have a standardized written form are in more danger of extinction than languages that do, so literacy in an Indigenous language may even be crucial for its survival.[10] Surprisingly, even literacy programs that are relatively unsuccessful can help to change people's attitudes and contribute to a renewed sense of pride in their language.[11] Literacy in a language brings with it prestige, and conversely, lack of a written form can signal both to speakers and outsiders that it is not a "real" language.[12] However, the connection between standardization and literacy is not direct, and literacy does not necessarily require a standardized orthography. Innu-aimun has had various written forms for over 200 years and many Innu have been literate during that period, ironically only losing their ability to write their own language after school became compulsory in the 1950s and '60s.[13]

Literacy is also connected to language revitalization in that school-based revitalization programs usually require it.[14] Once literacy is established, it can be used for the documentation of traditional knowledge and for writing diaries, letters, lists, recipes, and so on.[15] Tshaukuesh's diary is an example. More recently, Innu-aimun seems to be widely used by Innu on social media and for texting. These informal venues suit the conversational exchanges typical of social media, hovering as they do between oral and written with their informal abbreviated style and insertion of video clips and other oral and visual forms.

The development of literacy can lead to a flourishing of literary work in Indigenous languages, which can be further supported with publication, prizes, and recognition. The Inuktut Writing Prize, which provides financial support as well as a residency and mentorship, is intended to foster the "protection, promotion and revitalization of Inuktut [through] creating Inuktut literature and increasing the everyday use and understanding of Inuktut."[16] Work can be submitted in any of Nunavut's Inuktut languages, either in syllabics or roman orthography, thus recognizing diversity of language and writing styles. The annual Indigenous Voices Awards also offer substantial monetary awards across nine categories in recognition of exceptional emerging Indigenous writers working in Indigenous languages as well as English or French.[17] In South America, the Peruvian Academy of the Quechua Language (Academia Peruana de la Lengua Quechua) supports and values writing in Indigenous languages by awarding literary prizes.[18] There are also Indigenous language publishing houses and others that occasionally publish works in Indigenous languages.

While standardization and related support can increase the prestige of a language and the social status of its speakers, it can also have a negative impact on diversity within the group. It can even impede literacy and contribute to language loss by privileging some forms of the language, which may lead to stigmatization of others and subsequently of their speakers.[19] Teaching literacy itself, with or without standardization, can be divisive in other ways, too, since it may threaten or at least lead people to question the role of oral tradition in the culture.[20] Some community members may also worry that they will lose control of who has access to their stories if they are written down, and others may be disillusioned if they believe that literacy will save their language and then it does not.[21] It may help but it is not enough on its own, and it brings other challenges such as the need for trained teachers and funding.[22] Yet another challenge is the question of whether or not there is actually a need for literacy in a given Indigenous language, and the answer to this is not as obvious as one might think.

The concept of local literacies frames literacy not just as a set of standard technical practices but as an aspect of community identity, taking different forms in different contexts. Lenore Grenoble and Lindsay Whaley make the point that "the local literacy is or will be in competition with the language of wider communication, which is more widely used and better established."[23] When literacy is already reasonably strong in the dominant language, it is difficult to shift thinking toward using the Indigenous language in written contexts. However, for the Innu, whose territory spans English-speaking Labrador and French-speaking Quebec, the fact that the "language of wider communication" is not the same in all regions may create a significant need for literacy in the Indigenous language, since Innu do not have another shared language known to all.

There may also be affective and aesthetic needs for literacy in Indigenous languages. One Innu acquaintance mentioned that he rarely reads in Innu-aimun, except for poetry, which he loves. Perhaps the reason is that his high level of literacy in both English and French meets all of his other reading needs. Literacy is not just a technical skill that can be applied the same way to any context. It is a practice—aesthetic, spiritual, and technical—and it is used differently for different purposes. At times this means that the language in its written form is used only to meet certain specific needs. Poetry in Indigenous languages along with other literary writing and song lyrics might have affective and aesthetic dimensions that cannot be found elsewhere.[24]

It is helpful to think about literacy in the plural, as a range of literacies that are appropriate for different social contexts and used in various different ways in a given community. The best-known kind, functional literacy, refers to the basic competence with written text that enables one to vote, use an ATM, and read straightforward information such as product labels. The concept of functional literacy as the end goal of a literacy program has been critiqued, most famously by Paolo Freire, who argues in his classic *Pedagogy of the Oppressed* that literacy has to be community based and used as a means of fighting oppression, as defined by the community.[25] However, if there is a dominant or colonizing language, such as English, and a readily available means for attaining literacy in that language, such as compulsory schooling, it is not at all obvious why functional literacy in the Indigenous language would be necessary. If there is no perceived need for it, it may be seen as superfluous, since basic literacy tasks would probably be carried out in the dominant language. This is what Francis seemed to be suggesting when he struggled to find a need for Tshaukuesh's book in Innu-aimun and could only come up with the idea that outsiders wanting to learn the language might read it. Tshaukuesh herself, however, despite her misgivings, believed it was important as a contribution to preserving the language and culture for future generations: "I'm always writing my journal. When I'm gone, my journal will still be here. It's an important story, deserving of respect."[26] Writing a diary was a need that could only be met through literacy in her own language; she wondered who would read it but she continued to write it. The idea that there are multiple literacies recognizes that different kinds of literacies meet different needs, from functioning at the grocery store to using a computer or a cell phone to learning a new language or writing one's own story in the language that is most personally meaningful.

Tomson Highway suggests that affective and cultural dimensions of writing, at least when used for theatrical production, can play a key role in saving Indigenous languages. Upon releasing Cree versions of two of his plays, he encouraged Indigenous playwrights and actors to work in Indigenous languages, "because if anybody in this country is capable of saving those languages from extinction, it's the writers."[27] Highway also wrote about language survival in an essay about his experiences at residential school: "And even if our mother tongue was forbidden ('on pain of getting strapped on your bare buttocks') by the Church and the Government that ran such places right across the country ('to assimilate the Indians into *our* culture'), we still could speak it, *if* under cover of night and darkness and rope-thick intrigue (like French spies in a Hitler movie). That is to say, we had formed, without our knowing it, a kind of 'resistance movement' of the Cree language. And it worked; the language survived."[28]

This story reminded me of the code talkers in the Second World War who used Cree, Navajo, and other Indigenous languages for the military as codes that were never broken. The niece of one of the Cree code talkers, Adele Laderoute, believes that their story may also play a role in saving Indigenous languages by inspiring people through films such as *Cree Code Talker* (2016) and *Windtalkers* (2002). Laderoute comments, "The more the story is told, the more people will hear it—and hopefully it will galvanize the younger people to learn their language. It is important to keep the Cree language alive and this story enforces this."[29] While the code talking of the Second World War was based on oral language transmitted by radio and telephone rather than through literacy in an Indigenous language, the idea of a "resistance movement" of language does suggest thought-provoking possibilities. The ability to write in a language known only to your community can be applied not only to spying in wartime or whispered exchanges between children in residential school but also to establishing a special sense of community online and avoiding the well-documented surveillance of various internet platforms.[30] Posts or exchanges in an uncommon language such as Innu-aimun would be almost impossible for the U.S. National Security Agency or internet companies like Facebook and Google to surveille.

Decolonizing Language Teaching

Lynn Drapeau described the situation for Innu teachers before standardization and the challenges presented by the variations in spelling, especially since these teachers not only had to teach but also to create most of their own materials:

> Knowing that their spelling system was highly inconsistent, teachers were discouraged at the thought of producing reading materials since they knew that one day, perhaps in the near future, they would have to change most of it. The disparity of spelling habits among the teachers naturally caused a great deal of confusion among the pupils, who came to believe that [Innu-aimun] classes were futile or at least not serious. Indeed, one must remember that any students, taught to read and write in a European language with a rigorous orthography, develop high expectations about the nature of the writing system, whether it is their own language or a second language. Continuous groping and frequent disparities in spelling habits on the part of the teachers are readily noticed by students and entail considerable disillusionment.[31]

I thought about my own early teaching career in late French immersion, a program that existed because of parental lobbying and the economics and politics of the Official Languages Act. It was pre-internet and we had no curriculum and few books. The books we did have were far too advanced for students just beginning in the language but required to follow the same curriculum as their English-language counterparts nonetheless. For health, we were given the English-language textbook and told to teach it in French, to students who knew next to no French. The history textbook was in French, but I later learned that it was a book designed for francophone senior high school students, and we were expected to teach from it to grade seven students who did not speak the language. In the first year of the program, teachers—many of whom were recently qualified and had no experience—spent hours every night making up all the materials and activities for the next day. I had two-year-old twins, and it was my first year teaching. Most nights I ended up in a sleep-deprived haze of tears and exhaustion. And yet that was nothing compared to what Indigenous teachers of language and literacy have to deal with. For one thing, we were supported by the Official Languages Act. There was funding for travel, activities, resources, and teacher development. There were endless French-language materials we could use, even if it took time to select, adapt, and modify them. And still it was hard. Indigenous language and literacy teachers have to do all of what we had to do but with very few resources and the additional challenges described by Drapeau above (keeping in mind that "producing reading materials" frequently means conceptualizing, writing, designing, and printing or putting online most of the curriculum) and often in contexts where people have complex and deeply painful feelings about the language because of a history of colonizing stigma and residential schools.

In 2019, the Canadian Parliament passed Bill C-91: An Act Respecting Indigenous Languages. The Act is intended to support the implementation of the TRC's Calls to Action 13, 14, and 15, which "aim to reclaim, revitalize, strengthen and maintain Indigenous languages in Canada."[32] If the Act has anything like the impact of the Official Languages Act, it will change the linguistic face of Canada once again, and standardized writing systems will undoubtedly play a major role in the process.

Identity, Modernism, Ideology, and Standardization

A writing system can be closely tied to identity.[33] This is a key reason why the standardization of an Indigenous language has to be based on consensus rather than on a top-down imposition.[34] Linguist Anne-Marie Baraby describes the process of standardizing Innu-aimun as "long and arduous, taking 25 years to arrive at a consensus satisfactory to representatives from all the communities."[35] Thanks to that process, there has been an officially recognized common spelling system since 1997 and, with its more recent approval by Innu school boards, it seems likely to be ever more widely accepted.

The idea of standardization is very old. Chinese writing was first standardized during the Qin Dynasty over 2,000 years ago.[36] Because many characters are associated with meaning rather than sound (as with an alphabetic or syllabic writing system), standardization often enabled speakers of very different dialects to communicate with each other. Several other orthographies have also had standardized forms for at least 1,000 years. It has been argued that standardization of writing in European contexts has its roots in seventeenth- and eighteenth-century philosophical projects of modernity. Standardized writing was intended to institute "a democratic, universally accessible public space" in which language is neutral and belongs to everyone and no one.[37] Ironically, this particular project is based on the belief that some ways of saying something are correct and others are not, and often the decision to emphasize one or more varieties or dialects over others. Declaring that "the only fully standardized language is a dead language,"[38] Milroy and Milroy suggest that standardization is primarily ideological, both because it requires decisions about which forms (and whose forms) to privilege and because it represents a certain modernist way of understanding the world, a world view that values "universality, rationality and progress" over "particularity, emotion and tradition."[39] Standardization is based on the assumption that uniformity and categorization are good things, indeed, that they must be imposed.[40] This idea is demonstrated visually in linguistic maps representing each language with a different colour or pattern neatly filling in bounded spaces, thus erasing multilingualism and varieties of language within a territory.[41]

My family was once selected to complete the long-form census and one of the questions was about the first language of the family, with the instruction to "choose only one." We alternated every day among three languages, two of which—French and English—were also constantly spoken in the community, not just in our home. We listed all three on the paper form and added a note to explain why and to reject the assumption that it was possible to truthfully choose a single answer to the question. Presumably, so did others, as this question had changed by the next census to allow more than one first language per household. Real people's linguistic lives, and their feelings and attitudes toward the languages they use, are complex.

I grew up writing in English and then French, and learning to be meticulous in the spelling and grammar of both. I was used to bilingualism from an early age but I never really questioned the value of having a written standard until much later. When I started thinking about it in relation to Tshaukuesh's writing and her reaction the first time she saw it standardized, I felt differently. Suddenly, standardization of writing, a process I had always taken for granted, represented the erasure of diversity, emotion, and the rich particularity of individuals and small groups.

Probably the most common uses of reading and writing in Innu-aimun outside of school work and official documents are comments on social media and texting. Spelling is often improvised. I have never seen the superscript "u" of standardized Innu-aimun used in online conversations, for instance. It accurately represents the sound of a barely vocalized "u" at the end of a word, but it takes several keyboard formatting actions to produce it in most word processing programs. Furthermore, many social media interfaces accept only "plain text"; on Facebook, for example, producing a superscript "u" requires an elaborate nine-step process involving downloading an online superscript converter and submitting your text to be converted. I don't really think it matters that people don't do this (although it does matter that Facebook makes it so difficult for those who want to write their language in standardized form). After all, most online conversations are informal and spelling is not usually policed in any language the way it often is in other contexts. However, it does highlight the diversity of contexts for literacies and the practical limits of some forms of standardization.

Meanwhile, and perhaps ironically, social media and texting in English are moving away from standardization. That may not matter either. Linguist David Crystal describes the popular belief that texting both reflects and shapes declining standards of literacy and quotes the British journalist John Humphrys, who wrote that texters are "vandals who are . . . pillaging our punctuation; savaging our sentences; raping our vocabulary."[42] Crystal has shown that people can still easily read texts written in various creative and abbreviated ways, with the title of his book on the topic, *Txting: The Gr8 Db8*, being a good example. There are still strong expectations in more formal contexts that writing will follow established rules and conventions, but these can vary quite widely in terms of grammar, spelling, and vocabulary across dialects, especially between North American and British usage, which are actually more different than we tend to think.

Assuming a community wants a writing system, there are many things to be considered in choosing an appropriate one. Hul'q'umi'num' and hən̓q̓əmin̓əm̓ are two dialects of a Salish language of southwestern British Columbia. Hul'q'umi'num' uses Roman orthography with apostrophes in combination with various letters to represent glottal stops and clicks, which means the language can easily be used on social media and for other online purposes and texting as well as in more official contexts. Hən̓q̓əmin̓əm̓ uses a writing system based on the International Phonetic Alphabet, which emphasizes the distinctiveness of the language. The system includes numerous phonetic characters such as ə, ƛ, and ʕ that cannot easily be used in online or many official contexts.[43]

Earlier in this chapter I quoted Chelsea Vowel on the importance of standardized spelling for her children's Cree names.[44] She emphasized that she wanted future generations to know what the names meant. This is another argument in favour of standardized spelling, to avoid ambiguity in both present and future. If writing is closely tied to identity, the writing of names is at the very heart of that closeness. Names were often changed or misspelled, and in many cases lost forever, during the era of residential schools and the placement of Indigenous children in homes outside their communities and linguistic groups. This was so widespread that one of the TRC's Calls to Action is "to enable residential school survivors and their families to reclaim names changed by the residential school system by waiving administrative costs for a period of five years for the name-change process and the revision of official identity documents, such as birth certificates, passports, driver's licences, health cards, status cards, and social insurance numbers."[45] This is an important step, but there are still official challenges to the spelling of some Indigenous names today.

In 2014, Shëné Gahdële-Valpy gave her baby daughter a Chipewyan name, Sahɑ̨́į́ʔɑ̨ May Talbot. When she tried to register it with the Northwest Territories government to get a birth certificate, it was rejected. Like hən̓q̓əmin̓əm̓, the Dene language of Chipewyan uses a phonetic alphabet. The character "ʔ" represents a glottal stop, a sound that cannot be represented in roman orthography (though Hul'q'umi'num' found a way around that by using an apostrophe). Some dialects of English have a glottal stop but use the same standardized spelling as other dialects, thus making the stop solely an oral feature of the dialect. However, in Chipewyan, unlike English, eliminating the stop in writing would change the meaning, thus raising the same problem Chelsea Vowel had with the non-standard version of her daughter's name. Gahdële-Valpy refused to register her daughter's name without the correct spelling for over a year but finally gave in and agreed to use an apostrophe instead of ʔ because without a birth certificate she could not get medical care for her daughter unless she paid for it herself.

The Northwest Territories' language commissioner, Shannon Gullberg, has said that not allowing names spelled with Dene orthography would violate the Northwest Territories Official Languages Act.[46] However, while the territory made two other changes to its Vital Statistics Act in 2017, to allow single names based on traditional Indigenous cultures and to recognize gender changes and non-binary gender, as of the writing of this book it has not removed a requirement that names be written in standard Roman orthography.[47] Thus it still does not recognize names in the standardized orthographies of several Indigenous languages of the territory. Commenting on this, Gahdële-Valpy said that her daughter's name should be recognized everywhere in Canada: "It should be everywhere. This is our homeland and this is our opportunity to rebuild our languages for everyone."[48]

Seven

Listening

"Nin Tshaukuesh tan etin niuitsheuan tshema nistuatamen innu Natim tshipa mishinimatin ekun iame."

I puzzle for hours over the message from Tshaukuesh that popped up on my phone, frustrated that after all this time working together, I still cannot even understand a simple text. The black Helvetica stares back at me opaquely from its flat grey background. It does not help that Innu-aimun is a polysynthetic language with words composed of multiple parts. What speakers of many other languages—languages as different from each other as English and Chinese—would think of as a sentence can be a single long word in Innu. Although there is an Innu-aimun–English dictionary,[1] it is not always informative, at least to me, because the words change as different components are added, and even if I could figure out the components, there's more than one spelling system. The dictionary uses standardized Innu-aimun but Tshaukuesh does not. I have literally lost sleep over this text, staring at it, picking out the bits I do understand. "This is Tshaukuesh, how are you, my friend? . . . Innu . . . you could . . . okay, good-bye." I'm not sure about the "my friend" part. Her spelling is different from what I think it would be, but it seems close. I desperately want to reply in Innu, but finally I give up and call her to admit I can't understand her message and ask her what it means. "Oh," she says airily, "it means: 'I wish you could read Innu! If you could read Innu I would text you all the time.'"

Later, as we're working together editing her book, I see that Tshaukuesh has written about the text:

Tshaukuesh and Elizabeth working together at Jessica Tellez's house in Halifax. Photo by David Openshaw.

> May 22, 2017
> Sometimes I feel very sad that it's so hard to communicate. I got a computer but nobody has time to show me how to use it. Most of all, I wish my friends could read Innu-aimun. This morning I sent a text in Innu-aimun to Elizabeth. It said, "Hello, my friend. I hope you can understand this. It's me, Tshaukuesh. I wish you could read Innu so I could write you all the time." I was thinking about my friend Frank Gibson too. He can't read or write Innu either. But anyway, sometimes when it's quiet in my house, after my grandson goes to school, I sit down and I write my diary in Innu.

Research Relationships

January 2008. We sit side by side at Robin's polished Victorian dining table and slowly, painstakingly, Tshaukuesh explains what she has written. I am not yet used to the way she speaks and unfamiliar with the context, so I often misunderstand her. Sometimes she phones somebody in her family to ask them to explain, or Francis helps when he comes to pick her up. Mostly, I listen. It is surprising how calming it can be to give up any sense of control and just try to understand, yet we so rarely do that. I think the only reason I am able to do it now is that I know so little and, if we are going to make a book, I have no other choice.

When Tshaukuesh and I began working together, we were already comfortable with each other, since by then I had interviewed her about her life and work and also joined her on her walk, traversing the snow-covered landscape of Innusi together by day and sharing meals and a tent by night. But we still needed to find a method for working together. Some things are serendipitous. I can explain the method we developed, but the circumstances that enabled it to function came together by chance. Tshaukuesh's friend in Goose Bay, Robin McGrath, offered me a place to stay and a table to work at. I flew to Goose Bay from St. John's and the next morning Tshaukuesh appeared. Robin produced meals (hot meals, Tshaukuesh would emphasize, with as much Indigenous meat and fish—country food—as possible).

Tshaukuesh's husband, Francis, drove her back and forth each day on the rough and often icy road from Sheshatshiu. And we got to work. At first I made audio recordings, but I soon realized that I could type as fast as she talked because she paused often to think about how to explain in English. After a few days, I exchanged my recorder for a laptop. I am glad I made the early recordings, though, because they document the place we started from and how little I knew.

I was only able to travel to Labrador two or three times a year for a week or so at a time, but when I was there we worked intensively. I was away from all my other responsibilities, and being at Robin's house meant we didn't have the interruptions we would have had at Tshaukuesh's, with her large family and many responsibilities. My lack of language and cultural knowledge was obviously a serious disadvantage, but surprisingly it also had a positive aspect. We could not just email each other. Nor could I just take the written stories away and translate them. We had to sit down together hour after hour, day after day, and that meant that Tshaukuesh could revise, clarify, and add new material as she told me what she had written. Having a listener allowed her to edit her stories.

Nine years later, I am trying to remember what those early sessions were like. It is easy to bring vividly to mind the smell of Robin's bread baking, the endless pots of Red Rose tea, the sound of our spoons clanking against ceramic mugs and the wind in the trees outside; harder to retrieve the conversations because our way of talking to each other and writing together has evolved so much since then. I bring up one of the early recordings on my laptop and click the play icon: "I am organize for the walk," she says, "You know sometimes when you talk about something, 'that's what we should do.' And the people he break it, what you say . . . he didn't want to do it . . . 'no, no,' like that. He didn't want to do what I'm saying."

She is telling me about trying to persuade people to walk with her in nutshimit when she first had the idea for the walk. She believes so deeply in the value and importance of traditional ways of life, of being on the land, of *living* on the land. But it's hard, it takes enormous effort and physical and emotional strength. People "broke it" by saying it was impossible, they couldn't do it because they smoked or they had diabetes or a heart condition.

I can sense how difficult it was for her to communicate with me in those early days and I feel frustrated myself by my inability to understand her language.

"I want to close here," she says. "Did I close?"

"You mean, is this the close of the page?" I ask.

"Did I say, did I say close?" she repeats.

"I think so," I say, referring to the fact that we have finished translating this diary entry. "That's the end of this page."

"I mean I want to close here. I want to say something here."

"Oh, you want to say something else. This is not in the diary but you want to add it to finish the story. Is that right?"

Gradually, as we work together, we begin to understand each other. I learn that by "a close" she means she wants to add a reflection or some concluding thoughts, and when she says "the people" she usually means the Innu. I acquire a few words of Innu-aimun and a notion of the spelling system. These are details. The gradual accumulation of knowledge is crucial and underlying it all is simply listening. But what does that mean? Petrilli and Ponzio distinguish between listening and wanting to hear.[2] Listening is opening ourselves up toward the Other, responding, offering hospitality. Wanting to hear is more possessive, less reciprocal. It defines, judges, classifies. In Petrilli and Ponzio's view, translators have an ethical responsibility to acknowledge the rights of others over their own, which they call semioethical responsibility. The semioethical translator is "a listening device" who practises "hospitality towards the word of the other."[3]

Petrilli and Ponzio's conceptualization of translation as listening was inspired by the philosopher Emmanuel Levinas, one of the first European philosophers to consider what it would mean to have an ethical relationship with the Other. In his philosophy, an ethical encounter would require one not to judge or classify but to recognize that the Other is ultimately unknowable, and yet be willing, despite this, to learn. It is not through identification with the Other or through mastery of what they tell us that we will learn, but through recognizing that their experience is different, unique, and irreducible, and yet still listening attentively, being open, committed to our responsibility toward them. Only through this kind of listening can we come to understand things differently. Such listening is not only about attending to the words that are spoken, important though they may be, but also to the embodied presence of the Other, which exceeds spoken words.

Levinas has been critiqued for being apolitical in his focus on individual relationships (thus discounting the possibility of solidarity and resistance) and for being Eurocentric. However, Simone Drichel suggests that his ideas can be useful in postcolonial contexts if we read him against the grain, deconstructively. She reminds us that there is no ethics without a politics and, regarding Levinas's focus on one-to-one relationships, that these relationships can inform a just socio-political order.[4] Sharon Todd applies Levinas's ideas to the more overtly political context of social justice education, asking how the development of such a relationship can contribute to a larger sense of responsibility. She writes that "justice depends on our capacity to be moved, to have ourselves shaken up to the point where the lives of others matter."[5] Can the one-on-one act of collaborative translation as listening play a role in this shaking up? And can the re-mapping, the walking with, the visual counter-narratives—all the different kinds of translation work described in the preceding chapters—enhance our capacity to be moved? I think the answers to these questions are obvious. There are no certainties in this kind of work, but it requires a commitment of time and effort, a sharing of joy and pain and the simple acts of daily life that are what relationships are made from.

I had been working with Tshaukuesh for several years when my university colleagues and I were informed that we had to complete a multiple-hour, online course on research ethics developed by the Tri-Council, a joint agency representing Canada's three main research funding bodies.[6] The course, known as the TCPS-2: CORE, had to be completed before we or our students could submit any further proposals for ethics review. This meant that none of us could do our jobs without it. I was resentful at this waste of my time, at the insulting assumption that I, after more than thirty years of doing research and supervising students, needed to complete an oversimplified and commodified series of modules on research ethics. However, I had a student who was almost ready to submit her thesis proposal for ethics review, so I opened the first module and worked through it until I got to this:

> You are making a documentary about life in a nomadic culture in another country. You are working with a team of local historians, anthropologists, and cultural geographers who have built a relationship with the community. You are all invested in creating a record of a way of life that is rapidly disappearing and respecting the traditions of the community. The elders have given permission for the documentary to take place but they will not sign consent or release forms and they will not allow any members of the community to do so. In this culture, asking for a signature after a verbal agreement has been made is considered disrespectful. Your translator is a member of the community and you discuss several strategies with him.[7]

This scenario was followed by three proposed strategies that respondents were required to rank in order from best to worst: get the translator to sign on behalf of the community, give the elders gifts to persuade them to sign, or videorecord them agreeing orally. I think the one that was preferred by the test designers was to videorecord them, but what if community members were also opposed to that? Even if the elders of this hypothetical dying culture accepted that option, wouldn't this insistence on documentation still imply that we didn't trust them? Couldn't it damage the relationship that the team had so carefully built? As for the other two options, I could not figure out which one the module designers might have thought would be better than the other. Both were clearly manipulative and coercive. And then there was the monolithic statement about "in this culture," as if all of these people (whose culture was dying anyway) think and act as one (and none of them could conceivably *be* a local historian, anthropologist, or cultural geographer). How do these notions of what might be ethical, and the idea that ethical responses might be summarized in single lines and ranked hierarchically, relate to what actually happens, which is relational and takes place over time, often years? How do they relate to listening?

I went back to the opening page of the module and reread it:

Upon completion of this module you will be able to:
- describe the guiding principles of research ethics
- recognize ethics violations
- evaluate strategies for creating ethical research designs[8]

These are still the stated outcomes for the TCPS-2. An outcomes-based approach is common in public school curriculum design and in many web courses, but it is not well suited for the kind of learning that requires creativity, critique, or affective engagement, especially when paired with multiple choice questions. This introduction is followed by a slideshow about the infamous 1971 Stanford Prison Experiment, which has been shown to have been shockingly unethical as well as methodologically unsound.[9] As I worked my way through the long series of slides and commentary from Philip Zimbardo, the principal researcher in that study, my anger grew: at the cruelty of the experiment and the detached way Zimbardo describes what happened, as well as at the time I was wasting. At the end of the series there were two questions that could only be answered with yes or no: "Were whatever results the researcher got from this study worth the conditions the participants endured? If you were in charge of determining whether this study was consistent with research ethics guidance, would you approve it as it was originally designed?"[10]

How could they even think these questions were worth asking? I emailed the chair of our ethics review board, who responded that ethics review submissions had improved in the last few years. It was not clear how this was related to the TCPS-2 since it was a new requirement but that seemed to be his implication. After a couple of exchanges, it was obvious that he did not see the problem and was dismissive of my concerns, so I emailed the Tri-Council, as sponsors of the TCPS-2, about the question that had stymied me. To my surprise, I received a reply right away asking to set up a phone call. During the call, the woman I spoke to agreed that the question was flawed and explained how I could simply skip ahead without answering. Presumably she had requested a call because she had not wanted to put this in writing. The question was later modified slightly so that one of the proposed solutions was to negotiate with the elders rather than to offer gifts. Apart from that, it is unchanged, and the tone and structure of the modules in general is still disturbingly deterministic and lacking in nuance. I would have simply refused to do the course and carried on with my work, but my student's proposal would not have been accepted for ethics review if I had not completed it and she would not have been able to finish her degree. I decided to do my own experiment: Now that I understood how to skip over material in the modules, I answered the questionnaires at the end of each one without reading any of the content. When I had finished, I was able to download the certificate of completion, a meaningless credential. I later found out that some colleagues had received the certificate without even answering the questions at all by simply clicking from slide to slide through the modules.

I was dismayed at how much time I had put into this, at the thought of students who might get the impression that this was really how one should think about research ethics, and at the framing presentation of the Stanford Prison Experiment as research that could conceivably be considered ethical. Later, my colleague Robin Whitaker sent me her review of *The Ethics Rupture*, a collection of essays written in response to "a near collective dismay, discomfort and disorientation about the process known to social science researchers as 'research ethics review.'"[11] As I read her discussion and then the book itself, I learned that the ethics review process has caused social science researchers in some cases to choose topics or groups to research that will not cause difficulties when reviewed, which means that potentially important but sensitive areas are left unexamined. Others "feel compelled to choose between abandoning core disciplinary methods [such as ethnography or arts-based methods that are more likely to be questioned by ethics review panels], misrepresenting what they actually plan to do, or simply not applying for clearance."[12] What I find most troubling is the sense that on the one hand, ethical research can be contained and controlled through often simplistic rules and formulas, but on the other, this same research is fraught with potential dangers. Paradoxically, these dangers can (and must) be mitigated through complicated paperwork and committee oversight, thus shifting the moral responsibility from the actual researcher to a bureaucracy that, as van den Hoonaard and Hamilton point out, is not overseen by anyone else.[13] The TCPS-2 modules contain much thought-provoking and informative material that could be a basis for a rich series of discussions, but the way they are presented and the certificate is awarded does not leave room for it, let alone for listening and opening up to the embodied presence of the Other.

Writing Together

"February 27th 1996." I translate the date of the diary entry aloud, as I have already learned the months of the year, and then read the first sentence of the entry in Innu-aimun, basic words but I don't know them yet: "Ume kashikat."

"Means 'today,'" Tshaukuesh explains. "The days everybody moving, just want to do something. It's gonna something."

"Something's gonna happen?" I ask.

"Yeah. Election. Election go wrong. You know election?"

"Oh, there's an election."

"Yeah, mmm-hmm. The people at Band Council, the chief, the workers and the chief . . . everybody exciting movement. This election is not very, is not very good. It's not very nice what the people doing. Just like election come . . . Innu people start getting nervous: 'Oh, they're gonna have election again, now the people they're gonna be drunk.' A lot of young children they want to drink alcohol, drugs . . . it's not very nice because it's ah . . . someone they're gonna have money and then buy drugs or alcohol. It's not very nice."

The connection between the election and money sounded like bribery, but I wanted to be sure and to understand how it worked before I attempted the written English version. "Why do they have money when there's an election? Where do they get the money?"

It seemed Tshaukuesh was not sure either, or was hesitant to tell me. "Um, I don't know. Maybe Band Council is looking for money. Looking for the money, almost like donations. Maybe he went to see her friend, business people, and maybe business people said, 'You're a good man. I wish you win again.'"

"So they . . . so they give them money?"

"Yeah. Mmm-hmmm. Sometimes the people give them money. Just like, just like you buy, you buy people."

"Oh, you bribe them."

"Yeah. That is lots going on that is not very, is not very nice. . . . I know they start already, it's not even, it's not even election yet, but they start already. We had a lot of problems, lot of problems, all kinds of problems. Only one thing I'm happy what happened today. The people moving, lot of wants to do something. Like before election, just like everybody you don't do nothing. You stay in the house and nobody, nobody show up."

"They're apathetic."

"Is that what it mean?"

"They're apathetic, yeah, they don't feel like doing anything or going anywhere."

"Yeah, that's the one. And the people, I don't see him do something. Now this election coming, a lot of people move around, happy, proud. I wish, I wish our people, Innu people moving all the time."

"You wish they still had energy even when there isn't an election?"

"Yup, that's right. Like today, everybody, everybody happy to do something, everybody proud. That's what I'm thinking."

As I look at her words transcribed on my screen I think how poorly the written form captures the eloquence of the way she speaks. I cannot communicate her intensity and concern, her struggles and my own to find the right words. The final version in the book reads:

> It's an anxious time with an election coming, because some people start drinking. Sometimes they bribe the young people with money for alcohol and drugs. The election hasn't even been declared yet, but they've started already.
>
> An election causes a lot of problems but there is one good thing about it: people are energized. Before they started talking about an election, everybody was apathetic; they stayed home and nobody showed up for meetings. Now people are on the move, excited, dynamic—though I do worry that some of them just want alcohol and drugs. Still, I wish our people would have this kind of energy all the time. That's what I think.[14]

As we worked, Tshaukuesh was able to edit orally, adding more information and "closes," or concluding statements, and sometimes deleting material that was repetitive, unimportant, or private. There are some examples of that as well in the early recorded material: "No, is not so important," "okay, don't type that one," and "same story, same thing." "Don't type that either. Okay." Bit by bit, we got used to each other's ways of speaking and working. I learned more Innu-aimun and more about the culture, place names, and history. Tshaukuesh got to know which Innu words I understood and used them without explanation.

After Francis died in 2013, I started staying with Tshaukuesh in Sheshatshiu or in a rented cottage across the river, in walking distance from her house, since she no longer had a ride to Goose Bay. By then we had a well-established working routine so we carried on, but it slowed us down having to plan and prepare meals, and we missed the sociable suppers at John and Robin's house where Francis often joined us, as well as his knowledgeable and incisive help with translations when we got stuck. And Tshaukuesh was grieving the ineffably greater loss of her life companion. "I miss ninapem," she said, "I miss my husband."

But we carried on.

When Tshaukuesh and I began working together, she set some ground rules. First and most important, her name and her name only would be on the cover. Her story had been told time and again and she had done countless interviews, but she had rarely been named as the author. She wanted to speak for herself. Gayatri Spivak famously asked whether the subaltern can speak.[15] In some ways, "subaltern" seems an odd word for Tshaukuesh, a woman who is such a powerful force, who has spoken so widely and been the subject not only of books and articles but of documentaries and countless media interviews, who has won national awards, who is consulted over and over on environmental issues and Indigenous health and traditional life. Her courage and eloquence have inspired generations of environmentalists and activists. Yet Spivak's definition of a subaltern is useful for thinking about the extent to which Tshaukuesh's voice has or has not been heard by those who make decisions that will have an impact on all of us: "Subalternity is the name I borrow for the space out of any serious touch with the logic of capitalism or socialism."[16] This could be through lack of literacy or knowledge of colonizing languages and would mean also not having access to dominant or resisting discourses. Spivak's work is particularly interesting to me in light of her unceasing struggle to support subaltern peoples. This has always seemed to me extraordinarily hopeful, given her conclusion that the subaltern cannot speak, or at least cannot be heard by those in power. This hopefulness, combined with her assertion that "pedagogy as political interpretation must be seriously considered," seems especially relevant to Tshaukuesh, who constantly reminds us that she is a teacher and who is so determined to speak to the world on behalf of Indigenous peoples and the environment.[17] Spivak also writes that changes to laws, relations of production, health care, and educational systems cannot happen without "the mind-changing one-on-one responsible contact" essential to becoming "transnationally literate."[18] Because of her lack of access to dominant institutions and languages, and lack of literacy in those languages, Tshaukuesh must use people like me to disseminate her knowledge. Thus, to return to the earlier discussion of Levinas's focus on the individual relationship, and Petrilli and Ponzio's semioethics of translation, perhaps the individual relationship is not at all apolitical in postcolonial collaborative translation contexts.

Tshaukuesh knew that others had published her stories, but she could not read English so she had no way of knowing what they said. In addition, as far as she could see, she had not been given credit since her name was not on the covers of those stories. She was indeed credited in the narration and the citations (at least the ones I am aware of) in the way that most academics and journalists would consider ethical and appropriate, but she did not know about these conventions and they were *her* stories. I told her that my name would have to be somewhere in the book since I would be the co-editor and co-translator, but it was fine with me for her name to be the only one on the cover. That was good, she said, as long as we agreed on the cover. "These are Innu stories," she said, "not Akaneshau stories." "Okay," I said. At an earlier stage of my career, I could not have said "okay" so easily. I knew the project would take years and I would have needed an author's credit to get tenure.

A few years later, when we began to talk about publishers, I asked her for her opinion. "You have your meshkanau and I have mine," she said. "Your meshkanau is books and mine is the land." I chose University of Manitoba Press because they had been so interested in the project, contacting us after one of my students mentioned it to their editors at a conference and then staying in touch for several years, and because they specialized in Indigenous and northern stories. However, everything *in* the book had to be the way Tshaukuesh wanted it, and this sometimes involved a lot of time and many exchanges. At other times, though, things came together almost magically. As we prepared the manuscript for submission, we still had not found the perfect way to end. We wanted something upbeat but not overly optimistic, something that reflected Tshaukuesh's determination but also the daunting realities described in the book. Tshaukuesh often asked family members or friends to email me with ideas and stories; she would dictate and they would transcribe or translate. Although she worried about her lack of computer skills, she almost made up for it in her ability to find scribes. I was concerned about missing something important that she might have sent me, so I went back through years of emails to check. In 2011 Robin had sent me a message from her with this story:

> I was walking by myself one beautiful day. The dogs were behind me and I had my tea and biscuits and I wasn't afraid of anything, not wild animals, nothing. When I got to the marsh I sat down for a rest and a cup of tea, just me and the dogs. The trees were swaying in the wind, all different kinds of trees. It looked as though they were dancing. I wondered why I was all alone, why people didn't want to walk with me when I'm trying to protect the land and the animals, our culture, our children, our way of life. There'll always be money, but if the land is gone, it's gone. I hope people will understand this one day. In the meantime, I'll just keep trying to make a good meshkanau for future generations. I feel as though the dancing trees are my friends, as if they're saying to me, "Don't worry. We're here and we know you care about us. Don't cry in your heart. We're still here, still dancing." It was a clear day and I could see the mountains. Then I put my thermos away again and started walking.[19]

I thought it had the perfect combination of loss, longing, and resolution. It was also atmospheric, with the animate trees as companions, the vast boreal forest, and the contrasting coziness of a cup of tea with biscuits. I emailed it to Kanani and asked her to see what Tshaukuesh thought of using it as the ending for the book. We did not always have the same aesthetic sensibility or the same ideas of what made a good story. But Kanani emailed back almost right away with three words: "She loves it."

Technical Dialogue

In 1988, I participated in what we called a computer conference—a very early form of social media using software that enabled members of the group to participate in asynchronous conversations from remote sites. It was set up as an optional part of a doctoral course in which we were learning about poststructuralist theory. We called the conference Sam's Café and began with a scenario where various intellectuals and others (including a fly on the wall, the cantankerous cook, and so on) applied the theory and its difficult language to texts and events that interested us. I wrote about that experience in a course paper in which I explored the philosopher Martin Buber's idea of technical dialogue as a way of working toward what he called genuine dialogue.[20] In Buber's concept, there are three kinds of dialogue: monologue, in which two people talk in the presence of each other but really to themselves; technical dialogue, in which the speakers do truly listen to each other but only to achieve a practical purpose or common goal; and genuine dialogue, in which Buber says there is a "change from communication to communion."[21] Genuine dialogue may sometimes even take the form of silence, but a silence in which the participants turn toward each other and are deeply attentive. What I was interested in at the time was the way we used technical dialogue in the computer conference to try and understand a rather difficult theory through playful use of the medium of computer conferencing, and how we sometimes achieved something much more connected and perhaps even profound. Working together online to solve two problems, one theoretical and one about how to use the online communication tools that were then fresh and exciting, seemed to create a space where trust, friendship, and mutual support were possible. It is not that technical dialogue inevitably leads to genuine dialogue, but it can.

I often thought about technical dialogue while I was working with Tshaukuesh. I am not sure we would have connected in the same way if we had not begun using our limited common language to reach practical goals, first as we walked in nutshimit and later working together to complete her book. Given the language challenges and cultural differences between us and the history and present of colonization, it would have been difficult. But our first conversations, apart from the radio interview, were about things like what kind of branches would be best for insulating the floor of the tent and why ice is better than snow to melt for tea. Later on, as we worked on the translation of the book, concentrating on finding the right meaning, the perfect word or turn of phrase, and explaining its context was strangely relaxing. I suppose the intense focus led to what some people call "flow," a state in which we lose self-consciousness and sense of time, and experience intrinsic reward for an engrossing task or activity.[22] Technical dialogue and the experience of flow, along with shared commitment to our goal, led to an opening to each other and an ongoing effort to communicate through both technical and genuine dialogue. It is not transferrable or scalable. But I do think an understanding of the concept of technical dialogue and the way it can enable more profound connections is a useful methodological insight for other researchers.

Last year, Camille Fouillard sent me an article by Julie Vaudrin-Charette, a Quebec scholar who grew up in Innusi, near Pessamit. She too was interested in Innu writing, particularly the poetry of Joséphine Bacon, which focuses on resilience and the land. Vaudrin-Charette felt a love and a longing for the same land that Bacon wrote about, her home too, yet she knew it was unceded Innu territory and she was not Innu. Vaudrin-Charette suggested that her translations of Bacon's poetry could be thought of as "tiny threads, containing possibilities to expand" or as whispers that could create intimacy and foster listening and learning, "open[ing] conversational spaces about how we relate to each other as a moment of ethical renewal."[23]

Bacon translates her own poems from Innu-aimun into French and Vaudrin-Charette works from the French versions, bringing them over into

English. Her translations focus on staying as close as possible to Bacon's French versions rather than trying to produce a parallel but differently poetic English version. As discussed in Chapter 3, these are very difficult decisions. If one thinks of a translation as a "possibility to expand" and the "opening of a conversational space," a way of listening, perhaps staying very close to the original is the best strategy. The advantage Tshaukuesh and I had was that the conversational space between us was already open through our ongoing technical dialogue, and thus the translation could be a much more iterative process. However, the point of literary translation is to broaden the possibilities for communication between cultures, not just individuals. I tried to "invoke wonder," as Burtynsky phrased it, while staying as true as possible to the details of Tshaukuesh's accounts and to the poetics of her voice through careful listening: technical dialogue that ideally would merge into genuine dialogue between us and, later, with readers. At the same time, I was also compelled to be quite literal as I attempted to represent as accurately as possible the basic meaning of what Tshaukuesh told me and to make the end result broadly accessible while still retaining a sense of an Innu world, nutshimit and Innu-aitun. I tried to write in a voice that was colloquial and reminiscent of spoken language, since Tshaukuesh had no literary models and did not give the impression of following traditional storytelling protocols but rather of addressing herself to a friend, or at times in prayer to a spirit and at other times to herself in memos and lists. I had read about translating Rumi, Sei Shônagon, Homer, Sappho: classical texts by unknowable long dead writers. However precise and scholarly or imaginative and contemporary the translation, they remain unknowable. But I was translating a living person, one I knew personally and thought of both as a friend and a public figure whom I admired enormously. Yet she too was in a sense unknowable, as I was to her, our cultures and language backgrounds too different for me to simply ask her to explain every nuance or for her to realize what I was not getting. Technical dialogue allowed us to get to know each other.

Listening to Indigenous Languages

Culturalism, or epistemological dominance, is a focus of critique in various fields, including Indigenous studies, and in postcolonial, decolonial, and critical race theories.[24] This dominance plays out in many different ways in relation to what counts as worthwhile knowledge; for instance, the way our legal and governmental systems, research protocols, and practices are structured to prioritize the written over the oral and certain kinds of empirical evidence over others such as storytelling, performance, and lived experience. Sophie McCall has shown how storytelling, unlike traditional documentary evidence, depends on a relationship in which the listener as well as the teller plays a role. Using the example of the 1996 Royal Commission on Aboriginal Peoples (RCAP), she explains how the commissioners, because they were focused on making recommendations and thus on managing and containing the testimonies, missed an opportunity to enact a shared history by truly listening in a way that acknowledged their own roles in Canadian–Indigenous relations.[25] Similarly, in research, if our focus is on managing or categorizing what we hear and observe, we may miss important opportunities. Following Gillian Whitlock and Dori Laub, McCall emphasizes the dynamic relationship between speaker and listener as fundamental to reconciliation and indeed to the very existence of the story, because "a story without a witness is virtually incommunicable: it is little more than charred remains, a burnt out shell . . . It is the witness's responsibility to affirm the existence of the fugitive pieces."[26]

We listen, or we don't, but we must also think about which languages we listen to and why. Culturalism has led to English and French being the official languages of Canada, and this affects what research can be funded. Each time Tshaukuesh and I submitted a proposal for funding we had to explain why I was writing on Tshaukuesh's behalf. Understandably, the funders were concerned about a non-Indigenous researcher receiving funds for an Indigenous elder's project, but Tshaukuesh writes only in Innu-aimun. I wanted to write an explanatory note that I was applying because grant reviewers cannot read Innu-aimun. Indeed, I did write those notes, though I framed them a little more diplomatically. In the end, we were very well supported by several agencies, including the Social Sciences and Humanities

Research Council (SSHRC), Canada's largest official funding body for research in these areas, but there were more hoops to jump through than there might have been for other types of research. Applications cannot be submitted to SSHRC or Canada Council (another government funding source) in Indigenous languages, thus excluding many holders of Indigenous knowledge. Clearly, the widespread use of English and other colonial languages such as French and Spanish has allowed Indigenous peoples to communicate and organize across groups. However, it has also marginalized those who communicate solely or primarily in Indigenous languages, and has played a key role in the demise of many languages.

The requirement that funding applications must be in an official language is largely unexamined. The SSHRC website states that Indigenous research is a priority and that it works to "ensure that Indigenous research incorporating Indigenous knowledge systems (including ontologies, epistemologies and methodologies) is recognized as a scholarly contribution." SSHRC's guidelines also affirm that "Indigenous knowledge is rarely acquired through written documents, but, rather, a worldview adopted through living, listening and learning in the ancestral languages and within the contexts of living on the land."[27] Obviously, it would be very challenging to accept submissions in Indigenous languages, yet it would also support and make space for Indigenous knowledge and research. As well, it would make a public statement about the significance and value of the languages. It would be an act of decolonization and it is not impossible. The TRC Calls to Action include several calls relating to language, among them a recommendation that degree and diploma programs in Indigenous languages be created.[28]

Fred Metallic's PhD thesis is a more encouraging example of Indigenous language in an academic context. Written entirely in Mi'kmawi'simk and untranslated, the thesis, successfully defended at York University in 2009, is titled "Mi'gmawei Mawio'mi: Goqwei Wejguaqamultigw?"[29] York University now accepts theses in Indigenous languages as long as they have supervisory support. One of the reasons the university agreed to accept the thesis without a translation was to assert the value of the language itself and the premise that culturally contextual meanings could not always be carried over into English.[30] Metallic says that he was inspired to do doctoral work after being a witness to police brutality, humiliation, theft and trespassing during the 1981 raids on Mi'kmaw salmon fishers by Quebec provincial police and fisheries officers.[31] Then Quebec Minister of Recreation, Hunting and Fishing Lucien Lessard, who ordered the raids, said in response to questions as to why he supported francophone Quebec sovereignty but not Indigenous sovereignty, "You cannot ask for sovereignty because to have sovereignty one must have one's own culture, language and land."[32] It was an echo of the arguments in the 1960s that were used to exclude Indigenous peoples from the Official Languages Act. For Fred Metallic, it was about "the right to tell the story about our historical occupation in this territory, and the right to talk about what happened to our people and how we want to move forward . . . That story historically has been told by non-Indigenous researchers . . . Unless language is protected in law, it's not going to receive the attention or the resources necessary to preserve it."[33]

The act of listening to Indigenous languages and seeing them in written form, even for those who don't understand them, is also meaningful in its own right. The public presence and recognition of these languages says they are alive, they matter, and the rights of the people who speak them matter. Tshaukuesh often speaks publicly in Innu-aimun with an interpreter. The consecutive interpretation is time-consuming and can seem cumbersome, but that too makes a significant statement. Let the audience take the time to hear the language and to experience the speaker's comfort and eloquence in her own language rather than forcing her to struggle with theirs.

Language and the Land

Tshin ka minin
tshetshi taian,
tshin ka minin
tshetshi tshissenitaman,
tshin ka minin
tshetshi eka unishinian
uitamui kashikat
tanite tshe ituteian

tshetshi mishkaman
meshkanau anite ka mitimeht
nimushumat.

You who taught me
to be,
you who gave me
knowledge,
you who showed me the way,
tell me today
where I should go
to find
the path
of our ancestors.[34]

Thus writes Innu poet Joséphine Bacon. Tshaukuesh's political struggles, her walks on the land, and the work on her book all have this pedagogical purpose, to create a space for young people to learn their own paths and the paths of their ancestors. She writes often of the routes her ancestors walked and her keen interest in visiting the sites where they travelled and hunted. She also uses walking to educate young people about how to live in nutshimit. This includes skills such as finding their way without a map, recognizing traces left by animals that indicate they are nearby and may return, using the language and the names of places in meaningful contextualized ways as they travel; and values like sharing and respect for the land, its inhabitants, and its spirits. While documentation, writing, cartography, and other forms of recording are important, there is no substitute for actually spending time in nutshimit, walking on the land, paddling the rivers and learning the stories through direct encounters with each other and with significant sites and activities, through listening.

As we have seen in Chapter 2, Michelle Lelièvre suggests that Indigenous walks, despite their diverse goals, have in common that they all call into question the bias toward sedentism, offer dynamic ways of thinking about land, and have the potential to reshape relationships and alliances in settler states.[35]

The Indigenous Humanities group of Battiste, Bell, Findlay, Findlay, and Henderson elaborates on the idea of knowledge of the land as fundamental to education and research, arguing that Indigenous place-based knowing should be central to the humanities. While a focus on place may seem to be at odds with a critique of the bias toward sedentism, it is not if place itself is understood as they conceptualize it—as a living organism—and our engagements with it as dynamic. Understanding place in this way would offer, among other things, a research agenda focused on respectful and sustainable ways to do what all humans do: "mark our place and progress across time and space,"[36] through a "non-acquisitive cartography"[37] that is needed now more than ever. Dougald Hine reminds us that "much of the ritual and story by which humans have found their bearings in the world has at its heart the cultivation of awareness and gratitude for the deaths of the animals and plants that give us life."[38] He sees our current fossil-fuelled economy as breaking that cycle, in that fossil fuels are formed from millions of years of death and yet are used up in only a few generations, causing more death through climate change, habitat destruction, and roadkill as they are used. We are no longer part of that cycle of life and death; we no longer try to restore what we have taken. Even if we did, how could we compensate for so much death? Hine concludes, "Committed to dependence on these vast underground reserves of death, the only response that remains to such questions is to silence them, to extinguish the ways of living which embody them, to make them unthinkable."[39]

As I come to the end of this chapter, I struggle to bring together all the ideas and questions that weave their way through it: trying to show through examples how Tshaukuesh and I developed a method for translating her writing, a method based on listening; the value of listening to Indigenous languages, whether or not we understand them; some of the challenges of learning an Indigenous language when one only knows unrelated colonizing tongues; how not knowing each other's languages well could actually be conducive to careful listening; how technical dialogue could also play a role in spinning "tiny threads" toward genuine dialogue and opening up toward the words and presence of the Other; how one-on-one relationships can be political; ways of thinking about research ethics and dismaying trends in ethics review; how the conventions and ethics of journalism and academe may not mesh with those of Indigenous elders and how carefully we might need to pay attention to each other on this; and how we must listen to the living land.

While I was writing this chapter, I attended a research presentation where I learned that in a sample of out-of-school youth in Nunavut, the probability of having dropped out of high school is 12.6 percent lower for respondents who spent time on the land relative to those who didn't. In a published report on the study, the researchers wrote: "We interpret this to reflect the value of learning the contemporary practices of one's people and closeness to one's culture."[40]

In another study, reported on in the same presentation, among a sample of First Nations, Métis, and Inuit respondents, the high school graduation rate is 14.2 percent *lower* for those speaking an Indigenous language relative to those not speaking one.[41] The authors suggest that "while the current emphasis on Aboriginal language instruction is important for cultural revitalization in the North, this could come at the cost of lower high school graduation rates if proper supports for bilingualism are not provided."[42]

I asked the authors what they thought might be the reasons behind the startling discrepancy in the effects of knowing a language compared to spending time on the land. They had several ideas: that speaking the language may also be correlated with resisting colonial systems such as school in the first place (another example was that rigid schedules were similarly resisted); that parents who want their children to be high achievers in the world outside their traditional one often will not place them in language classes, as they think it will make them less competitive; that time on the land also correlates to having the resources to get there—owning a skidoo or a boat, having funds to buy gas and equipment—so the correlation with success in the other study probably relates to economic class; and that schooling in the Indigenous language is often phased out after grade two, three, or four. This is frequently because of lack of resources or trained teachers but also says a lot about what is seen to be important (or possible) by people who control schools. The result is that children stop using the language just as they are beginning to develop literacy in it. They can still do short core language classes once or twice a week, but this is not enough: they need intensity and continuity, and the lack of emphasis and resources gives the impression that it does not really count for much. We know that residential schools were responsible for devastating language and cultural loss, but we do not often talk about how *most* schools are antithetical to Indigenous languages.

These paradoxical research findings sit oddly here at the end of a chapter about listening. Yet they are compelling and disturbing, and I keep thinking they *are* relevant. If this chapter is about listening to language and the land, what do the findings tell us about that? I want to end with two Innu poets who say quite different things about language, the same two poets who spoke Innu jubilantly in the streets of Paris, who write profoundly about their attachments to their own land and to language: Joséphine Bacon and Natasha Kanapé Fontaine.

The poem by Joséphine Bacon quoted above has another verse. It continues:

Tshin ka minin
tshetshi akua tutaman aimun,
tshin ka minin
tshetshi tutaman aimun
tshe patshitinaman,
nitshissẹniten tshuapamin ute etaian.

Tshinatuenitamatin tshetshi uitshin.

You who made me
guardian of the language,
you who told me to follow your words,
I know you can see me.

I beg you to help me.[43]

Kanapé Fontaine describes her amazement on seeing a video of herself at her fifth birthday party speaking Innu and realizing that not long after, when starting school, she began communicating exclusively in French.

Language is a vast territory. It is one of those necessary invisible latitudes of physical territories that we know. Each language carries the vibrations of its own land; each language belongs to the land that brought it into being. The same goes for culture. . . . I speak French because I had no choice. And yet French will be my weapon of mass destruction against colonialism, that outrageous attitude that permeates everyday life. This weapon will refine my thinking, enlarge my memory, enfranchise my opinions and my speech. . . . The French language will be my weapon of mass reconstruction. My words will be the colour of my blood.[44]

Eight

Songs

What are we going to do?
No marten.
What can we do?
No caribou.
...
What are we going to eat?
Where can we hunt?

—PHILIPPE MCKENZIE, "TANITE MACK TSHE TIAK" (WHERE CAN WE HUNT?)[1]

I play Chloé Sainte-Marie's cover of Innu singer-songwriter Philippe McKenzie's song "Tanite Mack Tshe Tiak" for Tshaukuesh, curious to know what she thinks of it.[2] A few lines in, she spontaneously begins to translate the Innu words into English. Sainte-Marie's version of the song is plaintive and Tshaukuesh's soft voice and tentative interpretation exactly echo the mood. It is very moving. I ask her to do it again so I can record it, but it loses some of its impact in the repetition. We try several times but just cannot recapture the moment. Still, I keep the recording and listen to it from time to time, thinking about that and other evocations of Innusi. Singer-songwriter Florent Vollant, of the Innu musical duo Kashtin, describes the topics and inspirations of his songs: "I've always told stories of the North. Very much so. I tell the stories of the North, I tell the stories of the people who live there, I tell the stories of that space, I tell many stories

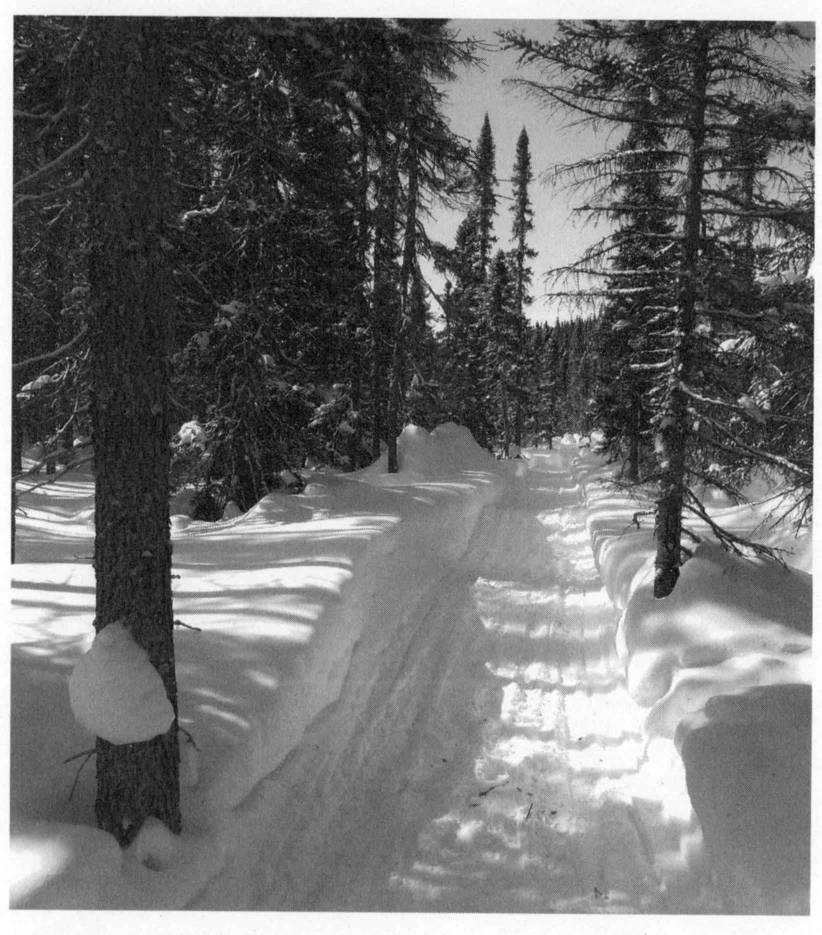

"One warm line": A snowmobile trail in nutshimit. Photo by Melissa Tremblett.

about nomads . . . their gestures, their dreams, their movements, their travels; I also tell stories of their past, where they come from . . . The Innu."[3] Ethnomusicologist Véronique Audet elaborates more generally that Innu popular music plays a key role in asserting Indigenous identity and pride as well as in cultural renewal, transformation, and social healing. She also notes that this is rooted in knowledge of the land and of being Innu.[4]

This chapter is not primarily about Innu music, however. It is about how some non-Innu popular musicians have interpreted Innusi and the North. I consider specific much-loved songs and their possible contribution to structures of feeling that are part of ongoing colonization. I offer the vignette and comments above as a contrast to what follows, and I conclude the chapter with another Innu song, "Tshinanu."

"Si tu savais comme on s'ennuie à la Manic"

Georges Dor's plangent song of love, loss, and longing, "La Manic," has become a classic of Québécois popular music, sung more recently to huge acclaim in Quebec by Leonard Cohen: "Si tu savais comme on s'ennuie à la Manic, tu m'écrirais bien plus souvent à la Manicouagan."[5] Cohen translated the opening lines as "If you knew how life drags on at La Manic, you'd write to me a lot more often at La Manicouagan."[6] He said he was working on an English translation of the whole song, but as far as I can find out, he never completed it.[7] Perhaps it was impossible, even for such a great poet and one who understood the sensibility of francophone Quebec quite well. Perhaps the two cultural contexts were incommensurable. If so, how much greater is the translation gap between English or French and Innu-aimun, for the lands where the Manicouagan dam was built belong to the Innu. The song takes the form of a letter from a construction worker on the dam, built in the 1960s and still one of the world's largest, to his beloved in the urban South. The song isn't really about Innu land but about the loneliness of life on a massive construction site far from home. Yet the words contrast the isolation of that place in the forest with what the narrator sees as the more vibrant and comforting urban life to the South:

"Dis-moi c'qui s'passe à Trois-Rivières
Et à Québec
Là où la vie a tant à faire
Et tout c'qu'on fait avec
Dis-moi c'qui s'passe à Montréal
Dans les rues sales et transversales . . ."

"Tell me the news from Trois-Rivières
And from Quebec
Where life is full and fully lived,
And from the grimy criss-cross streets
Of Montreal . . ."
(My attempt at translation, though I hesitate to try
where Leonard Cohen apparently decided not to.)

Manicouagan is part of the traditional territory of the Pessamit Innu. The dam there was built during Quebec's Quiet Revolution and was an important symbol of economic and technological power, part of a reinterpretation of francophone Quebec, which had long been dominated by an English-speaking minority. In the highly successful cultural and political conscientization movement that was growing as the dam was built, the rejection of anglophone domination often meant emphasizing francophone homogeneity rather than diversity, replacing one set of cultural tropes and mythic memories with another, and reworking Québécois understanding of community, identity, and relationships with other regions (some might say nations). A notion of francophone Québécois as underdogs poised to overthrow an oppressive anglophone elite underlay much of the re-visioning and rethinking. This binary opposition of francophone/anglophone and the ongoing struggle for francophone autonomy sometimes made it difficult for other histories to be told, since they might have disrupted the Québécois cultural and political project. While this remembrance and the counter-memories produced in response to it helped drive the movement to cultural autonomy—and the rich cultural renaissance that was part of it—it also excluded other stories, other lives, most notably those of Indigenous peoples.

In both Canada and Quebec, exclusions were also enforced culturally through structures of feeling. For many Québécois in the 1960s, the Manicouagan dam was part of a narrative of prosperity and power, nationhood. Georges Dor's song was part of that narrative too, even though it focused on the loneliness and isolation of the workers. What it wasn't about, however, was Innu land and culture, the rich lives that were lived in that northern place. Those lives were invisible in that moving and powerful song. It is easy to critique stories that are obviously exclusive, racist, or overtly harmful; much harder to think analytically about stories that touch us deeply and that are compellingly told. Understanding them as structures of feeling can help and so can understanding our own responses to them.

At supper at my friend Marie's house one evening, another guest is originally from Matapedia. She mentions something about Manicouagan that I do not quite catch. "What's that?" I ask. "Oh, it's a hydroelectric project," she says, misunderstanding my question. When I say I know that and I know the beautiful song "La Manic," she tells me, "My father was a bucheron, a lumberjack. He worked on the dam at La Manic. Sometimes he was away for months at a time and they were so lonely there. People make fun of lumberjacks and look down on them. They say 'parler comme un bucheron, jurer comme un bucheron, manger comme un bucheron' as terms of disdain. But they worked so hard! And without them, we wouldn't have had the electricity." I suddenly remember another friend, Hélène, from my university days. She was from Montreal and her father was in public relations for Hydro-Québec, editor of their in-house magazine. I had the impression it was a very significant and successful job, which surprised me—editing a magazine for an electricity company did not seem like such a big deal to me. I did not realize how central Hydro-Québec was to Quebec in the 1970s.

La Manic is the site of several dams, most notably the Daniel-Johnson dam, Manic-5, one of the world's largest. The vast island in the centre of the reservoir is officially named after René Levasseur, chief engineer on the dam, and the mountain at its centre after a missionary, Louis Babel. Neither of them was Innu. Large sections of the island were made into an ecological reserve after challenges from the Innu and environmental groups.[8] The names of the missionary and the engineer are still the ones found on maps and public documents, marking their memory. In a digital photo essay, Natasha Kanapé Fontaine recounts her return to Lake Tetepiskat in the Manicouagan reservoir area with her father. He had not been there since 1977. She had never been there. But it was their ancestral territory, in Innusi.

To mark my presence
in the world
on the lake
among trees and forests
and shields
tundras hills and herds
me too I existed
me too mark me
on your geography of memory[9]

"Rocks and Trees"

Tshaukuesh wrote this in her diary, about a visit from a mining executive: "So many things we've lost: our river, our animals, our land, our health. I invited an utshimau from Emish[10] to come to my house, and when he came I told him, 'One day you'll finish working and you'll go back where you came from. I don't know where you came from: Halifax, Toronto? You'll retire and you'll get a cheque every two weeks, and my people will still be here and our land will be destroyed.'"[11] Wendell Ferguson's "Rocks and Trees"[12] uses slant rhymes, unexpected images and brilliantly minimalist descriptions of scenes along Highway 17 in northern Ontario to evoke a reality that many of us from the South—like the utshimau who visited Tshaukuesh and the narrator of "La Manic"—have known briefly as we passed through or worked, planting or cutting trees, mining, building dams, visiting.

Though I dearly love this land,
I've stood all I can stand,
Of rocks and trees, trees and rocks.

Rocks and trees, trees and rocks,
Reams and reams of endless trees and tons of rocks;
The whole north is just proliferous
With metamorphic and coniferous,
Rocks and trees, trees and rocks.
Rocks and trees, trees and rocks;
Motel signs, hydro lines and a flattened fox;
Oh, construction site machinery
Is a welcome change of scenery,
From rocks and trees, trees and rocks . . .
Here's a break.
It's a little lake . . .
As I gaze down to the bottom
I can see it's filled with rotten,
Rotten trees and rotten rocks![13]

When Tshaukuesh and I were working with the maps described in Chapter 1, she also said something about all the submerged rocks and trees: "When we cross the bridge on the way to Churchill Falls we look down and see all the rocks and trees under the water, we think about how that was our land all along the river. We never dreamed it would all be destroyed. If our ancestors had known, it would have broken their hearts."[14]

Ferguson emphasizes his knowledge and love of the land on his website: "The rugged beauty of the land up there has inspired both paintings and poems. As a musician I have travelled this road many times, many many many times."[15] He was not just a brief visitor. And there really is love in these lyrics: that is exactly what makes it so difficult to think about the structures of feeling they might produce and the way they contrast so dramatically with Tshaukuesh's writing about the same rocks and trees. We cannot really know what effect they will have, though. They might inspire wonder, too, with their humour and the sense of vastness they create. Kathleen Stewart has pointed out that structures of feeling are similar to what she calls "ordinary affects." Following Raymond Williams and Roland Barthes, she highlights their potential to shape our thinking and feeling, to pressure us to react in certain ways, to make connections we might otherwise not have made, for better or for worse. She stresses that the meanings they produce are different from semantic or symbolic meanings, "more fractious, multiplicitous, and unpredictable ... not the kind of analytic object that can be laid out on a single, static plane of analysis."[16] Yet they are feelings that profoundly affect both public and intimate life, and Stewart suggests they might help us to think through things differently than we would with more abstract concepts like neoliberalism or globalization. From her vantage point in 2007, she gives two examples that are almost eerily prescient of compelling issues as I write this in the context of the Black Lives Matter movement and COVID-19 in 2020: the politics of affect can influence what happens in the split second when a policeman decides to shoot a man because he is Black, and they can also turn someone's daily life from endurable to not with a seemingly small thing like a shift in a child's school schedule.[17] In juxtaposing writing by Innu women with the words (and music) of the songs presented here and my own reactions to both, I am trying to follow Stewart's advice to pay "close ethnographic attention to pressure points and forms of attention and attachment."[18]

There is also wonderful humour and love for the North in Wade Hemsworth's "The Blackfly Song," brilliantly animated in a National Film Board version with backup vocals by Kate and Anna McGarrigle, another song about the rigours of life in the North for Akaneshau from the South.[19] Hemsworth has stated that the song was originally written in Labrador in 1949, though it recounts a survey trip on the Little Abitibi, a tributary of the Abitibi River, for the Ontario Hydro-Electric Power Commission:[20]

> ... the unemployment office said they'd see me through
> To the Little Abitibi with the survey crew.
> ...
> "They want to build a power dam and we must find a way
> For to make the little Ab flow around the other way."
>
> And the blackflies, the little blackflies
> Always the blackfly, no matter where you go
> I'll die with the black fly a-pickin' on my bones
> In north Ontar-i-o.

"The Blackfly Song" humorously evokes a nightmare land, swarming with stinging insects, a land where the role of the Akaneshau is to get a paying job, to endure, and to make the rivers "flow around the other way." Yet similar northern landscapes have a different meaning for Tshaukuesh. While acknowledging the hardships of life in nutshimit, including the swarms of blackflies, she writes elegiacally about similar scenes, imagining the lives her ancestors lived on the land and remembering her own nomadic childhood. Her evocations of the rocks, trees, and flowing rivers of the boreal forests of Innusi come from a very different kind of ordinary affect:

> July 22 [1994]
> Every time I'm on this train, I look out the window at the route my parents walked, year after year. The Innu have travelled across this land for thousands of years. When I look at the vast territory they traversed, I think about the hardships they endured and how resilient they were. And they didn't even think it was hard. For them, their way of life was their well-being and their strength. They weren't under pressure but they never stopped working, except when they were sick. They never had to pay their children to help them.[21]
>
> August 7 [1995]
> I'm looking out [the train window] at the Mishta-shipu, where I often paddled with my parents as a child. There were many rapids, some of them very dangerous, and big mountains. It's a winding river, so they often had to stay close to shore or make a portage, carrying all their gear until they could safely get back into their canoes again. There must have been swarms of blackflies and mosquitoes too, and people with large families probably had to cope with two canoes as well as all their gear. But to compensate, their campsites were always in beautiful locations, and once they reached the highlands it was easier, though they still had many challenges. That was their way of life. They never complained. They never gave up.[22]

> April 10 [1999]
> Today I was thinking about how I hadn't walked on our land for so many years, but all those years I was thinking, "I want to go, I want to go. I want to walk where my ancestors walked, where I walked with my parents when I was young." I can see my mom and dad, my brothers and my sisters, all of us so happy, walking in nutshimit. When my father found a good hunting place with plenty of animals, we'd stop and camp for a couple of months. And then we'd move on.[23]
>
> June 12, 2008
> [In a letter to Premier Danny Williams, arguing against the construction of a new dam and inviting him to come on a canoe trip with her so she can show him] how beautiful the river is, everything so beautiful, trees, river, mountains, long beach, rocks, so beautiful.[24]

Danny Williams never did go to meet with her but in an essay about the river, Tshaukuesh expressed her concerns in more detail: "I often think about life before Patshishetshuanau was flooded, and I imagine the people camping along the shore and paddling down the river. How they used to tell their families and their children stories of the past, how beautiful the land was, and how the river would be there for them to live on and to use forever. But now that's not true. I feel that all the work I've done, trying to save the land and the river was in vain."[25]

Tshaukuesh's sense of profound loss of a beautiful world and way of life contrasts sharply not only with the hydro lines and construction sites comically evoked by Hemsworth and Ferguson but also with a different vision of nutshimit. Both Abitibi-Témiscamingue and Manicouagan are now marketed as ecotourism destinations, showing a change in the perception of what a wilderness is but still with the emphasis (though much less explicit and, at the same time, no longer satirical) on making money from the land: "Get a new lease on life in Abitibi-Témiscamingue, an untouched paradise in western

Québec that's teeming with cultural treasures and adventure possibilities. From the depths of the mine to the dazzling sun on the suspended footbridge, and from traditional Anishinabek dance to emerging music, the region offers an endless variety of stimulating experiences." The Anishinabek people and their history are included in this marketing with the explanation that "traces of the Anishinabek people date back 8,000 years, and this Algonquin First Nation continues to be a thriving presence in the territory today." There is also an emphasis on enjoying "Abitibi-Témiscamingue's pristine lands safely and enjoyably, without harming the environment." The mines, dams and construction sites, rocks, trees, and blackflies are transformed in this narrative to "lush forests dotted with 22,000 lakes and rivers."[26]

As for Manicouagan, even the dam has become a draw for tourists, who are invited to "visit the Jean-Lesage Generating Station (Manic-2) and Daniel-Johnson Dam (Manic-5), the world's largest multiple-arch-and-buttress dam, for free."[27] Here, the only mention of Indigenous peoples is a reference to the Innu Essipit craft boutique, although the Conseil des Innus de Pessamit is a partner in the development and promotion of the area as an ecotourism destination.[28] Manicouagan-Uapishka was designated a UNESCO Biosphere Reserve, one of the world's largest, in 2007. According to the regional tourism website, this designation "honours and underlines the community's will to build a model of belonging and sustainable development. The RMBMU is proving itself to be collectively empowering, a reflection of the territory and an invitation to excellence, as well as social and business innovation."[29]

There are several very different ideas, then, of what these places are: The ancestral lands of Tshaukuesh and Natasha Kanapé Fontaine, demanding but beautiful landscapes with good hunting and thousands of years of history. The powerful dams built by Hydro-Québec, or more precisely, by the father of my friend Marie's dinner guest and a multitude of other bucherons, lonely and looked down upon, immortalized in Georges Dor's "La Manic"; developments promoted by people like my friend Hélène's father to create structures of feeling, ordinary affect that gave the Québécois the confidence to overthrow anglophone domination and run their own affairs. The "untouched paradise" and "lush forests" of Abitibi-Témiscamingue and the Manicouagan-Uapishka Biosphere Reserve, the latter "a model of belonging and sustainable development." Sites for social business innovation, ecotourism, and getting a new lease on life. These ideas could be seen chronologically, each one superseding the last, but in many ways they all continue simultaneously as different ways of defining and understanding Innusi, its inhabitants, and its historical and actual significance in the world. Finally, another excerpt from Kanapé Fontaine's photo essay:

> . . . So many times I've imagined myself burning the
> mining companies
> blowing up hydroelectric dams
> melting the motors of those machines made to dig into us
> . . .
> is there still something to build
> a breath
> that will be neither the margin nor the world
> . . .
> even the salmon knows from its genes
> to return to the source of its birth
> even seven generations after.
> . . .
> Here I don't fear dying.[30]

"One Warm Line"

Perhaps the most powerful song of all for many English-speaking Canadians, Stan Rogers's "Northwest Passage" affects many of us with its haunting beauty and memorable refrain. It is about driving alone along the routes of early European explorers, each verse ending with a refrain in which a man traces "one warm line through a land so wide and savage / [to reach] a northwest passage, to the sea." It is soul stirring, that idea of the solitary adventurer on his lonely quest across the land, but it also carries a storyline in which Akaneshau survive, conquer, and humanize a vast and empty wilderness. That storyline is so powerful in the national consciousness that two very different national leaders, former prime minister Stephen Harper, a business-oriented Conservative, and former governor general Adrienne Clarkson, liberal supporter of the arts, both suggested it should be the national anthem, a song to reflect the psyche of the people.[31] But for Indigenous peoples, the land was never savage; they have traced countless "warm lines" through it for millennia and they continue to do so (as do animals, Tshaukuesh would probably add). In *Maps and Dreams*, Hugh Brody relates how Atsin, an Athapaskan hunter, responded to Brody's mapping project emphatically with "too many, too many," which Brody took to mean that "he could never, even in a hundred interviews, mark down all the places he had hunted and travelled."[32] And indeed, the maps from the project are covered with lines, and Brody describes them as "a strong affirmation of the peoples' enduring presence on the land."[33]

Benedict Anderson suggests in *Imagined Communities* that "the most important thing about language is its capacity for generating imagined communities, building in effect *particular solidarities*."[34] One of the ways this happens is through unisonance, a term Anderson uses to describe a shared response to certain narratives, songs, and poetry that evoke a powerful sense of community. He suggests the singing of a national anthem or other well-known and loved songs about nationhood as examples. "Northwest Passage" is a compelling example of a call to unisonality, "the echoed physical realization of the imagined community."[35] This idea has been critiqued, for example by Gopal Balakrishnan, who argues that there has to be "the possibility of sacrifice," usually through war, a call to arms, for there to be the strong nationalistic sentiments Anderson attributes to shared language.[36] However, perhaps for settler-colonizers the idea of a sacrificial history in which lone adventurers and explorers risked their all to gain and tame the land creates a sense of sacrifice via songs like "Northwest Passage."

In Anderson's analysis, community is based on excluding others, and this song poetically excludes all the inhabitants of Innusi except male European adventurers and their followers, arguably more effectively than Canada's official national anthem. Originally written in French, "O Canada" has been sung in many languages, including Cree, Inuktitut, and other Indigenous languages, as well as in English and French. The Toronto Symphony Orchestra performed it with various singers in the twelve most widely spoken languages in Canada, with Cree being the only Indigenous language in that category.[37] At times the song seems to be more divisive than unifying, with ongoing debates about gender parity and Christian religiosity in the lyrics.[38] The French version is more explicitly Christian than the English one, with the line "Il sait porter la croix" (He knows how to carry the cross). However, unlike the English version, the French has not been modified since 1880, perhaps because it is not very significant in nationalist francophone Québec; and nor is "Northwest Passage." No unisonance there. I'm thinking also of Paolo Pietropaolo's *Ode to the Salish Sea*, the interweaving of Stz'uminus elder George Harris speaking in Hul'qumi'num with the voice of monarchist Keith Roy and that faint and haunting rendition of "God Save the King," as described in Chapter 1. No unisonance there either. But "La Manic" could be the unofficial national anthem of Québec with its powerful evocation of the North, of the lives of the bucherons, of Hydro-Québec, and a nation taking control of its own destiny.

The singer-songwriter Evalyn Parry eloquently opens up the concept of unisonance in her musical essay "To Live in the Age of Melting: Northwest Passage," which features the songs "Northwest Passage" and "Lady Franklin's Lament." She draws a parallel between the vagus nerve, which travels through the human body and "circles the heart," and the warm lines "innervating and connecting" the places of the land we live on. Parry writes: "You can trace the lines on a map of a country, chart the way to the heart of a country, explore, stake a claim, go down in history, write your name on a spot on the map, claim you found it but does that make it yours? What does discover mean? To be pointed in the right direction by someone who will not be named, someone who knows the frozen land like the back of their weathered hand, someone about whom no song will be written."[39]

"The Parting Glass"

There is another category of songs that often produces unisonance: drinking songs. The traditional Scottish song "The Parting Glass," revived in the mid-twentieth century by the Clancy Brothers and Tommy Makem, captures an ineffable tenderness toward humanity, flawed, damaged, vulnerable. Commenters on YouTube versions (of which there are many) write about weeping and being profoundly moved as they sang it or heard it sung at funerals and farewells. Interestingly, in relation to the theme of unisonance and national anthems, one commenter also suggested that this song could be Ireland's unofficial national anthem. It is strange how the stories about alcohol are different in different communities. For certain groups, these stories are quite central to how they imagine themselves and how they organize their socializing, their grief, their celebration, and their everyday relaxation. "The Parting Glass" is a deeply moving song for many, one that often even sums up the lives of their loved ones who have died. Just one of a huge category of songs that romanticize drinking alcohol, though a particularly beautiful one. A version of it, performed by Face Vocal Band, made the rounds on social media a year or two ago.[40] Half a dozen men of different ages walk into a bar and seat themselves sombrely at the counter. They are dressed in clothing that could be contemporary semi-formal dress for men in an artistic milieu but that also evokes working-class Ireland of perhaps the 1950s: dark tweed jackets, white shirts, some open necked, some with ties, a flat cap. Interestingly, there is no alcohol shown in the video but we know it is a bar, not a diner, because of the words of the song:

> Of all the money that e'er I spent
> I've spent it in good company
> And all the harm that ever I did
> Alas it was to none but me
> And all I've done for want of wit
> To memory now I can't recall
> . . .
> So fill to me the parting glass
> Good night and joy be with you all
> Oh, all the comrades that e'er I had
> They're sorry for my going away
> And all the sweethearts that e'er I had
> They'd wish me one more day to stay

But since it falls unto my lot
That I should rise and you should not
I'll gently rise and softly call
Good night and joy be with you all

"All the harm I've ever done, alas it was to none but me." But the harm done by drinking is rarely just to the drinker, for we are all connected. Tshaukuesh often wrote about alcohol in her diary. The most horrifying and heartbreaking entry of all is from February 15, 1992: "Last night something terrible happened in Utshimassit. A house burned down and six children who were left alone there died. The parents were out drinking. This is a huge tragedy. Alcohol is killing us more than ever. We've lost our way of life."[41] That same year, on November 8, as Tshaukuesh and her husband, Francis, set out for addictions counselling in Ontario, she wrote: "Sometimes I still feel angry, though, when I think about how strong a dependence on alcohol can be and how it changes the behaviour of men, how it controls them. It's merciless. I detest it. Alcohol destroys us—our bodies, our children, our culture. If alcohol didn't exist, we would never have experienced such poverty here on earth."[42] Tshaukuesh and Francis were successful in freeing themselves from the control of alcohol. However, she continued to write about the immeasurable damage it does to individuals, families, and communities, as in this entry on March 14, 1998: "When the moon first came up this evening, it was red. After a while it started to change into a brilliant ball of silver light. I felt so happy looking up at it, and I thought about what a beautiful night it was and how nice it would be to go outside for a long walk. Then I thought about the day and felt sad because we saw a lot of drunks on the road. Alcohol is a big problem in Sheshatshiu. I detest it. It's destroying us."[43]

Thomas King has written about the stories we tell about alcohol in one of his most powerful essays. As a coda to a story about the devastation wrought by fetal alcohol syndrome, he notes, "The stories we tell about alcohol are romances. Wine is for lovers, single malt scotch for successful entrepreneurs, beer for young nubile women and virile young men."[44] He goes on to tell other stories about the environment and social justice, how we think we are good people but really we often do not want to talk about difficult issues, not because we don't care about them but because we care more about our own comfort and the things that insulate us from hardship and struggle. For many of us, whether we have a drinking problem or not, alcohol is one of those things. In public discourse, song, and story it is associated with conviviality, celebration, comfort, and companionship in grief.

Substitute Indigenous singers for seemingly Irish ones in the "Parting Glass" video that went viral, however, and it might be interpreted differently. Yet alcohol has probably caused as much grief and misery in Irish communities as in Indigenous ones. Many Indigenous communities have found ways of celebrating, grieving, and telling their stories that do not involve alcohol. So have many Islamic and some Christian communities. Yet Muslim and Pentecostal students at our university have told me that there is nowhere on campus for them to socialize in the evening where alcohol is not served. And that is partly because of the stories we tell and the songs we sing, the ways they shape our ability to imagine how we relax and how we celebrate.

Of course, songs are not the whole answer to this problem. Even stories are not the whole answer. As King put it, "We wrote knowing that none of the stories we told would change the world. But we wrote in the hope that they would."[45] Innu singer-songwriter Philippe McKenzie said something similar about songs: "Music leads to reflection. You don't change the world through song but it does have an impact on our conscience."[46] Songs that produce unisonance in large groups of people through their heart-aching beauty have a particular power. We should be careful what we sing.

"Tshinanu"

"Tshinanu" can be translated as "This Is Us," "All of Us" or, more specifically, "All of Us Innu." Véronique Audet notes that the song, by Florent Vollant of Kashtin, is often sung at Innu political, social, and cultural events, where it effectively functions as an Innu national anthem.[47] Many Innu groups perform it, and the rapper Samian of the Abitibiwinni First Nation collaborated with Kashtin on a hip hop remake in 2010.[48] The liner notes to the original CD *Kashtin* elaborate on the song's theme: "Over time,

'Tshinanu' has become a national anthem symbolizing the new generation of Innu. Without naming them, the song recognizes our grandfathers, our rivers, our children and our portages. 'Tshinanu' also names a territory. It's as if we could see all of our land at once, all laid out before us."[49] Vollant performed "Tshinanu" in 2004 at the St. Jean Baptiste celebrations on the Plains of Abraham in Quebec City. Unlike Philippe McKenzie and some other Innu singers, Kashtin generally took an apolitical stance. However, singing this song of Innu strength, pride, and sovereignty at an event celebrating Québécois sovereignty seems like a political statement, or perhaps just an inside joke, since most listeners at that event would not understand the words:

Tshinanu ui tshissenitetau
Tshinanu, tshinanu
Tshinanu uauapatetau
Tshinanu, tshimeshkanaminu
Tshinanu, tshitauassiminuat
Tshinanu, tshimushuminuat
...
Tshinanu, tshishipiminu
Tshinanu, tshitassinu
Ai ai! Ai ai! Ai ai! Ai ai! Ai ai! Ai!
Tshinanu, tshitapuenanu

It's up to us to know
All of us
All of us
It's up to us to see
All of us, our routes
All of us, our children
All of us, our grandfathers
...
All of us, our rivers
All of us, our land

Ai ai! Ai ai! Ai ai! Ai ai! Ai ai! Ai!
All of us, we are in the right.[50]

Nine

Wilderness

> In the old days, the Innu were resourceful and knew how to make everything they needed—snowshoes, canoes, toboggans, drums, everything. They were very independent and full of energy. Everyone made a contribution. They respected the land and never destroyed it or took more than they needed, just enough to live, just enough wood for tent poles and to keep the tent warm so the children would be healthy and comfortable. Sometimes they took a little extra if they were sick and they needed the kinds of tree branches they used for medicine, or they'd take some wood to make traps for uapush, mashk^{u}, nitshik^{u}, amishk^{u}, atshakash, or uapishtan. We just cut a few trees, not everything like the Akaneshau do.[1]

Tshaukuesh goes on to describe the various small ceremonies practised every day as reminders to keep this balance. For example, writing about how fish is prepared for eating, she explains that they always clean the fish immediately, noting that "the reason for this is that it shows respect for the animals. The animal spirits know the hunters are looking for them, but they understand we need to eat and so they give us something as long as we respect them."[2]

One of the things I have tried to do in this book is to show the trajectory of what I have learned, not only through the thought and writing of Tshaukuesh herself and our work together, nor through scholarly sources

Tshaukuesh's tent in nutshimit. Photo by Ryan Wood (Instagram: @ryanwoodphoto).

alone, but also through all the small actions of daily life that contribute to thought and discourse: informal discussions over coffee, casual reading, radio and social media, and daily life walking on the land and in the city. I have no conclusions, just a continuation of that stream of ideas and a life lived in conjunction with them. Over the years I worked with Tshaukuesh, I gradually outlined tentative chapters and added ideas, notes, and quotations where they seemed to fit. As I organized the material, I knew I wanted to return to the idea of wilderness and how to write about it.

As I read through that first draft of this final chapter, it seemed to me more like an old-fashioned commonplace book: a quote from Tshaukuesh about Penipuapishkᵘ, the mountains of her childhood world; another from Tomson Highway on the lakes and stars of nutshimit; an excerpt from my introduction to *Nitinikiau Innusi* about translating the word "nutshimit"; definitions of wilderness by various writers; references to an article and a film about the toxic legacies of abandoned mines; notes on the U.S. Wilderness Act; a revisiting of ideas about how nature writing might persuade people to do things differently, to keep the land alive; Tuck and Yang on giving back the land, all of the land; a quotation from Rumi (funny how he crops up everywhere); questions about how humans cope in crisis—and I write this now in a time of pandemic, a pandemic created, most likely, by humans encroaching too far and too violently into wilderness. As science writer David Quammen put it, these are the points we could learn from COVID-19:

> 1. Prepare for the worst, while hoping for the best.
>
> 2. Zoonotic spillovers will keep coming, as long as we drag wild animals to us and split them open.
>
> 3. A tropical forest, with its vast diversity of visible creatures and microbes, is like a beautiful old barn: knock it over with a bulldozer and viruses will rise in the air like dust.
>
> 4. Leave bats, in particular, the hell alone.[3]

In some ways, this is the perfect context for writing about wilderness. I make myself a cup of tea and try to see patterns or a storyline, something that can bring all these threads and all the stories of this book together into some coherent final words. One thing that strikes me in Quammen's statement, appealing though it is as a series of soundbites (and it does contain much good advice), is that it is not the fact of killing wild animals that is the problem; it is, much more broadly, our relationships with wildness. It is the fact that so many humans have lost respect for it. We do not have ceremonies to remind us to keep things in balance. We take too much. Traditional Indigenous people did and do kill wild animals but they are usually very careful to take only as much as they need, as Tshaukuesh describes in the diary excerpt at the beginning of this chapter.

Last winter I signed up for a MOOC on nature writing from the University of Iowa, a chance to do some reading and writing on the topic and to learn something about how a MOOC might work in practice.[4] As it turned out it was an extraordinarily enriching experience, though also a difficult and frightening one, because it was through the course readings that I first truly realized the scope and immediacy of climate change. Of course, I had known for years that we were heading in a reckless direction and that we had to change our ways, and I had been involved in various kinds of activism, but somehow I had not quite understood how imminent collapse may be. Now, as we negotiate lockdowns, quarantines, vaccines, and variants with no way of knowing how long this will last or what the outcome will be, it seems as though in taking the course I was also preparing for COVID-19. After one particular set of readings, I spent several days, perhaps weeks—I cannot remember now—in abject terror. I thought that terrible fear would be with me for the rest of my life. I could hardly bear to see my grandchildren—my four-year-old grandson wearing his catboy costume at the playground whispering to me, "They think I'm the *real* catboy!" I tried to share his fun and pretend everything was normal, but all I could think of was the desolate future that awaited him. Surprisingly soon, however, I adjusted to this new understanding of what our future might be.

Writing has always been the mode of activism that comes most easily to me, but the enormity of what we are facing, and the unlikelihood of humans being able to make the required massive societal changes in time, made it seem futile. Still, I thought often about Tshaukuesh, who has gone to prison so many times for peaceful resistance, who never gives up. I have not written enough, perhaps, about how inspiring she is, about her leadership as the Innu took on NATO, one of the most powerful organizations in the world, and how she continues to this day in her dedication to protecting the land. However daunting it all is, we cannot give up. We have to try. The alternative is unthinkable.

The Melting North

The articles that led me to despair and then to reassess how to live, or how to face life, were the following:

"Greenland Is Melting," by Elizabeth Kolbert
"The Invisible Catastrophe," by Nathaniel Rich
"Blue Capitalism," by Maya Weeks
"Cleaning a Continent," by Wendy Trusler and Carol Devine
"Rotten Ice," by Gretel Ehrlich
and most of all, "How to Write about a Vanishing World," also by Elizabeth Kolbert.

Elizabeth Kolbert offers two approaches to writing to keep the land alive, or as Tshaukuesh put it in the alternative title she had suggested for her book, the one we did not use, less catchy but more accurate, to *try* to keep the land alive. One approach is to "narrate the [smaller, somewhat more manageable] disaster as a way of trying to avert it" (for example, trying to save coral reefs by educating people about them). The other is "straight up despair," in which there is no point in writing about any smaller-scale event without "dealing with climate change, which is to say . . . completely revamping the world's energy systems."[5] She concludes that scientifically speaking, the latter is the only option, because local conservation and restoration efforts are doomed to failure as the climate continues to warm.

The Arctic is warming four times as fast as the rest of the world.[6] As Kolbert describes, the thawing Greenland Ice Sheet is one of the effects of this. A NASA study reveals that it is now melting on average seven times faster than it was in the 1990s. Between 1992 and 2018, the sea rose by 11 millimetres, which may not seem like much but as the lead author of the study, Andrew Shepherd, points out, "As a rule of thumb, for every centimeter rise in global sea level, another 6 million people are exposed to coastal flooding around the planet."[7] If the trend to melt ever faster continues, 400 million coastal people will endure flooding by the end of this century. According to the NASA authors, half the ice loss is caused by warmer air and the rest by a combination of ocean warming, ice shedding, and iceberg calving.[8] Meanwhile, here in Newfoundland and Labrador, tourists and locals alike rejoiced at bumper iceberg years. The icebergs were spectacular—crystal mountains, pinnacles and spires, azure pools and valleys. I posted photos of them on social media like everybody else but I could never understand why they seemed to bring such joy when they meant that the Arctic was melting. Last year there were hardly any though, and it is likely that this will be more and more frequent until there are none at all.[9]

There have been other periods of dramatic climate change during the time when humans have lived on earth. Known as Dansgaard-Oeschger (D-O) events, after the two scientists who discovered them through the study of ice cores from Greenland, these are periods when average temperatures have risen as much as fifteen degrees in fifty years. There have been twenty-five of these events in the past 115,000 years.[10] No one knows for sure what caused them, but we know our ancestors survived them somehow. They all happened during prehistoric times and this is significant because it means that the people who came through D-O events lived close to the land in small groups and could simply move on. Presumably other living things also moved, adapted, or disappeared.

Tshaukuesh had to reroute her walk years ago, away from the trail to Enipeshakimau that the Innu had walked for millennia, because it crossed and recrossed the winding Uapush-shipiss and the ice was no longer reliable. A bit further north, in the Labrador Inuit territory of Nunatsiavut, one in twelve people has fallen through ice, two-thirds are afraid to travel on it, and half say they have lost access to traditional hunting routes because of warming, according to a recent survey.[11] Innu and Inuit knowledge of the ice comes from thousands of years of experience, but now they cannot always rely on it and a mistake can mean life or death. The inability to hunt and fish also means they have to eat expensive, poorer-quality food if they can afford it or go hungry if they cannot. Like Tshaukuesh, people in Nunatsiavut have adapted. They are now using "smart komatiks" and "smart buoys" to measure ice thickness.[12] These are developed and built locally and contribute to the local economy as well as helping people to hunt and travel safely. People carry on the best way they can. They change their routes, they use new technologies, they tell different stories. People in the North in particular have always been flexible in order to survive.

The Greatest Nature Essay Ever

Several of the authors of those essays that changed my life proposed ways forward through writing. Gretel Ehrlich quotes biologist E.O. Wilson: "It's our chance to practice altruism," to discipline ourselves, to cooperate—to which Ehrlich adds that what we need is "an open exchange in which sentience shapes the eye and mind and results in ever-deepening empathy."[13] Maya Weeks and Nathaniel Rich in their respective articles advocate telling stories that persuade people to live differently[14] and helping people understand the crisis.[15] But I'm getting ahead of myself.

In an earlier module of the MOOC from the University of Iowa, we were challenged to nominate the "greatest nature essay ever" after reading Brian Doyle's short essay on that topic. I nominated Tomson Highway's "The Time Tomson Highway went to *Mameek* and Survived to Tell the Tale." It is, as I describe in Chapter 6, about surviving residential school, but it is also about the world of Highway's childhood in nutshimit. I thought about it often as I tried to find the best way to represent Tshaukuesh's loving descriptions of nutshimit and Innu-aitun in English. Doyle suggests that the greatest essay ever "would begin with an image so startling and lovely and wondrous" that you would stop everything and read it, thinking "*this is why I read nature essays, to be startled and moved like that, wow.*"[16] Highway's essay begins with a circuitous and comical explanation of how he got his unusual name. This explanation also sets the scene in Cree territory in northern Manitoba half a century ago, and the second paragraph begins in sharp contrast to the meandering of the first: "I was born in a snow bank." Only in the third paragraph (and his paragraphs are long) does Highway produce the first wondrous image. It begins with his parents on the journey during which he was born, "a journey that, by the way, passed through the most extraordinarily beautiful landscape anywhere on Earth; I know, I've seen it myself many times since (and plan, in fact, to die there). Hundreds maybe even thousands of lakes unseen by humans (except by us) with hundreds maybe even thousands of islands, encircled, all of them, by golden sand beaches or flat slates of granite that slide like plates into the water and, of course, are covered by ice and snow in winter."[17]

Doyle also says that "there's no shouting, no persuasion, no eloquent pirouetting . . . no call to arms . . . [just] a feeling eerily like a warm hand brushed against your cheek, and you sit there, near tears, smiling, and then you stand up. Changed."[18] I always want to write a call to arms, but Highway's essay ends where it began, with more about the origin of his name. In between, though, in only eleven pages, it takes his family on a long journey in northern Manitoba by snowshoe and canoe, lit by "ten trillion stars if not even more, the arc of the dome they hung from flawless in shape, the only sound in the universe . . . a ripple, paddles dipping."[19] It also takes him through the trauma of residential school—yes, in only eleven pages—and even that is treated with poetry and humour, and an emphasis on survival. It is what Eve Tuck would call an abundance narrative.[20] I love Highway's humour and hyperbole, his poetic rhythms and vivid images, his entrancing stories. And perhaps what I love most about this particular essay is the way it makes wilderness homelike and desirable, not in a domesticating way that requires it to be tamed but in the idea that it is already home.

Tshaukuesh uses less description, though the people and stories in her writing do seem to me to bring her world vividly to life in a different way. Her stories too evoke the wilderness as home. I think that is one of the most profound things I learned in the time I spent with her in nutshimit and the years we worked together: how wilderness can be home, *is* home for many. As we worked on the translation, I had to remind myself that while I had in mind readers who did not know Innusi, Tshaukuesh's primary goal was to leave a record for the Innu. As she wrote in the prologue:

> Before the protests, I couldn't have imagined I would ever be able to do all the things I've done . . .
>
> I've wanted to make my own book for so many years. I'm slow and it's hard work but I never gave up because this is very important. I want to see it before I die. It will be my legacy for my children, my grandchildren, my great-grandchildren, all my descendants . . . I didn't want to see the children lose our language, Innu-aimun, or our culture, and I could see that it was already happening. I hate to think that my journals could just lie there forgotten. I want people to remember this story . . . We can't go back to the old ways completely, but we must pass the knowledge and skills on to our children and grandchildren.
>
> I began this work by studying and writing my journal. It felt so good to do that and it gave me strength. I want to help other women to be strong too.[21]

Her prologue contrasts with my "outsider's" introduction to the book, where I wrote:

> Until I walked in nutshimit with Tshaukuesh, I could never have imagined how cozy it would be inside a tent in the wilderness at −30°C or how happy we would be: insulated by fir boughs and caribou skins, listening to the crackling of the fire in the rusty stove, breathing the scent of resin and wood smoke, illuminated by the flame of a single candle, the stories and laughter gradually subsiding as people drifted off to sleep; and then in the morning, waking up to the soft murmur of voices, the hiss of the kettle, the comforting smells of frying fish and bannock. Nor could I have

> known what it would be like to travel with a small band of people pulling all my belongings on a toboggan over frozen marshes and lakes, along forest trails and up into the mountains, under brilliant sunshine and through snowstorms; hunting and fishing for food, chopping chunks of ice from the river to melt for tea; the delicious warmth and comfort of it after a long day of walking on snowshoes. We had only each other to depend on, and though we did have a satellite phone for emergencies and occasional skidoos arrived carrying visitors, the outside world seemed very far away.[22]

I emphasized the contrast between our approaches, our sense of audience, but only now, as I revisit the two pieces, do I notice that both Tshaukuesh and I began with "I couldn't have imagined . . ." In her case, this refers to her activism, her travels, her engagement with the world outside nutshimit: the military, prison guards, politicians, reporters, academics, people from many cultures and perspectives, and to writing a book; in mine, to travelling in nutshimit and learning from her and from the Innu. We had this in common, our amazement at what we experienced in worlds outside our own when we found the courage to venture into them, though for very different reasons. We also had in common a sense of the significance of her story and the desire to make it available for people to read and for posterity.

To return to Doyle's criteria and the idea of opening with "a wondrous image": Tshaukuesh begins by describing crossing rotten ice and reaching the other side safely, and I with walking on the land with snowshoes and toboggan. Both are potentially wondrous images, I think, so the question is more whether we conveyed them well enough. And well enough for what? I am reminded of Edward Burtynsky's idea, discussed in Chapter 4, of invoking wonder so people will think and talk about those places. And, following Doyle again, "No call to arms. But you stand there. Changed." It is a daunting goal to change people but, as with doing anything at all, you have to try, and to keep in mind the way small impacts can gradually gather momentum. This means being part of a community, and considering whom you want to be in community with as you use whatever skills you have toward the kind of change you hope for. In terms of writing, it means thinking not only about readers but about other writers, and about which conversations you want to be part of. One aspect of this, as Daniel Heath Justice emphasizes, is "that we not continue to replicate the closed circuit of white heteropatriarchy in affirming the same group of voices over and over again."[23] I have written about Elizabeth Kolbert's and Brian Doyle's ideas on how to write about nature because they do seem important to me and because I want to show the trajectory of my learning, some of which came from the MOOC which featured their work. Kolbert's, in particular, were life changing for me because they confronted me with what I had long resisted understanding, and with the need to write anyway, in spite of, *because* of that. And both of them and all the readings from that MOOC influenced my ideas about *how* to write. I realize Kolbert and Doyle are not necessarily members of "the closed circuit of white heteropatriarchy" Heath Justice is referring to but his reminder was still timely, and I went back to Robin Kimmerer and Thomas King on stories.

Kimmerer describes her book *Braiding Sweetgrass* as "a braid of stories meant to heal our relationship with the world. This braid is woven from three strands: Indigenous ways of knowing, scientific knowledge, and the story of an Anishinabekwe scientist trying to bring them together in service to what matters most . . . healing stories that allow us to imagine a different relationship, in which people and land are good medicine for each other."[24] And King emphasizes over and over again the responsibility of the storyteller (and, by extension, the artist, the writer, the filmmaker, the translator—any cultural worker who seeks to make change through their art). King tells us that "stories are wondrous things. And they are dangerous."[25] He also writes, "There is a part of me that has never been able to move past these stories, a part of me that will be chained to these stories as long as I live."[26] This is the power of art, in its strongest forms.

Translating Wilderness

There were still more references and notes in my original draft for this chapter: an excerpt from the *National Observer* about the destruction of the Brazilian rainforest juxtaposed to a revisiting of Burtynsky; a piece by Kea Krause about how unfettered development in Montana has left it with an estimated 20,000 abandoned mines and all their detritus and poison; a note to myself that Canada has a similar number, huge for a whole vast country, unimaginable for a single American state. About the history of Montana, Krause wrote: "Copper companies were left to pursue their own interests without regulation . . . piles of rock, often the size of city blocks, were set on fire and allowed to burn for days. Smelting was just as noxious, producing excesses of smoke and another form of waste called slag, a muddy slush that would then get dumped from factories into nearby waterways. Silver Bow Creek, which runs through Butte, became a flowing mine-waste disposal site."[27] I kept thinking about the Indigenous peoples who lived there, who would have to deal with what remains, and looked them up: Assiniboine, Blackfeet, Chippewa, Cree, Crow, Gros Ventre, Kootenai, Little Shell Chippewa, Northern Cheyenne, Pend d'Oreille, Salish, and Sioux. I know nothing about their histories and experiences; I am not sure either that these are the names they call themselves. But I do know something about mines and dams in the North, and one source of my knowledge is the film that provided the figures I had noted along with Krause's article. I had seen *Guardians of Eternity: Confronting Giant Mine's Toxic Legacy* (2015) with Tshaukuesh and been struck by her ability to understand exactly what it was about, despite her lack of fluency in English. The film tells the story of an abandoned gold mine that has left the Yellowknives Dene First Nation living with arsenic trioxide contaminating their land for eternity.[28] Two of my colleagues, John Sandlos and Arn Keeling, speak in the film about their research on the Toxic Legacies Project.[29] I remembered two numbers from the film: there are around 22,000 contaminated mining sites in Canada, and you can't safely pick blueberries within a twenty-kilometre radius of Giant Mine. The Yellowknives Dene worry about how to let future generations centuries from now know that. These are not narratives of abundance on the surface. They are about appalling damage and destruction, but they are lifted into a different sphere by the courage and commitment of the people left with this contamination and the care they have, not only for each other but for all future generations, for eternity. We are all living with devastation and all we have really is our care for each other and for the damaged earth.

Our care for each other has global implications. In another of the pieces patched into my draft, the article about the Brazilian rainforest, Rufo Quintavalle argues that we must understand the needs of the roughly fifteen million people who live there, many of whom are desperately poor, in the context of our own involvement in global demand for products like beef, aluminum, and soy. We have to change our own patterns of consumption and support more sustainable forms of development and trade with local farmers. It is not helpful, in fact potentially deeply harmful, to imagine the Amazon rainforest as an uninhabited wilderness free of human intervention, since imagining it that way leads to the idea that it can be exploited by outsiders.[30]

The next section of my notes is about conceptualizations of wilderness: Cynthia Sugars's idea that there are two ways of understanding it in early Canadian literature. In one, it is inhabited by savage creatures (animal and human) to be conquered by European adventurers; in the other, it is a "new" world, empty, unfamiliar, and "unhaunted."[31] Two different imaginings of wilderness, both of which lead to the same tragic conclusion: land is there to be dominated, either because it is empty and for the taking or because it is savage and must be tamed. Eve Tuck and K. Wayne Yang, in their well-known article "Decolonization Is Not A Metaphor," offer a definition somewhere between the two,[32] one in which the wilderness is a place where the settler "can make a new 'home' and that home is rooted in a homesteading worldview where the wild land and wild people were made for his benefit."[33]

Jocelyn Thorpe, in *Temagami's Tangled Wild*, suggests that the concept of empty wilderness enables not only exploitation but also exclusion. Struggles to protect "pristine" land sometimes end up pitting environmentalists against Indigenous people and others who live there.[34] In the United States, the Wilderness Act provides a legal definition of wilderness: "A wilderness, in contrast with those areas where man and his own works dominate the landscape, is hereby recognized as an area where the earth and its community of life are untrammeled by man, where man himself is a visitor who does not remain."[35] We do not have such a law in Canada and we do not seem to have an official definition of wilderness, or at least there is no entry for it in the lexicons of the Canadian Environmental Protection Act or the Canada National Parks Act. The National Parks of Canada Wilderness Area Declaration makes the more open-ended statement that designated areas "that exist in a natural state or that are capable of returning to a natural state are declared to be wilderness areas."[36] However, a similar idea of wild lands that are separate from humanity dominated the formation of national and provincial parks throughout the twentieth century. I learned the word "expropriation" as a teenager in the 1970s, during the bitter struggle between people living in the area that had been designated for Kouchibouguac National Park in New Brunswick and the government. Whole villages were bulldozed, and there were confrontations with police and park visitors for years as some residents refused to leave the areas they had lived in for generations.[37] Partly in response to this painful experience, from the year 2000 the National Parks Act has stipulated that land will not be acquired through expropriation, and the establishment of new parks must be negotiated with local peoples. Thus Akami–Uapishkᵘ–KakKasuak–Mealy Mountains National Park Reserve, most of which is in Innusi, is jointly managed with the Innu and Inuit and, as part of the agreement, both Indigenous and non-Indigenous traditional users continue on the land.[38]

Poet and essayist Don McKay explores the word itself, wilderness, and how it works on our imaginations: "'The Wilderness,' once we mentally attach the article and capital letter, slides toward a packaged commodity—already noble, untamed, inspiring, teeming, tragic, romantically wounded (tubercular, shell-shocked); already picturesque, endangered, vanishing."[39] He goes on, however, to suggest a somewhat different understanding of the word, one in which wilderness is "the capacity in all things, even tools, to elude us, to outfox the mind's appropriations"; the wildness still inherent in something made of wood or stone. Everything on this earth came from it in some original form, and if we could just remember that, the wildness in things is "simply the persistence of otherness, the disturbing, thrilling awareness that there really is a world outside language, which, creatures of language ourselves, we translate with difficulty."[40] If the climate crisis and this pandemic teach us anything, it is to respect that otherness, to be humble, to know we can never master nature. Writers, artists, translators of all sorts can only try, as McKay puts it in another essay, to "answer the inappellable," which "doesn't mean solving the mystery; it means setting it to music."[41] We live by the stories we tell, and the setting of the mystery to music may help us find a way to the stories we need now, stories in which humans both belong to that mystery and leave it alone.

In the introduction to *Nitinikiau Innusi,* I wrote: "In any good story or any meaningful piece of research, something is at stake. Nutshimit is what is at stake in this book: nutshimit; Nitassinan—the land of the Innu; and Innu-aitun—Innu life and understanding of the world."[42] "Wilderness," in any of the senses presented here, does not map easily onto the Innu word "nutshimit" because, as I understand that word, nutshimit never loses its recognition of wildness, yet it is also home. However, the Innu concept of nutshimit does offer another way of thinking about what Akaneshau often call wilderness. If we can think of it as a place to respect and love, one in which we accept the inappellable while also knowing it is home to a multitude of living things, and that we all depend on its balance, we might find a way forward.

We cannot fix things. Our children's lives will not be better than our own. They will almost certainly be much worse in many ways, more precarious, more daunting. However, as American author Roy Scranton writes, our capacity to make sense of our existence through the stories we tell can make almost any life bearable and enable us to survive. We need stories that guide us to accept our fate and our limitations, and that draw on multiple perspectives, on the wisdom not just of other traditions but other species and entities: "We need to learn to see not just with Western eyes but with Islamic eyes and Inuit eyes, not just with human eyes but with golden-cheeked warbler eyes, coho salmon eyes, and polar bear eyes, and not even just with eyes at all but with the wild, barely articulate being of clouds and seas and rocks and trees and stars."[43]

Wildness and the inappellable seem to be themes for our time. There is also this, from Gretel Ehrlich:

> We have to stop pretending that there is a way back to the lush, comfortable, interglacial paradise we left behind so hurriedly in the twentieth century. There are no rules for living on this planet, only consequences. What is needed is an open exchange in which

> sentience shapes the eye and mind and results in ever-deepening empathy. Beauty and blood and what Ralph Waldo Emerson called "strange sympathies" with otherness would circulate freely in us, and the songs of the bearded seal's ululating mating call, the crack and groan of ancient ice, the Arctic tern's cry, and the robin's evensong would inhabit our vocal cords.[44]

Is this where translating words and worlds has led me? Ehrlich cites Emerson, but Tshaukuesh and every Indigenous elder have always taught strange sympathies, only they, perhaps, would not use the word "strange" since the world of the tern, the salmon, and the polar bear is not strange to them. As I mentioned in Chapter 3, Tshaukuesh translated her accounts of what the animals told her for Akaneshau with the caveat, "I know the animals can't talk but . . ." But they can. And we must listen as we live with the consequences of our misapprehension and destruction of wilderness. Listen and learn.

Peter C. van Wyck describes his writing as "an argument against the certainties of academic work."[45] He says he is bewildered, a word that seems appropriate to end this discussion of wilderness. Not lured *into* the wilderness, but seeing through its eyes, believing in it, letting it heal.

Trying to Keep the Land Alive

I thought about Tshaukuesh's alternative title for her book: "I Try to Keep the Land Alive." We can only try. In this time of pandemic, when so much travel and industry has shut down and the price of oil has dropped drastically, people are staying home. Two things the pandemic has brought into focus are how much we travel and the impact of humans on what used to be wilderness. I learned a lot about bats in the first few weeks of pandemic lockdown. With somewhere between 900 and 1,200 different species, they make up about one-fifth of the mammal population of the world. Like bees, they play a crucial role in pollination. They also disperse seeds and eat huge numbers of crop-destroying and (ironically) disease-carrying insects. But humans are encroaching on their territory in once-remote areas to make way for agriculture and urban expansion.[46] This destruction of wilderness threatens the bats, obviously, and it also threatens humans through loss of these crucial functions and through the transmission of viruses that were less likely to cross species lines in the past because our territories did not intersect so much with theirs, or, more precisely, because we did not destroy theirs.

Meanwhile, our unprecedented ability to travel means that viruses can be transmitted incredibly quickly even to the most remote places. Tshaukuesh writes about how Innu people never used to get sick. At first I thought this might be a romanticization, but in fact, traditional diets and active living meant that they did not have heart disease or diabetes and were generally very healthy. Many Innu did die after early contacts with Europeans, but they avoided viruses when they stayed in nutshimit, exposed to very few outsiders, taking only what was needed from the wilderness, and never forgetting to show their respect and gratitude for what they did take. Paradoxically, if the confined space of the reserve is the opposite of nutshimit, the vast reach of globalization may be the opposite of wilderness. As millions of people fly around the world for holidays or work and home again, viruses travel with them in both directions, incubated in the planes they travel in and disseminated upon landing. When the pandemic began to hit Canada, more than a million Canadians were repatriated; one in every thirty-seven people was out of the country, not counting all the people who were travelling within its borders.[47]

According to an article on the World Economic Forum website, around 100,000 flights take off and land every day. A simulation map shows them, so dense they are solid colours over Europe and the United States, swarming like hornets over the rest of the world. Even more disturbingly, the authors conclude that air traffic capacity should be *boosted* in the parts of the world where it is less dense.[48] Yet we know we must reduce emissions, and we saw dramatic reductions in levels of carbon dioxide, nitrogen dioxide, methane, and carbon monoxide as governments limited flying and other forms of fossil-fuelled travel and people stayed home.

Disasters can be catalysts for lasting change. They can bring people together. But the environmental gains could quickly be erased as the world returns to business as usual.[49] We can only try to learn from this pandemic how to keep the land alive, and why we should. As if we didn't already know.

Acknowledgements

This book is the second of a two-book project, the first being Tshaukuesh Elizabeth Penashue's *Nitinikiau Innusi: I Keep the Land Alive*. Many of the same people who helped bring that book to life contributed to this one too. I want to begin by thanking three people I forgot to include in the acknowledgements of the first book: Xiaolin Xu, who helped me find some wonderful archival photos; Joan Butler, who painstakingly transcribed and typed the original Innu diaries; and Lorraine Carpenter, who read a draft of the manuscript and provided meticulous notes and many thoughtful suggestions and questions. Lorraine did not live to see this acknowledgement. I did thank her in person, but I am so sorry I did not acknowledge her in the first book.

With immense gratitude I also thank the funders of the project: The Social Sciences and Humanities Research Council of Canada (SSHRC), the J.R. Smallwood Foundation, Intangible Cultural Heritage Newfoundland and Labrador, Mamu Tshishkutamashutau—Innu School Board, the Newfoundland and Labrador Arts Council, and Memorial University's Canada Research Chair in Aboriginal Studies.

Peer reviewers are usually anonymous but in this case the reviews became more of an ongoing conversation and I eventually learned the identities of the two reviewers. Peer review at its worst can be dire but at its best it is an extraordinarily enriching experience, and this was definitely peer review at its best. I am endlessly grateful to Valerie Henitiuk and Vanessa Andreotti for the ways they encouraged me to think harder and more deeply about many aspects of this book. The University of Manitoba Press's past director David Carr, current director David Larsen, editors Jill McConkey and Glenn

Bergen, and copy editor Maureen Epp were also enormously knowledgeable, helpful, and encouraging. I could not have had a better publisher.

I learned a lot from all the translators and linguists who contributed to written versions of substantial sections of *Nitinikiau Innusi* or provided informal explanations and interpretations of specific words and concepts. Their work also helped me to understand many of the ideas I explore in *Exactly What I Said*. I thank Joséphine Bacon, Kanani Davis, Laurel Anne Hessler, Marguerite MacKenzie, José Mailhot, Bart Penashue, Francis Penashue, Jack Penashue, Max Penashue, and Angela Penashue Rich. I also thank Henry Ike Rich, a different sort of translator, who helped me understand Innusi through mapping, as did all the contributors to the "Pepamuteiati Nitassinat" website.

I am also grateful to many friends, colleagues, and family members: Marie Wadden for introducing Tshaukuesh and me to each other; Patricia Chagnon and Camille Fouillard for giving me marvellous Innu books; Rita Auffrey, Camille Fouillard, John Joy, Robin McGrath, Heather McLeod, Jessica Tellez, Dorothy Vaandering, and Marie Wadden for thought-provoking conversations about this work; Margot Maddison-MacFadyen for help with an early draft; Mario Blaser, Sonja Boon, Daniel Coleman, Ana María Fraile, María Hernáez, RM Kennedy, and Fiona Polack for opportunities to develop the ideas in some of the chapters through various workshops, symposia, and publications; Jennifer Anderson for a wonderfully supportive writing partnership and, along with Camille Fouillard, for generously reading and commenting on drafts; David Openshaw, for endless patience as he listened to me read the entire manuscript aloud, and some parts two or three times; Sheila Yeoman, Ilse Jean, Dominique Jean, and David Openshaw for always being there.

Finally, thank you to the Penashue family. I made many mistakes on this learning journey and I humbly apologize for all of them, but I also thank you for all your hospitality, generosity, and openness. I especially want to remember Francis, from whom I learned so much, and to thank Tshaukuesh, to whom this book is dedicated. As she once told me, my meshkanau is books and hers is the land but, obviously, I could never have written this book without her.

Notes

Introduction

1 From the transcript of an interview for Yeoman, "The Least Possible Baggage."

2 Enipeshakimau is known in English as Pants Lake. I use Innu place names except in direct quotations or excerpts from interview transcripts where English names were used. I discuss the reasons for doing this in Chapter 1. For the most part, I use standardized spelling but occasionally I use Tshaukuesh's orthography if we could not find a standardized version or if she seemed to feel strongly about her version, as she did with Enipeshakimau (standardized version is Enakapeshakamau).

3 Mika et al., "The Ontological Differences between Wording and Worlding."

4 I now know the names of these places in Innu-aimun and something about their history, but I didn't when I wrote this diary. The Innu name is Atatshi-Uinipek^{u}, which is a more accurate description, since it means "cut off from the sea."

5 Penashue, *Nitinikiau Innusi*, 189.

6 Earlier publications include Penashue, "Innu Games," "A Winter in Hospital," "Like the Gates of Heaven"; and Penashue and Gregoire, "Nitassinan: Our Land, Our Struggle." Tshaukuesh's stories had also been featured in Brody and Markham, *Hunters and Bombers*; Wadden, *Nitassinan*; and Yeoman, "The Least Possible Baggage," as well as in many other interviews and reports.

7 Most younger Innu say "Nitassinan" but Tshaukuesh and many elders prefer Innusi.

8 Eve Tuck and K. Wayne Yang critique the very concept, arguing that "reconciliation is about rescuing settler normalcy, about rescuing a settler future." See "Decolonization Is Not a Metaphor," 35. In their view it focuses on what the impact of decolonization will be on the colonizers. In contrast, Aimée Craft and Paulette Regan suggest that reconciliation is itself a decolonizing process involving "everyday acts of resistance, resurgence and solidarity, coupled with renewed commitments to justice, dialogue and relationship building." Craft and Regan, *Pathways of Reconciliation*, 1.

9 Simon, Rosenberg, and Eppert, *Between Hope and Despair*, 5.

10 Bacon, *Bâtons à Message/Tshissinuatshitakana*, 131. Unless otherwise noted, all translations into English in this book are my own.

11 Quoted in Tymoczko, Baer, and Massardier-Kenney, Introduction to *Translators Writing, Writing Translators*, 8.

12 Ahmed, "Making Feminist Points."

13 Tuck, Yang, and Gaztambide-Fernández, "Citation Practices Challenge."

14 In the documentary film *Hunters and Bombers*.

15 Williams, *Marxism and Literature*.

16 Venuti, *The Translator's Invisibility*.

17 Van Wyck, *The Highway of the Atom*, 151.

18 Ibid., 150.

19 McCall, *First Person Plural*, 75.

20 Penashue, *Nitinikiau Innusi*, xxvii.

21 Paul, *We Were Not the Savages*.

22 Jonah, "Reconciling Chignecto."

23 Hiller and Harris, "Newfoundland and Labrador."

24 Aylward and Joe, "Beothuk and Mi'kmaq," 126–27.

25 Lawrence, "Unrecognized Peoples and Concepts of Extinction," 297.

26 King, "'I regret it.'"

27 Truth and Reconciliation Commission, *What We Have Learned*, 4.

One - Mapping

1 In the following transcript of conversations, some place names are in English, some in Innu-aimun. The transcript has been edited to standardize and clarify Tshaukuesh's English somewhat, as she asked me to do, but I left the place names in whichever language she used for them. The English names she uses are not necessarily official names found on maps, and some Innu names are on the maps we were using.

2 Although the marsh was frozen solid, it was better to camp at one end or the other since there would be trees at the edges to give protection from wind.

3 It is generally preferable to walk on frozen waterways or marshes because they are flat and unobstructed, so this was an exception.

4 A community meal or party with dancing to celebrate the hunt. According to Innu singer-songwriter Florent Vollant it also has a strong spiritual aspect in which the spirits of the animals are celebrated and people might have visions. (Quoted in Bénédicte Filippi, "Kamanitushinanut—L'Esprit Innu," *Ici Côte-Nord*, Radio Canada, 21 June, 2019. https://ici.radio-canada.ca/nouvelle/1188381/langue-innue-esprit-innu).

5 According to the Innu place names website *Pepamuteiati Nitassinat*, the river is named after the Baikies, a settler family who had a camp there (Pekiss or Pekissiu being based on an Innu pronunciation of their name). Pekissiu-shipiss is called the Susan River in English.

6 Cree and Petshish are two of Tshaukuesh's numerous grandchildren.

7 Innu Nation and Sheshatshiu Innu First Nation, *Pepamuteiati Nitassinat*.

8 Government of Canada, "Canadian Geographical Names Database."

9 Penashue, *Nitinikiau Innusi,* 150.

10 While such methodologies have yet to become a norm, many researchers do use them, such as Hugh Brody in his *Maps and Dreams*, in which people told stories as they drew maps, and Stephanie Springgay and Sarah E. Truman in *Walking Methodologies in a More-Than-Human World*.

11 NoiseCat, "Armageddon in Our Bones, Utopia in Our Souls."

12 Belcourt, *Mapping Routes*.

13 From the transcript of a 1984 conversation that was posted at the Innu Nation website but seems no longer to be available there; quoted in Sider, *Skin for Skin,* 195–96.

14 This account is from Sarah Nelson's petition to King George III, 1789.

15 Jollie, preface to *Edward Jollie Reminisces*, n.pag.

16 Gaudry, "Maps."

17 Ibid.

18 Tytelman, "Place and Forest Co-management," 132.

19 Global Forest Watch, Peru.

20 Longrigg, "Money and Maps."

21 Indigenous Mapping Workshop, Inuvik and Perth.

22 Innu Nation and Sheshatshiu Innu First Nation, *Pepamuteiati Nitassinat.*

23 Innu Nation, "Innu Place Names Website a Worldwide First."

24 Harron, "Landmark Achievement."

25 King, *The Truth about Stories*, 100–101.

26 Mika et al., "The Ontological Differences between Wording and Worlding."

27 Harley, *The New Nature of Maps,* 163.

28 Labrador Research Forum, Happy Valley-Goose Bay, NL, 1–3 May 2019. https://labradorresearchforum.ca.

29 Tuck and Yang, "Decolonization Is Not a Metaphor."

30 Others have also made this point; for example, Daniel Heath Justice wrote, "Many of the stories about Indigenous peoples are toxic, and to my mind the most corrosive of all is the story of Indigenous deficiency." Justice, *Why Indigenous Literatures Matter*, 2.

31 Eve Tuck, "Research on Our Own Terms."

32 There were others but I only wrote down the points that seemed most relevant to our project. I found out later that a colleague, Max Liboiron, had taken much more detailed notes, available online at https://civiclaboratory.nl/2019/05/03/research-on-our-own-terms-by-eve-tuck-a-thread-by-a-listener/. Eve Tuck herself has also written about some of these ideas in more detail in Tuck, "Suspending Damage."

33 Engel, "Decolonial Mapmaking." Tshaukuesh's daughter Kanani is working on the Innu-aimun version of *Nitinikiau Innusi*, and we hope also to have a French version.

34 Engel, "Decolonial Mapmaking."

35 Grace, *Canada and the Idea of North*, 88.

36 Justice, *Why Indigenous Literatures Matter,* 137.

37 Belcourt, "Reclaiming Ourselves."

38 Sugars, *Canadian Gothic*, 14.

39 Grace, *Canada and the Idea of North*, 85.

40 Ibid., 85.

41 Creates, *Marlene Creates*, exhibition shown at The Rooms, St. John's, NL, 12 October 2019—2 February 2020, https://www.therooms.ca/exhibits/past-exhibit/marlene-creates-places-paths-and-pauses.

42 Grace, *Canada and the Idea of North*, 90.

43 Conseil tribal Mamuitun, Québec et Canada, (2004), 31; cited in Fortier, "Une lecture sociologique."

44 Regroupement Petapan, "Innu Assi."

45 Lacasse, *Les Innus et le Territoire*, 248; quoted material is my translation of the original French.

46 Fontaine, *Shuni*, 102, my translation of the original French.

47 Anderson, *Imagined Communities.*

48 Kusugak, "Nunannguaq."

49 "More Information on Labrador Innu Place Names," in Innu Nation, *Pepamuteiati Nitassinat.*

50 Venuti, *The Translator's Invisibility*, 264.

51 Grace, *Canada and the Idea of North*, 87; referring to the map in Rudy Wiebe, *Playing Dead.*

52 Harron, "Landmark Achievement."

53 Utshimassit was the name of the place where the Mushuau Innu lived before relocating to Natuashish.

54 Grace, *Canada and the Idea of North*, 244.

55 Van Wyck, *The Highway of the Atom*, 67.

56 Ibid., 127.

57 Harron, "Landmark Achievement."

58 As I write this, I'm forced to think about the complexity of names and renaming, because the George River has several names and so does the Naskaupi. The George travels through the territories of two different Innu groups as well as Inuit territory. It is known in Inuktitut as Kangirsualujjuap Kuunga (River of the Great Bay) or Kangertialuksoak River; in Innu-aimun as Mushuau Shipu (River without Trees, River of the Barrens, or Tundra River), Metsheshu (or Mitshishu) Shipu (Eagle River), or Pupun Nikau Shipu. The Naskaupi River is also called Meshikamau Shipu. Tshaukuesh calls them, respectively, Mushuau-shipu and Naskaupi-shipu. See Fédération québécoise du canot et du kayak, *Guide des parcours canotables*; Government of Canada, "Rivière Georges"; Innu Nation, *Pepamuteiati Nitassinat.* The name George River was given to this already multi-named body of water in 1811 by two Moravian missionaries, Benjamin Gottlieb Kohlmeister and George Kmoch. In their diary, they recount raising a Union Jack and renaming the river to honour King George III, who had approved their land grant in Labrador. See Coady, *The Lost Canoe*, 129–30.

59 Roy, "Visualizing Labrador," 26.

60 Ibid., 26–27.

61 Ibid., 28.

62 Canadian Dam Association, "Dams in Canada."

63 The complete list of names and attributions to the authors being celebrated are explained and shown on a map in Commission de toponymie du Québec, "Le jardin au bout du monde."

64 "C'est peut-être pourquoi, au Québec, les symboles perçus de la domination de la majorité francophone par les Anglais sont renommés. Ceci représente un effort de décoloniser le paysage familier du Québec du Sud." Matthew Coon Come in a letter to Louise Beaudoin, Minister of Culture and Communications; cited in Desbiens, "*Le jardin au bout du monde*," 7.

65 Indeed, the entire James Bay project was part of that movement, which is far beyond the scope of this chapter; for an excellent analysis, see Desbiens, *Power from the North*.

66 Wyatt, "What Do You Call 101 Hidden Islands?"

67 Geopoetics, "What Is Geopoetics?"

68 Magrane et al., *Geopoetics in Practice*; Cresswell, "Beyond Geopoetics"; and Nassar, "Geopoetics."

69 "Nous étions persuadés que le territoire était anonyme, complètement vierge." Chouinard, "La Commission de toponymie maintient son projet," 1. Caroline Desbiens also notes that this project "should not be confused with the approach of the Commission de toponymie in general, which, in numerous other cases, has sought to be critically reflective and to make efforts to maintain Indigenous place names in Quebec" ("ne saurait être confondu avec l'approche globale de la Commission de toponymie qui, dans de nombreux autres dossiers, a cherché à mener une réflexion critique et à œuvrer pour le maintien des toponymes autochtones sur le territoire québécois"). Desbiens, "*Le jardin au bout du monde*," 13. Please note that Commission documents, including several about Indigenous place names, are available online in French as PDFs.

70 Desbiens, "*Le jardin au bout du monde*." In thinking about the Crees' apparent rejection of the invitation to submit lists of existing names, we should remember that the Innu Nation place names project "Pepamuteiati Nitassinat" took thirty years to complete and that northern Indigenous communities have huge responsibilities in relation to their size as they work to defend and manage their communities, land, and water; address the traumas of cultural loss and colonization; and seek ways of building a healthy and prosperous future.

71 Wyatt, "What Do You Call 101 Hidden Islands?"

72 Desbiens, "*Le Jardin au bout du monde*," 12.

73 Desbiens, *Power from the North*, 218.

74 Ibid., 220.

75 Cruikshank, "Encountering Glaciers," 64.

76 Desbiens, *Power from the North*, 217.

77 "Une réécriture dialogique du paysage, et donc l'invention d'une poétique de l'espace métissée." Desbiens, "*Le Jardin au bout du monde*," 13. Desbiens is writing in the context of Quebec but her ideas seem to apply also to Canada and other colonial nations.

78 Fontaine, in *Nin e tepueian*.

79 Desbiens, *Power from the North*, 221.

80 Cynthia Hammond, profile on Academia.edu: https://concordia.academia.edu/CynthiaHammond.

81 Hammond, "The Gathering of Earth," 104.

82 Ibid., 95.

83 Pietropaolo, *Ode to the Salish Sea*.

Two - Walking

1 Penashue, *Nitinikiau Innusi*, 118.

2 Ibid., 132.

3 Ibid., 133.

4 Ibid., 148.

5 Kusugak, "Nunannguaq."

6 Penashue, *Nitinikiau Innusi*, 130.

7 Stanley Vollant, quoted in Rubenstein, "The Walking Cure," 39.

8 Penashue, *Nitinikiau Innusi*, 124.

9 Li, "Effets des forêts et des bains de forêt (shinrin-yoku) sur la santé humaine."

10 Bakolis et al., "Urban Mind."

11 Song et al., "Psychological Benefits of Walking."

12 Li, "Effect of Forest Bathing Trips."

13 Sherwood, "Getting Back to Nature."

14 Penashue, *Nitinikiau Innusi*, 109.

15 Ibid., 137.

16 For a recent generalist review of much of this literature, see O'Mara, *In Praise of Walking*.

17 Tsing, Mathews, and Bubandt, "Patchy Anthropocene," S188.

18 On the topic of not being able to walk, the word "walk" itself is considered by some not to be inclusive of all forms of moving through the world at a human pace. However, in the documentary film *Examined Life* (2008), disability rights activist Sunaura Taylor says that she "goes for a walk" and uses that word to describe what she does, although she uses a wheelchair. I follow her lead in using the word in this chapter. I have also been thinking about the arguments outlined here regarding walking and creativity and would not like to be too categorical about this, either. The human brain, body, and spirit often find extraordinary ways to compensate for losses, sometimes even making them into strengths. I do not have the expertise to discuss this in detail, and there is much that is still not known. For example, Oliver Sacks wrote that until the 1980s or later, most neurologists believed that the nervous system was "fixed and invariant, with 'pre-dedicated' areas for every function." However, he asks, how could that theory "explain learning and the effects of practice? How could it explain the reconstructions and revisions of memory we make throughout our lives? How could it explain the processes of adaptation, of neural plasticity?" Sacks, *On the Move,* 357.

19 I use the term "landscape" as it is frequently used in cultural anthropology, archeology, and geography: to refer to a place or region and the relationships between people and other living things, sites, and objects on the land there. Árnason, Ellison, Vergunst, and Whitehouse suggest that the term "goes beyond land" and brings together "physical, cultural, mental and material" aspects of a place (*Landscapes beyond Land*, x). They note that the term "seems productive because of its very ambiguity in presenting both material interactions and cultural understandings" (ibid., 3). Lelièvre uses the term "to refer to large-scale places . . . that hold meaning for individuals and collectivities because of their associations with particular places within those landscapes" (*Unsettling Mobility*, 181). Landscape is also political. As Coulthard and Simpson put it, "Our relationship to the land itself generates the processes, practices, and knowledges that inform our political systems, and through which we practice solidarity" ("Grounded Normativity," 254).

20 Oppezzo and Schwartz, "Give Your Ideas Some Legs."

21 Leisman, Moustafa, and Shafir, "Thinking, Walking, Talking," 94.

22 Quoted in Wadden, *Nitassinan*, 94.

23 Desbiens, "*Le Jardin au bout du monde*," 8. "Maîtres chez nous" was an expression coined by *Le Devoir* editor André Laurendeau, widely used during Quebec's Quiet Revolution of the 1960s and extremely ironic when used in reference to Innusi.

24 A NATO spokesperson speaking in the documentary film *Hunters and Bombers*, directed by Hugh Brody and Nigel Markham.

25 Penashue, *Nitinikiau Innusi*, 132–33.

26 Stanley Vollant, quoted in CBC News, "First Nations Doctor."

27 Penashue, *Nitinikiau Innusi*, 201.

28 Mailhot, *The People of Sheshatshit*, 152–53.

29 Lelièvre, *Unsettling Mobility*.

30 Ibid., 11 and 26.

31 Ibid., 49.

32 Ibid., 174–76.

33 McCall, *First Person Plural*, 69.

34 Nahanni, "The Mapping Project."

35 Brody, *Maps and Dreams*, 147.

36 McCall, *First Person Plural*, 54.

37 Sahtú Renewable Resources Board, "Dene Mapping."

38 Innu Nation, *Pepamuteiati Nitassinat*.

39 See, for example, van Wyck, *The Highway of the Atom*, regarding Dene elders and place names, and Penashue, *Nitinikiau Innusi,* regarding the Innu.

40 Howlett, "Ontario Settles Long-Running Land-Claims Dispute."

41 Wabanaki Water Walk, Facebook page.

42 The Peace and Friendship Treaty of 1752 provided for a treaty truck house to be built if the community felt it was necessary. In the context of the treaty, it was mainly intended to be a trading post, but in its twenty-first-century form it became a gathering place for the river protectors, a site to block and monitor the gas company, thus protecting the river, and a way of making the continuation of treaty rights visible. Mi'kmaw historian Roger Lewis suggests that building truck houses at "'usual' places of resort for Mi'kmaq people," as specified in the treaty, could help "re-establish the true extent of Mi'kmaq cultural landscapes." See Lewis, "What Is a Truck House?"

43 Grant, "Siding with First Nation."

44 Alton Natural Gas Storage L.P., "Alton Natural Gas Storage."

45 Lelièvre, *Unsettling Mobility*, 168.

46 Sundberg, "Decolonizing Posthumanist Geographies," 39.

47 Ibid.

48 Camille Fouillard, personal communication, 17 September 2020.

49 Walking Lab and Public Pedagogies Institute, *Journal of Public Pedagogies*.

50 Springgay and Truman, "Walking in/as Publics," 2.

51 Ibid.

52 Lund, "Landscapes and Narratives," 226.

53 Luka, "Walking Matters," 65.

54 Paths, or meshkanaua.

55 Recollet and Johnson, "'Why Do You Need to Know That?,'" 184.

56 Johnson, "Pathways to the Eighth Fire," ii.

57 Somerville, with Tobin and Tobin, "Walking Contemporary Indigenous Songlines," 13.

58 Ibid.

59 O'Neill and Roberts, *Walking Methods.*

60 O'Neill and Einashe, "Walking Borders."

61 Legat, *Walking the Land,* 175.

62 Ibid., 191.

63 Brody, *The People's Land,* 10.

64 Chambers, "Where Are We?," 125.

65 Quotations transcribed from the video *Mi'kmaq Resistance.*

66 Michelle Paul, transcribed from *There's Something in the Water.*

Three - Stories

1 Angela Antle, NL Reads 2020, St. John's, 27 February 2020. My transcription, used with Angela Antle's permission. For more information on the NL Reads event, see https://www.cbc.ca/news/canada/newfoundland-labrador/nl-reads-2020-books-announced-1.5339105.

2 However, the final winner was decided by an online vote in which *Nitinikiau Innusi: I Keep the Land Alive* came a close second.

3 Kapesh, *Eukuan nin matshimanitu innu-iskueu* (1976).

4 "Pour moi, choisir de réinscrire la parole d'An Antane Kapesh dans l'histoire littéraire du Québec est un acte décolonial et même révolutionnaire dans la littérature québécoise." Gill, "*Eukuan nin matshi-manitu innushkueu,*" 11.

5 Kapesh, *Eukuan nin matshi-manitu innushkueu* (2019): 14; my translation from Innu-aimun and French.

6 Penashue, *Nitinikiau Innusi,* 5.

7 Fontaine, préface to Kapesh, *Eukuan nin matshi-manitu innushkueu,* 6.

8 "Kie nipa minueniten tshetshi uapataman kutak innu tshetshi mashinaitshet e innushtenit." The French language translator, José Mailhot, renders the Innu original as "Et je serais heureuse de voir d'autres Indiens écrire, en langue indienne" (I would be happy to see other Indians writing, in their Indian language). This may reflect common usage in French in the 1970s when the translation was first published, or Kapesh's own desire to take back the names that white people called her. However, the original Innu-aimun uses the words "Innu" and "Innushtenit," which reference Innu or, more broadly, First Nations people. I should also note that I worked from the 2019 Mémoire d'encrier text in French and Innu-aimun. Meanwhile, Sarah Henzi's English translation was released by Wilfrid Laurier University Press shortly before my book went to press. Henzi translates from the French: "I would be happy to see other Innu people writing, in the Innu

language" and notes in her afterword that this revision had also been made in a 2015 French version published by the Saguenay Native Friendship Centre.

9 "C'est le colonialisme dans ce qu'il a de plus vicieux." Quoted in Villeneuve, "La colère d'An Antane Kapesh."

10 While the book may transcend contemporary genres, Valerie Henitiuk has suggested that it oddly resembles Sei Shōnagon's *Makura no Sôshi*, or *Pillow Book*, a zuihitsu from the Heian period of Japan dating from about a thousand years ago (Henitiuk, personal communication). Henitiuk describes zuihitsu as a writing form that makes a "striking series of leaps from one apparently random image, anecdote or list to another, which draw readers ever more deeply into a unique and uniquely engrossing reading experience." Henitiuk, *Worlding Sei Shônagon*, i.

11 "Il faut la faire notre littérature!" In an interview with Petitpas, "L'influence du livre *Je suis une maudite sauvagesse*."

12 Quoted in Heeney, "'In the Innu language, every word is an image.'"

13 Lacombe, "'Pimuteuat/Ils marchent/They Walk,'" 172.

14 Le Clézio, "Quel avenir pour la Romaine?"

15 "Je vais aller toutes récupérer ces mots-là puis je vais faire de la poésie avec ces mots pour qu'ils puissent continuer à vivre." Speaking in the documentary film *Je m'appelle humain*.

16 "La morale de l'histoire, envers toute l'Histoire, l'Haïtien aura fait entrer la femme innue dans une institution de la société dominante, lieu historique de la langue française . . . une femme innue portant l'héritage fabuleux de l'innu-aïmun, notre langue, comme un bagage sur le dos . . . Qui d'autre pouvait représenter la relation étroite entre la langue, la culture et l'entité-territoire ? Qui d'autre pouvait porter à point l'importance de la préservation des langues et des cultures que la femme autochtone aînée seule, fille indigène du territoire des Amériques, totalement ouverte vers le monde?" Fontaine, "Petit cahier d'un voyage."

17 Ibid.

18 "We spoke Innu in Paris." Ibid.

19 Justice, *Why Indigenous Literatures Matter*, 1.

20 Carter, "How Three Indigenous Authors Cut through the Noise of Social Media."

21 By my count, but it depends how you categorize them as some works mix languages.

22 Young, "The Digital Language Divide."

23 "Il y a deux sortes de saumons: l'utshashumeku qui a rejoint la mer . . . et le pipunamu qui n'a jamais quitté l'eau douce." Fontaine, *Kuessipan/À Toi*, 88.

24 Reder, "Book Review of Tomson Highway's *From Oral to Written*."

25 McCall, *First Person Plural*, 212.

26 Saladin d'Anglure explains that Nappaaluk had begun a collaborative process of transliterating the novel into Roman orthography and translating it into French with Father Lechat, and that he (Saladin d'Anglure) later took over this work. It became the focus of his PhD and resulted in a version that was published by the Association Inuksiutiit in 1984 and used in Inuit schools. He describes the collaborative process in some detail in the foreword (Saladin d'Anglure, foreword to *Sanaaq*, ix–x). Saladin d'Anglure later re-translated it for non-Inuit readers. That version was published in 2002 by Éditions Stanké, then translated from the French into English by Peter Frost for the 2014 University of Manitoba Press edition.

27 Martin, "Arctic Solitude," 16.

28 Ibid., 17.

29 Patsauq, *Hunter with Harpoon.*

30 Lutz, *The Diary of Abraham Ulrikab*; Pitseolak and Harley Eber, *People from Our Side*; Ayaruaq, *The Autobiography of John Ayaruaq*; and Nuligak, *I Nuligak.*

31 In an interview featured in Yeoman, "The Least Possible Baggage."

32 Johnson, "Inuk Director's New Film."

33 Ibid.

34 Chisholm, "The Enduring Afterlife of *Before Tomorrow*," 220.

35 Ibid., 212.

36 Ibid., 213.

37 Ibid., 222–23.

38 Isuma TV, "Zacharias Kunuk Interview."

39 Angilirq, interview by anthropologist Nancy Wachowich. Sadly, Paul Apak Angilirq died before the film was completed. He posthumously won best screenplay at the 2002 Genie Awards, where the film also won five other Genies including best motion picture.

40 Isuma TV, "Costume Interview."

41 Dimaline, *The Marrow Thieves*, 214.

42 Diaz, "Cherie Dimaline on Erasure."

43 Statistics Canada, "Census in Brief."

44 Eigenbrod, *Travelling Knowledges*, 142.

45 Neuhaus, *The Decolonizing Poetics of Indigenous Literatures*, 2.

46 Cariou, "Edgework," 35.

47 Lacombe, "'Pimuteuat/Ils marchent/They Walk,'" 160.

48 Ibid., 163.

49 Désy and Mestokosho, *Uashtessiu.*

50 *Aimititau/Parlons nous* can be translated as "Let's talk to each other." Here it refers to the title of the first collection of Indigenous–non-Indigenous poetic exchanges, which was followed by *Uashtessiu/Lumière d'automne.*

51 "*Aimititau* devient un incontournable de notre littérature commune. Une manière de nous dire que nous sommes égaux et que nous sommes capables de plus que de simples ou compliquées négociations, de bien plus que d'ententes ou d'entente. Nous sommes capables d'amour, avouons-le, et de rêver entre nous d'une métisserie fondamentale qui reposera sur des paroles échangées et partagées, bien qu'il soit évident qu'entre les communautés, il y aura toujours des différends." Désy, in Désy and Mestokosho, *Uashtessiu*, 12.

52 "Le mot 'métisserie,' c'est cette foi que, culturellement, on est capable dans les temps qui s'en viennent . . . de trouver des mots qui vont pouvoir nous définir tous ensemble, Autochtones et non-Autochtones." In Arsenault, "L'essai Amériquoisie."

53 "On ira voir cette fameuse grotte
là où les ours ont sommeillé des grands hivers
là où les grands froids ont pénétré nos os
là où je me suis endormie

une vie entière.
La route qui mène vers la grotte
est là quelque part
proche de ma poitrine
du côté gauche.
On ira ensemble . . ."
Mestokosho, in Désy and Mestokosho, *Uashtessiu*, 13.

54 Lacombe, "'Pimuteuat/Ils marchent/They Walk,'" 164–65.

55 Angilirq, interview by anthropologist Nancy Wachowich.

56 Nolette, "Partial Translation, Affect and Reception," n.pag.

57 Carol Maier, quoted in Tymoczko, Baer, and Massardier-Kenney, Introduction to *Translators Writing, Writing Translators*, 7.

58 Martin, "Arctic Solitude," 29.

59 Henitiuk, "Of Breathing Holes and Contact Zones," 57.

60 Vizenor, "Aesthetics of Survivance."

61 Vizenor, *Manifest Manners*, vii.

62 Tuck, "Suspending Damage," 93.

63 The term "Anthropocene" is more widely used but has been critiqued by many, perhaps first by environmental historian Jason W. Moore, who argues for "Capitalocene" on the grounds that humans are by no means all equally responsible for climate change. Rather, the capitalist system with its endless cycle of ever-growing production and consumption has led to the crisis and maintains unjust structures that mean that humans will also, at least in the short term, not be equally affected by it. Ecologist, urbanist, and journalist Aaron Vansintjan argues that the choice of which term one uses can affect how one decides to act, and that the term Capitalocene is more likely to lead to a strong climate justice movement. See Moore, *Anthropocene or Capitalocene?*; and Vansintjan, "The Anthropocene Debate."

64 Klein, "Dancing the World into Being."

65 Van Wyck, *The Highway of the Atom*, 16.

66 Henitiuk, "'My tongue, my own thing,'" 15.

67 Government of Canada, "Valerie Henitiuk: SSHRC Postdoctoral Prize."

68 See Henitiuk, "Going to Bed with Waley," 42.

69 Ibid.

70 Henitiuk, "The Single, Shared Text?," 34.

71 Jay-Rayon, review of *Literature in Translation*, 256.

72 Tymoczko, "Translation, Ideology and Creativity," 27.

73 Kamboureli, "Beyond ~~Understanding~~ Canada," 17.

74 Lacombe, "Leanne Betasamosake Simpson's Decolonial Aesthetics," 45.

75 Martin, "Arctic Solitude," 25.

76 Kamboureli, "Beyond ~~Understanding~~ Canada," 19.

Four - Looking

1 Penashue, *Nitinikiau Innusi*, 12.

2 Ibid., 55.

3 Tea dolls were traditionally made from smoked caribou skin stuffed with black tea, to be carried by a young child as they travelled across the land. The tea was gradually used up and the doll refilled when they were able to get fresh supplies.

4 Pedri-Spade, "'But They Were Never Only the Master's Tools,'" 107.

5 Ibid., 109.

6 Ibid., 108–10.

7 Smith, "Repeat Photography"; cited in Pedri-Spade, "Waasaabikizo," 51.

8 Pedri-Spade, "Waasaabikizo," 46.

9 Ibid., 51.

10 Ibid., 48.

11 Ibid., 51.

12 Penashue, *Nitinikiau Innusi*, 64.

13 Ibid., 41.

14 Ibid., 112.

15 Lewis, "On Leaving Only Footprints."

16 Creates, *The Boreal Poetry Garden*.

17 Harper, "Talking about Pictures."

18 Ibid., 21.

19 Ibid., 13.

20 Ibid., 22–23.

21 Edward Burtynsky, in Tremonti, "Anthropocene Project Highlights the Apocalyptic Beauty."

22 Jennifer Baichwal, in ibid.

23 Nehamas, *Only a Promise of Happiness*, 3.

24 Sartwell, "Beauty."

25 Benjamin Von Wong, in Jacobsen, "A Wave of Plastic."

26 Creates, *The Boreal Poetry Garden*.

27 Camille Fouillard, personal communication, 17 September 2020.

28 Tuck, "Breaking Up with Deleuze."

29 Tuck and Yang, "R-Words," 227.

30 Tuck, "Suspending Damage," 416.

31 Penashue, *Nitinikiau Innusi*, 20.

32 Ibid., 112.

33 Ibid., 31.

34 Rees, "Introduction: Today, What Is Anthropology?," 5.

35 Hirsch, *Family Frames*.

36 Ibid., 58.

37 Ibid., 65.

38 While it is true that the photographers were nowhere near as diverse as their subjects, Eric Sandeen reminds us that "the accusation of visual imperialism relies on the assumption of a kind of photographic essentialism: the thought that the only genuine portrait emanating from emotion-laden circumstances can be made by a photographer from that country." Sandeen, "The Family of Man in Guatemala," 129.

39 Ibid., 123–24.

40 Barthes, *Mythologies*, 122.

41 Ibid., 123.

42 *Honk If You Want Me Off The Road*.

43 Hanrahan, "Good and Bad Indians," 42.

44 Ibid., 48.

45 Penashue and Yeoman, "The Ones That Were Abused," 76; our translation from the original Innu-aimun.

46 Tymoczko, "Translation: Ethics, Ideology, Action," 455.

47 Venuti, *The Translator's Invisibility*.

48 Heim, "To Foreignize or Not to Foreignize," 83.

49 Williams, *Marxism and Literature*.

50 Said, *Culture and Imperialism*, 14.

51 Tymoczko, "Translation and Political Engagement."

52 Apter, *The Translation Zone*.

53 Berger, *About Looking*, 5.

54 Kimmerer, "Speaking of Nature."

55 Berger, *About Looking*, 26.

56 Laughland, "Everlyn Sampi."

57 Doris Pilkington Garimara, interview with Elizabeth Yeoman in "The Least Possible Baggage."

58 Tymoczko, "Translation: Ethics, Ideology, Action," 452.

59 Henitiuk, "Of Breathing Holes and Contact Zones," 57.

Five - Signs

1 "The Mines and the Dams," in Penashue, *Nitinikiau Innusi*, 169. A fish consumption advisory from Environment and Climate Change Canada states that lake trout and northern pike from the river should only be eaten once a week. See Environment and Natural Resources Canada, "Mercury: Fish Consumption Advisories." In April 2016, the Nunatsiavut (Labrador Inuit territory) Government released a report authored by researchers from Memorial University, the University of Manitoba, Harvard University, and the Nunatsiavut Government. The report examined a number of topics, one of which was the human health risks of methylmercury exposure from the Manitu-utshu (Muskrat Falls) hydroelectric project. Both Innu and Inuit use fish

from the area as an important part of their diet, in a region where store-bought food is extremely expensive and locally caught meat and fish is generally much healthier as well as more accessible to them. The researchers concluded that there would probably be significant bioaccumulation of methylmercury in the food web after flooding the reservoir, and that this could be mitigated by clear-cutting the area and removing topsoil. Following demonstrations, hunger strikes, and public pressure in 2016, the province agreed to ensure that mitigative measures are taken, but the area is now flooded and this was not done. For the full report see Durkalec, Sheldon, and Bell, *Lake Melville.*

2 See Penashue, *Nitinikiau Innusi*, 64.

3 Hanrahan, "Good and Bad Indians," 42.

4 Call to Action 14, in Government of Canada, "Language and Culture."

5 These words are my translation.

6 A Basque separatist organization responsible for hundreds of deaths between the late 1960s and 2010.

7 It seems worth noting in the context of this book about translation that Nancy Huston was the focus of a controversy in 1993 when she won the Governor General's Award for French-language fiction (romans et nouvelles). A group of Montreal publishers argued that the jury's decision should be overturned because the book, *Cantique des plaines*, was Huston's self-translation of its English version, *Plainsong*, and therefore only eligible in the translation category. Huston argued that the French version was not a translation but a re-creation or a re-writing, although she also described it elsewhere as a "version traduite," or translated version. See Huston, *Âmes et corps*, 25. The award was not overturned. For more on the controversy, see Senior, "Whose Song, Whose Land?"; and Klein-Lataud, "Les voix parallèles de Nancy Huston."

8 Tuck, "Research on Our Own Terms."

9 Willemsen and Bøegh, "Linguists Need Preservation of Languages."

10 Mika et al., "The Ontological Differences between Wording and Worlding," 24.

11 Tuglavina, "My Own Cultural and Language Experiences," 162.

12 Ibid., 175.

13 Truth and Reconciliation Commission of Canada, *Canada's Residential Schools: Reconciliation*, 12–13.

14 Haque, *Multiculturalism within a Bilingual Framework*, 4.

15 Ibid., 7.

16 Ibid., 30; quoting Jenson, "Commissioning Ideas," 39–40.

17 Haque, *Multiculturalism within a Bilingual Framework*, 240.

18 Ibid., 127.

19 Ibid., 117–19.

20 In *Just Watch Me*.

21 In Haque, *Multiculturalism within a Bilingual Framework*, 174.

22 See Emily Apter's account of the Arabic translator in Apter, "Translation after 9/11"; and broader discussion in Apter, *The Translation Zone*.

23 Mika et al., "The Ontological Differences between Wording and Worlding," 24.

24 Camille Fouillard, personal communication.

25 Cruikshank, *The Social Life of Stories* (quoting James Clifford, "Interview with Brian Wallis"), 98.

26 Penashue, *Nitinikiau Innusi*, 151.

27 The Innu-aimun-English dictionary also suggests this translation, but indicates "identification unsure." See Mailhot, MacKenzie et al., *Aimun Mashinaikan*.

28 Many of Carol Maier's views on teaching literature in translation have been consolidated in the two collected volumes that she has co-edited on the subject: Dingwaney and Maier, *Between Languages and Cultures*; and Maier and Massardier-Kenney, *Literature in Translation*.

29 This was also the question raised in relation to the controversy about Nancy Huston's Governor General's Award; see n.7, above.

30 CBC News, "Tomson Highway Releases Plays in Cree."

31 In Merrill, "Stephanos Stephanides on Memory Fiction." Merrill talks with Stephanides about the complexity of the notion of home and the creative and subversive nature of literary translation, as well as his film *Poets in No Man's Land* (2012).

32 Valerie Henitiuk, personal communication.

33 A similar critique was made of Arthur Waley, early twentieth-century translator of the Japanese *Tale of Genji*: that "his descriptions of Buddhism occasionally sound somewhat too Anglican for comfort." See Henitiuk, "Going to Bed with Waley," 42.

34 Thornton, "Rumi for the New-Age Soul."

35 Hassan Lahouti, in Azadibougar and Patton, "Coleman Barks' Versions of Rumi," 176–77.

36 Coleman Barks in *Soul Fury*; quoted in Thornton, "Rumi for the New-Age Soul."

37 Ali, "The Erasure of Islam."

38 Cited in Azadibougar and Patton, "Coleman Barks' Versions of Rumi," 176.

39 Ibid., 178.

40 Grossman, *Why Translation Matters*, x–xi.

41 See Archibald-Barber, "Native Literature Is Not Postcolonial," 14; and King, "Godzilla vs. Post-Colonial," 184–85.

42 Tymoczko, "Translation: Ethics, Ideology, Action," 456–57.

43 Ibid., 455–56.

44 Henitiuk, "Of Breathing Holes and Contact Zones," 54–56.

45 Cited in Massardier-Kenney, Baer, and Tymoczko, *Translators Writing, Writing Translators*, 7.

46 Apter, *The Translation Zone*, 3.

47 Grossman, *Why Translation Matters*.

48 Benjamin, "The Task of the Translator," 77.

49 Venuti, *The Translator's Invisibility*, 15.

50 Petrilli and Ponzio, "Translation as Listening."

51 Henitiuk, "'My tongue, my own thing,'" 33.

52 Tymoczko, Baer, and Massardier-Kenney, Introduction to *Translators Writing, Writing Translators*, 14.

53 These ideas are drawn from McCall, *First Person Plural*, 213.

54 All quotations in this paragraph from ibid., 212–13.

55 Maracle, "Indigenous Poetry and the Oral."

56 Mercredi, "Achimo."

57 Sinclair, "The Power of Dirty Waters," 210.

58 Ibid., and Sioui Durand, "Maurizio Gatti."

59 "Là d'où je viens, le français est une langue seconde. Très facultative. L'anglais vient loin derrière." Fontaine, "Ma parole rouge sang."

60 St-Amand, "Discours critiques pour l'étude de la littérature autochtone."

61 See Lacombe, "Leanne Betasamosake Simpson's Decolonial Aesthetics"; Henzi, "Littératures autochtones et traduction"; and Lacombe, Macfarlane, and Andrews, "Indigeneity in Dialogue."

62 Bacon is quoted in Lalonde, "Joséphine Bacon, poétesse innue."

63 Rita Mestokosho, interview recorded with Christophe Premat and Françoise Sule, 10 October 2009, and translated into English by C. Premat; quoted in Premat, "The Survivance in the Literature of the First Nations," 78.

64 Nolette, "Partial Translation, Affect and Reception."

65 Nolette, *Jouer la traduction*.

66 McCall, *First Person Plural*, 75.

67 Ibid., 189.

68 Moyes, "From One Colonial Language to Another," 65.

69 Ibid., 70.

70 Ibid., 76.

71 Fontaine, "Pour que nous puissions VIVRE."

72 Homer-Dixon, "We Need a Forest of Tongues."

73 Skutnabb-Kangas and Phillipson, "A Human Rights Perspective on Language Ecology."

74 Highway, *A Tale of Monstrous Extravagance*, 19.

75 Innu: "Kashikat pietamani eshinikatikauian SAUVAGESSE nimishta-ashinen. Kauapishit pietuki essishueti nenu aimunnu, nitishinishtuten kauapishit nanitam nuitamak[u] tapue eukuan nin tshitshue innushkueu mak kauapishit nuitamak[u] ninishtam anite minashkuat katshi ut inniuian . . . Tshima nanitam petuk kauapishit tshetshi ishinikashit SAUVAGESSE." Kapesh, *Eukuan nin matshi-manitu innushkueu*, 202.

French: "Je suis très fière quand, aujourd'hui, je m'entends traiter de Sauvagesse. Quand j'entends le Blanc prononcer ce mot, je comprends qu'il me redit sans cesse que je suis une vraie Indienne et que c'est moi la première à avoir vécu dans la forêt . . . Puisse le Blanc me toujours traiter de Sauvagesse." Ibid., 203; translation by José Mailhot.

Note that in the Innu-aimun original Kapesh leaves the word "savage"—"sauvagesse"—in French and capitalizes it.

76 "Sauvage, ça veut dire être libre entièrement." Bacon, in the film *Je m'appelle humain*.

77 Ibid.

78 Samson and Wilson, *Canada's Tibet*, 19.

79 Lacasse, *Les Innus et le Territoire*, 249.

80 Ruers, "The Uncanny."

81 Tanner, "Innu (Montagnais-Naskapi)."

82 Penashue and Yeoman, "The Ones That Were Abused."

83 See Carr, "Evidence for the Persistence of Ancient Beothuk."

84 "Innu, c'est notre nom, et ce nom nous appartient . . . ce nom, nous le portons depuis toujours." Lacasse, *Les Innus et le Territoire*, 247.

85 Ibid., 247.

86 Pastore, "The Beothuks."

87 Simon, *Changing the Terms*, 11.

88 According to Camille Fouillard.

89 Aylward, "The Beothuk Story," 282.

90 Anderson, *Imagined Communities.*

91 Kimmerer, "Speaking of Nature."

92 Ibid.

93 However, Kimmerer also cites Robert Macfarlane's *Landmarks*, a book about how English too was once intimate with all living beings. Writers like Macfarlane and artist Marlene Creates are trying to revive English's ancient connections to nature and the land. Just as the English language has almost lost many of these connections, Indigenous languages may lose them if life on the land is lost.

94 Kimmerer, "Speaking of Nature."

95 Andreotti, Ahenakew, and Cooper, "Epistemological Pluralism," 44.

96 Smith, *Decolonizing Methodologies.*

Six - Literacies

1 Drapeau, "Le développement de l'écrit en montagnais."

2 Vowel, "Giving My Children Cree Names."

3 Blake, *Shakespeare's Non-Standard English.*

4 Rawat, "NWT Orthography Backgrounder."

5 In Lane, Costa, and De Korne, *Standardizing Minority Languages*, 2.

6 Penashue, "Miam ka auieiat."

7 Battiste, "Bringing Aboriginal Education into Contemporary Education."

8 Lane, Costa, and De Korne, *Standardizing Minority Languages.*

9 Patrick, Murasugi, and Palluq-Cloutier, "Standardization of Inuit Languages," 137.

10 Baraby, "The Process of Spelling Standardization of Innu-aimun."

11 Grenoble and Whaley, *Saving Languages*, 117.

12 Hinton and Hale, eds., *The Green Book of Language Revitalization.*

13 Baraby, "The Process of Spelling Standardization in Innu-aimun," 200.

14 Grenoble and Whaley, *Saving Languages*, 102.

15 Hinton and Hale, *The Green Book of Language Revitalization*, 239–40.

16 NationTalk, "NTI: Inuktut Writing Prize Launched."

17 *Indigenous Voices Awards*.

18 Hinton and Hale, *The Green Book of Language Revitalization*, 239–40.

19 Grenoble and Whaley, *Saving Languages*, 102, 130.

20 Ibid., 102.

21 Hinton and Hale, *The Green Book of Language Revitalization*.

22 Grenoble and Whaley, *Saving Languages*.

23 Ibid., 113.

24 I wrote about this aspect of literacy in Yeoman, "The Meaning of Meaning."

25 Freire, *Pedagogy of the Oppressed*.

26 Penashue, *Nitinikiau Innusi*, 159.

27 CBC News, "Tomson Highway Releases Plays in Cree."

28 Highway, "The Time Tomson Highway Went to *Mameek*," 50.

29 Capuano, "Canada's Indigenous Soldiers Wove Unbreakable Wartime Code."

30 Toomey, "The NSA Continues to Violate Americans' Internet Privacy Rights."

31 Drapeau, "Decision Making on a Standard Orthography," 27.

32 Call to Action 13: What's Happening?, in Government of Canada, "Language and Culture."

33 Baraby, "The Process of Spelling Standardization of Innu-aimun," 201.

34 Ibid., 198.

35 Ibid.

36 Norman, *Chinese*.

37 Lane, Costa and De Korne, *Standardizing Minority Languages*, 3.

38 Milroy and Milroy, *Authority in Language*, 22.

39 Gal, "Visions and Revisions of Minority Languages," 223–24.

40 Milroy, "Language Ideologies and the Consequences of Standardization."

41 Gal, "Visions and Revisions of Minority Languages," 226.

42 Crystal, *Txting: The Gr8 Db8*, 7.

43 First Peoples' Cultural Council, "Orthographies."

44 Vowel, "Giving My Children Cree Names."

45 Truth and Reconciliation Commission of Canada, *Calls to Action*.

46 Bird, "Baby Named Sahaiʔa."

47 Government of Northwest Territories, "GNWT Introduces Changes."

48 Bird, "Baby Named Sahaiʔa."

Seven - Listening

1 Mailhot, MacKenzie et al. *Aimun Mashinaikan.*

2 Petrilli and Ponzio, "Translation as Listening."

3 Petrilli and Ponzio, "Translation, Encounter among Peoples and Global Semiotics," 8.

4 Drichel, "Face to Face with the Other Other," 38–39.

5 Todd, "Listening as Attending to the 'Echo of the Otherwise,'" 411.

6 The Tri-Council is made up of the Canadian Institutes of Health Research (CIHR), the National Sciences and Engineering Research Council (NSERC), and the Social Sciences and Humanities Research Council (SSHRC).

7 Government of Canada, "TCPS-2: Core," Module 1.

8 Ibid.

9 Le Texier, *Histoire d'un mensonge.*

10 Government of Canada, "TCPS-2: CORE," Module 1. (Note: This appears to have been removed from the TCPS-2 since I did the modules.)

11 Van den Hoonaard and Hamilton, *The Ethics Rupture*, 5.

12 Whitaker, review of *The Ethics Rupture.*

13 Van den Hoonaard and Hamilton, *The Ethics Rupture*, 6.

14 Penashue, *Nitinikiau Innusi*, 97.

15 Spivak, "Can the Subaltern Speak?"

16 Spivak, "Supplementing Marxism," 115.

17 Spivak, *In Other Worlds*, 170.

18 Spivak, *A Critique of Postcolonial Reason*, 383 and 378.

19 Penashue, *Nitinikiau Innusi*, 204.

20 Later published as Yeoman, "Sam's Café."

21 Buber, *Between Man and Man*, 6.

22 Csikszentmihályi, Abuhamdeh, and Nakamura, "Flow."

23 Vaudrin-Charette, "Reading Silenced Narratives," 154.

24 Battiste, "Bringing Aboriginal Education into Contemporary Education."

25 McCall, *First Person Plural*, 109–36.

26 McCall, *First Person Plural*, 128; see also Whitlock, "In the Second Person"; and Laub, "Truth and Testimony."

27 Government of Canada, "Guidelines for the Merit Review of Indigenous Research."

28 Truth and Reconciliation Commission of Canada, *Calls to Action*. Calls 10 iv, 13, 14 i–v, 15, 16 (p. 2), 61 ii (p. 7); 84 i (p. 9), and 85 i (p. 10). Call 16 is the one referred to here: "We call upon post-secondary institutions to create university and college degree and diploma programs in Aboriginal languages."

29 The English version of the title is roughly "How You've Come to Know Mi'gmaq and What We're Entitled To." See Jean, "Listuguj Remembers."

30 Bosenberg, "Mi'kmaq PhD Dissertation a Canadian First."

31 The raids are documented in *Incident at Restigouche*, Alanis Obamsawin's 1984 NFB film.

32 Quoted by Alanis Obomsawin in conversation with Lucien Lessard in *Incident at Restigouche*; English translation from the film.

33 Fred Metallic, quoted in Jean, "Listiguj Remembers."

34 Bacon, *Bâtons à Message*, 112.

35 Lelièvre, *Unsettling Mobility*, 165–73.

36 Battiste, Bell, Findlay, Findlay, and Henderson, "Thinking Place," 12.

37 Ibid., 17.

38 Hine, "Notes from Underground #7."

39 Ibid.

40 O'Gorman and Pandey, "Cultivating the Arctic's Most Valuable Resource," 21.

41 O'Gorman and Pandey, "Explaining Low High School Attainment," 302.

42 Ibid., 306.

43 Bacon, *Bâtons à Message*, 112.

44 Fontaine discusses her languages in "Ma parole rouge sang."

Eight - Songs

1 English version translated by Tshaukuesh.

2 Spelling from the original recording by McKenzie, available online at http://citizenfreak.com/titles/324773-mckenzie-philippe-indian-songs-in-folk-rock-tradition. Sainte-Marie's version is also available online at https://palmaresadisq.ca/fr/artiste/chloe-sainte-marie/album/nitshisseniten-e-tshissenitamin-je-sais-que-tu-sais/.

3 "J'ai toujours raçonté le Nord. Beaucoup. Je raconte le Nord, je raconte les gens qui habitent le Nord, je raconte l'espace, je raconte les nomades . . . leurs gestes, leurs rêves, leurs mouvements, leurs déplacements, je raconte leur passé aussi, d'où est-ce qu'ils viennent . . . Les Innus." From an interview with ethnomusicologist Véronique Audet, quoted in Audet, *Innu Nikamu*, 188.

4 Ibid., 135 and 188.

5 Cohen, "La Manic," performed at Colisée Pepsi.

6 In his acceptance speech during his induction to the Canadian Songwriters' Hall of Fame, 2006; available online at https://www.youtube.com/watch?v=AS2qxBvEP10, posted 19 November 2015 (accessed 7 August 2020).

7 Cohen, "La Manic," performed at Colisée Pepsi.

8 Gouvernement du Québec, "Réserve Écologique Louis-Babel."

9 Fontaine, "Tetepiskat."

10 Voisey's Bay, where a nickel mine was being developed.

11 Penashue, *Nitinikiau Innusi*, 201.

12 Ferguson, "Rocks and Trees." With gratitude to Wendell Ferguson and his publishing company Wen Hel Freezes Music for kind permission to quote extensively from his song.

13 In Ferguson, "Lyrics." Quoted with his permission.

14 From the transcript of our conversation while working with maps (see Chapter 1 for more of this conversation).

15 In Ferguson, "Lyrics."

16 Stewart, *Ordinary Affects*, 3.

17 Ibid., 15 and 4.

18 Ibid., 5.

19 *Blackfly*.

20 King and Fowke, "The Blackfly Song."

21 Penashue, *Nitinikiau Innusi*, 67.

22 Ibid., 87.

23 Ibid., 132.

24 Ibid., 172.

25 Ibid., 185.

26 Tourisme Québec, "Abitibi-Témiscamingue."

27 Tourisme Québec, "Manicouagan."

28 Ibid.

29 Tourisme Côte-Nord, "Manicouagan-Uapishka Biosphere Reserve."

30 Fontaine, "Tetepiskat."

31 Harper, "The Call of the North"; and CBC Radio, "Stan Rogers, Folksinger."

32 Brody, *Maps and Dreams*, 12.

33 Ibid., 149.

34 Anderson, *Imagined Communities*, 133 (emphasis in the original).

35 Ibid., 145.

36 Balakrishnan, "The National Imagination," 66–69.

37 Toronto Symphony Orchestra, "Our Shared Mosaic."

38 Milewski, "Changing O Canada."

39 Parry, "To Live in the Age of Melting."

40 Face Vocal Band, "The Parting Glass."

41 Penashue, *Nitinikiau Innusi*, 35.

42 Ibid., 50–51.

43 Ibid., 117.

44 King, *The Truth about Stories*, 158.

45 Ibid., 92.

46 "La musique porte à réflexion. Tu ne changes pas le monde avec la chanson, mais ça fait travailler la conscience." Philippe McKenzie, quoted in Tisseyre, "Innu Nikamu."

47 Audet, *Innu Nikamu*, 160.

48 Samian, *Face à la musique*.

49 "Devenue avec le temps un hymne national, Tshinanu symbolise la nouvelle génération d'Innuat. Tshinanu ça nomme sans leur donner de noms, nos grands-pères, nos rivières, nos enfants et nos portages. Tshinanu ça nomme aussi un territoire. Tshinanu c'est comme si on voyait tout d'un coup notre pays devant nous." Kashtin, *Kashtin*.

50 "C'est à nous à le savoir C'est nous, c'est nous C'est à nous à y voir C'est nous, notre chemin C'est nous, nos enfants C'est nous, nos grands-pères C'est à nous à le savoir C'est nous, c'est nous C'est à nous à y voir C'est nous, notre chemin C'est nous, notre rivière C'est nous, notre territoire C'est nous, nous avons raison." My translation from the Innu original and Véronique Audet's French version in *Innu Nikamu,* 190.

Nine - Wilderness

1 Penashue, *Nitinikiau Innusi*, 183.

2 Ibid., 138.

3 Triolo, "Why David Quammen Is Not Surprised."

4 MOOC stands for massive open online course—a course offered online with unlimited registration.

5 Kolbert, "How to Write about a Vanishing World," 129.

6 Voosen, "The Arctic Is Warming."

7 NASA Jet Propulsion Laboratory, "Greenland's Rapid Melt Will Mean More Flooding."

8 Ibid.

9 Mullin, "Still Waiting."

10 Kolbert, "Greenland Is Melting."

11 Mercer, "Innovation Award–Winning SmartICE 'Great Thing to Have in Nain.'"

12 For more information on smart komatiks and smart buoys, see https://smartice.org.

13 Ehrlich, "Rotten Ice."

14 Weeks, "Blue Capitalism."

15 Rich, "The Invisible Catastrophe."

16 Doyle, "The Greatest Nature Essay Ever."

17 Highway, "The Time Tomson Highway Went to *Mameek*," 46.

18 Doyle, "The Greatest Nature Essay Ever."

19 Highway, "The Time Tomson Highway Went to *Mameek*," 49.

20 Tuck, "Research on Our Own Terms." She elaborates on the theories behind this idea in Tuck, "Suspending Damage"; and Tuck and Yang, "R-Words."

21 Penashue, *Nitinikiau Innusi*, vii, viii, ix.

22 Yeoman in Penashue, *Nitinikiau Innusi*, xi.

23 Justice, *Why Indigenous Literatures Matter*, 241.

24 Kimmerer, *Braiding Sweetgrass*, x.

25 King, *The Truth about Stories*, 9.

26 Ibid., 9.

27 Krause, "What's Left Behind."

28 See also Keeling and Sandlos, "Ghost Towns and Zombie Mines."

29 Toxic Legacies Project, http://www.toxiclegacies.com.

30 Quintavalle, "Politics and People Fuelling Amazon Rainforest Fires."

31 Sugars, *Canadian Gothic.*

32 Tuck and Yang, "Decolonization Is Not a Metaphor," 6.

33 Sugars, *Canadian Gothic*, 11–12.

34 Thorpe, *Temagami's Tangled Wild*, 7–8.

35 Proescholdt, "What's Wrong with Monitoring Volcanoes in Wilderness?"

36 Government of Canada, "Wilderness Area Declaration Regulations."

37 Canadian Press, "Parks Canada Reaches Out."

38 For more information on park management, see Parks Canada, "Akami-Uapishk[U]-KakKasuak-Mealy Mountains National Park Reserve."

39 McKay, "Local Wilderness," 5.

40 Ibid.

41 McKay, "Great Flint Singing," 4.

42 Penashue, *Nitinikiau Innusi*, xxvii.

43 Scranton, *We're Doomed. Now What?*, 8.

44 Ehrlich, "Rotten Ice."

45 Van Wyck, *The Highway of the Atom*, 7.

46 Atit̓wa, "How Many Bats Are There in the World?"

47 Tunney, "More Than a Million Canadian Citizens."

48 Myers and Hutt, "This Visualization Shows You."

49 According to the International Energy Agency (IEA), this is already happening as this book goes to press. See IEA, *Sustainable Recovery Trucker*.

Glossary

allou. Breathing holes made by seals in the sea ice.

amishku. Beaver.

atshakash. Mink.

Capitalocene. Alternate term for Anthropocene, used to emphasize that climate change is not caused by all humans equally but rather by an economic system (capitalism) that promotes an endlessly growing cycle of production and consumption for the profit of a small number of individuals owning the means of production.

Innusi. Innu territory, a term mostly used by older Innu to refer to their land but sometimes used by others to refer explicitly to the reserve.

komatik. Labrador Inuktitut word commonly used in English in Labrador for a large sled with raised sides that can carry people and supplies and be towed by dogs or a skidoo.

low-level flying. Flying an aircraft lower than 500 feet or 150 metres above ground, often practiced by military pilots to avoid detection by an adversary or to carry out a surprise attack. Also used to fly beneath bad weather or to conduct search and rescue operations.

mashku. Bear.

meshkanau/meshkanu. Path, trail or road.

miikaans. Anishinaabemowin word with the same meaning as the Innu "meshkanau": path, trail or road.

Mi'kma'ki or Mi'gma'gi. Mi'kmaw territory.

MOOC. Acronym for massive open online course.

nipishapui. Tea.

Nitassinan. Literally "our land" or "our territory," the word is used by many Innu, especially younger generations, to refer to Innu territory. It is currently also used by non-Innu to refer to Innu land claims areas.

nitshiku. Otter.

nutshimit. Inland, on the land, in the natural world away from the reserve. See also discussion of this word and its connotations in Chapter 5, pp. 134–35.

pakueshikan. Bread or bannock.

shinrin-yoku. Known in English as forest bathing, it is a Japanese healing practice based on walking and being in the forest.

Siknikt. Region of Mi'kma'ki spanning the Chignecto Isthmus and adjacent areas of New Brunswick and Nova Scotia.

Sipekne'katik. Region of Mi'kma'ki to the east and south of Siknikt.

uapishtan. Marten.

uapush. Rabbit.

uishuaushkumuk. A kind of moss used for insulating footwear in winter.

utshimau. Chief, leader, boss.

Wabanaki forest. Also known as the Acadian forest, it is an intermediary between the boreal forests of the north and the mainly deciduous hardwood forests to the south. It covers much of the Gaspé Peninsula, New Brunswick, Nova Scotia, Prince Edward Island and parts of New England—the territories of the Mi'kmaq and Wolastoqiyik peoples.

zuihitsu. A traditional Japanese literary genre based on personal narrative and random thoughts and ideas, often in response to the writer's surroundings.

Bibliography

Ahmed, Sarah. "Making Feminist Points." *Feministkilljoys,* 11 September 2013. http://feministkilljoys.com/2013/09/11/making-feminist-points/ (accessed 30 April 2020).

Ali, Rozina. "The Erasure of Islam from the Poetry of Rumi." *New Yorker*, 5 January 2017. https://www.newyorker.com/books/page-turner/the-erasure-of-islam-from-the-poetry-of-rumi (accessed 19 February 2020).

Alton Natural Gas Storage Project L.P. "Alton Natural Gas Storage Project Update." 22 October 2021. https://altonnaturalgasstorage.ca/news/alton-natural-gas-storage-project-update/ (accessed 22 October 2021).

Anderson, Benedict. *Imagined Communities.* London and New York: Verso, 1983/2006.

Andreotti, Vanessa, Cash Ahenakew, and Garrick Cooper. "Epistemological Pluralism: Challenges for Higher Education." *AlterNative Journal* 7, no. 1 (2011): 40–50.

Angilirq, Paul Apak. Interview by anthropologist Nancy Wachowich. Isuma TV, 16 April 1997; uploaded 20 January 2010. http://www.isuma.tv/atanarjuat/interview-with-paul-apak-angilirq (accessed 6 August 2020).

Antle, Angela. Unpublished speech in defence of *Nitinikiau Innusi.* NL Reads 2020, St. John's, 27 February 2020.

Apter, Emily. "Translation after 9/11." *Transit* 2, no. 1 (2006). https://transit.berkeley.edu/2006/apter/ (accessed 9 July 2020).

———. *The Translation Zone: A New Comparative Literature.* Princeton, NJ: Princeton University Press, 2006.

Archibald-Barber, Jesse. "Native Literature Is Not Postcolonial." *English Studies in Canada* 41, no. 4 (2015): 14.

Árnason, Arnar, Nicolas Ellison, Jo Vergunst, and Andrew Whitehouse. *Landscapes beyond Land: Routes, Aesthetics, Narratives.* Oxford and New York: Berghahn Books, 2012.

Arsenault, Marie-Louise. "L'essai Amériquoisie: Entrevue avec Jean Dézy et Natasha Kanapé Fontaine." Radio-Canada, 20 September 2016. https://ici.radio-canada.ca/premiere/emissions/plus-on-est-de-fous-plus-on-lit/segments/entrevue/8959/ameriquoisie-metisserie-quete-identitaire-quebec-jean-desy-autochtones (accessed 28 July 2020).

Atitwa, Sundra Chelsea. "How Many Bats Are There in the World?," 15 January 2018. https://www.worldatlas.com/articles/how-many-bats-are-there-in-the-world.html (accessed 18 March 2020).

Audet, Véronique. *Innu Nikamu/L'Innu chante: Pouvoir des chants, identité et guérison chez les Innus.* Quebec City: Presses de l'Université Laval, 2012.

Ayaruaq, John. *The Autobiography of John Ayaruaq*. Ottawa: Queen's Printer and Controller of Stationery, 1968.

Aylward, Christopher. "The Beothuk Story: European and First Nations Narratives of the Beothuk People of Newfoundland." PhD diss., Memorial University of Newfoundland, 2014.

Aylward, Christopher, and Chief Mi'sel Joe. "Beothuk and Mi'kmaq: An Interview with Chief Mi'sel Joe." In *Tracing Ochre: Changing Perspectives on the Beothuk,* edited by Fiona Polack, 117–32. Toronto: University of Toronto Press, 2018.

Azadibougar, Omid, and Simon Patton. "Coleman Barks' Versions of Rumi in the USA." *Translation and Literature* 24 (2015): 172–89.

Bacon, Joséphine. *Bâtons à Message/Tshissinuatshitakana.* Montreal: Mémoire d'Encrier, 2009.

Bakolis, Ioannis, Ryan Hammoud, Michael Smythe, Johanna Gibbons, Neil Davidson, Stefania Tognin, and Andrea Mechelli. "Urban Mind: Using Smartphone Technologies to Investigate the Impact of Nature on Mental Wellbeing in Real Time." *BioScience* 64, no. 2 (2018): 134–45.

Balakrishnan, Gopal. "The National Imagination." *New Left Review* 211 (1995): 56–69.

Baraby, Anne-Marie. "The Process of Spelling Standardization of Innu-aimun (Montagnais)." n.d. http://jan.ucc.nau.edu/~jar/ILAC/ILAC_21.pdf.

Barthes, Roland. *Mythologies.* Selected and translated from the French by Annette Lavers. London: Vintage Books, 2009.

Battiste, Marie. "Bringing Aboriginal Education into Contemporary Education: Narratives of Cognitive Imperialism Reconciling with Decolonization." In *Leadership, Gender and Culture: Male and Female Perspectives*, edited by John Collard and Cecilia Reynolds, 142–48. Maidenhead: Open University Press, 2004.

Battiste, Marie, Lynne Bell, Isobel Findlay, Len Findlay, and James (Sákéj) Youngblood Henderson. "Thinking Place: Animating the Indigenous Humanities in Education." *Australian Journal of Indigenous Education* 34 (December 2004): 7–19.

Being Innu. Directed by Catherine Mullins. Green Lion Productions, 2007.

Belcourt, Christi. *Mapping Routes: Perspectives of Land and Water in Ontario.* Online art exhibition. ChristiBelcourt.com. http://www.christibelcourt.com/Gallery/gallerySERIESmrPage1.html (accessed 29 April 2020).

———. "Reclaiming Ourselves One Name at a Time." CBC News, 31 December 2013. https://www.cbc.ca/news/indigenous/christi-belcourt-reclaiming-ourselves-one-name-at-a-time-1.2480127 (accessed 29 April 2020).

Benjamin, Walter. "The Task of the Translator." Translated by Steven Rendall. In *The Translation Studies Reader*, edited by Lawrence Venuti, 75–83. London and New York: Routledge, 1923/2012.

Berger, John. *About Looking.* New York: Pantheon Books, 1980.

Bird, Hilary. "Baby Named Sahaiʔa Prompts Changes to Vital Statistics Act." CBC North, 13 June 2016. https://www.cbc.ca/news/canada/north/nwt-aboriginal-font-official-id-1.3630353 (accessed 15 November 2019).

Blackfly. Directed by Christopher Hinton. NFB/ONF, 1991. https://www.nfb.ca/film/blackfly/ (accessed 9 September 2020).

Blake, Norman. *Shakespeare's Non-Standard English: A Dictionary of His Informal Language.* London and New York: Continuum, 2006.

Bosenberg, Erin. "Mi'kmaq PhD Dissertation a Canadian First." *This: Progressive Politics, Ideas and Culture*, 12 May 2009.

Brody, Hugh. *Maps and Dreams.* New York: Pantheon Books, 1982.

———. *The People's Land: Inuit, Whites and the Eastern Arctic.* Vancouver and Toronto: Douglas and McIntyre, 1991.

Buber, Martin. *Between Man and Man.* Translated by Ronald G. Smith. Abingdon and New York: Routledge, 1947/2002.

Canadian Dam Association. "Dams in Canada." https://www.cda.ca/EN/Dams_in_Canada/EN/Dams_In_Canada.aspx?hkey=11c76c52-7794-4ddf-b541-584f9ea2dbe9 (accessed 27 June 2020).

Canadian Press. "Parks Canada Reaches Out to People Still Bitter over N.B. Expropriation." CBC News, 1 October 2007. https://www.cbc.ca/news/canada/new-brunswick/parks-canada-reaches-out-to-people-still-bitter-over-n-b-expropriation-1.690238 (accessed 5 April 2020).

Capuano, Lynn. "Canada's Indigenous Soldiers Wove Unbreakable Wartime Code with Native Languages." Government of Canada, 2019. https://ml-fd.caf-fac.ca/en/2019/08/32964 (accessed 30 June 2020).

Cariou, Warren. "Edgework: Indigenous Poetics as Re-placement." In *Indigenous Poetics in Canada*, edited by Neal McLeod, 31–41. Waterloo, ON: Wilfrid Laurier University Press, 2014.

Carr, Steven M. "Evidence for the Persistence of Ancient Beothuk and Maritime Archaic Mitochondrial DNA Genome Lineages among Modern Native American Peoples." *Genome* 63, no. 7 (2020): 349–55.

Carter, Sue. "How Three Indigenous Authors Cut through the Noise of Social Media to Become Online Activists." *Quill and Quire*, March 2017. https://quillandquire.com/omni/how-three-indigenous-authors-cut-through-the-noise-of-social-media-to-become-online-activists/ (accessed 8 January 2020).

CBC News. "First Nations Doctor Launches 3200 Km Trek." 11 October 2010. http://www.cbc.ca/news/canada/montreal/story/2010/10/11/innu-meshkanu-trek-quebec.html (accessed 9 October 2011).

———. "Tomson Highway Releases Plays in Cree." 8 November 2010. https://www.cbc.ca/news/canada/ottawa/tomson-highway-releases-plays-in-cree-1.895683?ref=rss (accessed 20 February 2020).

CBC Radio. "Stan Rogers, Folksinger, Storyteller, Proud Canadian, Part 2." *Rewind*, 7 July 2016. https://www.cbc.ca/radio/rewind/stan-rogers-folk-singer-storyteller-proud-canadian-part-2-1.3239078) (accessed 5 April 2020).

Chambers, Cynthia. "Where Are We? Finding Common Ground in a Curriculum of Place." *Journal of the Canadian Association for Curriculum Studies* 6, no. 2 (2008): 113–28.

Chisholm, Dianne. "The Enduring Afterlife of *Before Tomorrow*: Inuit Survivance and the Spectral Cinema of Arnait Video Productions." *Études/Inuit/Studies* 40, no. 1 (2016): 211–27.

Chouinard, Marie-Andrée. "La Commission de toponymie maintient son projet." *Le Devoir*, 19 September 1997, 1.

Clifford, James. Interview with Brian Wallis. In "The Global Issue: A Symposium," *Art in America*, July 1989, 86–87 and 152–53.

Coady, Lawrence W. *The Lost Canoe: A Labrador Adventure.* Halifax: Nimbus Publishing, 2008.

Cohen, Leonard. "La Manic." Performed at Colisée Pepsi, Quebec City, 5 December 2012. https://www.youtube.com/watch?v=DAiGIRBrY5w (accessed 9 September 2020).

Commission de toponymie du Québec. "Le jardin au bout du monde, poème géographique." *Toponymix* 17, August 1997. http://www.toponymie.gouv.qc.ca/ct/pdf/toponymix17.pdf?ts=0.5258698490273119 (accessed 27 June 2020).

———. *La toponymie des Cris*. Dossier toponymique 29, October 2003. https://toponymie.gouv.qc.ca/ct/pdf/La%20toponymie%20des%20cris.pdf?ts=0.5973532736659926 (accessed 27 June 2020).

Coulthard, Glen, and Leanne Betasamosake Simpson. "Grounded Normativity/Place-Based Solidarity." *American Quarterly* 68, no. 2 (2016): 249–55.

Craft, Aimée, and Paulette Regan, eds. *Pathways of Reconciliation: Indigenous and Settler Approaches to Implementing the TRC's Calls to Action*. Winnipeg: University of Manitoba Press, 2020.

Creates, Marlene. *The Boreal Poetry Garden*. Portugal Cove, NL, 2005–. http://www.marlenecreates.ca/works/2005boreal.html (accessed 15 June 2020).

———. *Marlene Creates: Places, Paths, and Pauses*. Art exhibition shown at The Rooms, St. John's, NL, 12 October 2019—26 January 2020.

Cree Code Talker. Directed by Alex Lazarowich. NSI Aboriginal Documentary, 2016.

Cresswell, Tim. "Beyond Geopoetics: For Hybrid Texts." *Dialogues in Human Geography* 11, no. 1 (2021): 36–39.

Cruikshank, Julie. "Encountering Glaciers: Two Centuries of Stories from the Saint Elias Mountains, Northwestern North America." In *Landscapes beyond Land: Routes, Aesthetics, Narratives*, edited by Arnar Árnason, Nicolas Ellison, Jo Vergunst, and Andrew Whitehouse, 49–66. Oxford and New York: Berghahn Books, 2012.

———. *The Social Life of Stories: Narrative and Knowledge in the Yukon Territory*. Lincoln: University of Nebraska Press, 1998.

Crystal, David. *Txting: The Gr8 Db8*. Oxford: Oxford University Press, 2008.

Csikszentmihályi, Mihály, Sami Abuhamdeh, and Jeanne Nakamura. "Flow." In *Handbook of Competence and Motivation*, edited by Andrew J. Elliot, Carol S. Dweck, and David S. Yeager, 598–608. New York: Guilford Press, 2005.

Dimaline, Cherie. *The Marrow Thieves*. Toronto: DCB Books, 2017.

Desbiens, Caroline. "*Le jardin au bout du monde*: Terre, texte et production du paysage à la Baie James/*Garden at the End of the World*: Land, Literature and Landscape in James Bay." *Recherches amérindiennes au Québec* 38 no. 1 (2008): 7–15. https://www.erudit.org/en/journals/raq/2008-v38-n1-raq3860/039739ar/ (accessed 9 May 2020).

———. *Power from the North: Territory, Identity, and the Culture of Hydroelectricity in Québec*. Vancouver: UBC Press, 2013.

Désy, Jean, and Rita Mestokosho. *Uashtessiu/Lumière d'automne*. Montreal: Mémoire d'Encrier, 2010.

Diaz, Shelley. "Cherie Dimaline on Erasure, the Power of Story, and *The Marrow Thieves*." *School Library Journal*, 2 November 2017. https://www.slj.com/?detailStory=cherie-dimaline-erasure-power-story-marrow-thieves (accessed 8 January 2020).

Dingwaney, Anuradha, and Carol Maier, eds. *Between Languages and Cultures: Translation and Cross-Cultural Texts*. Pittsburgh: University of Pittsburgh Press, 1995.

Doyle, Brian. "The Greatest Nature Essay Ever." *Orion Magazine*, 30 October 2008. https://orionmagazine.org/article/the-greatest-nature-essay-ever/ (accessed 1 April 2020).

Drapeau, Lynn. "Decision Making on a Standard Orthography: The Betsiamites Case." In *Promoting Native Writing Systems in Canada*, edited by Barbara Burnaby, 27–31. Toronto: OISE Press, 1985.

———. "Le développement de l'écrit en montagnais." *Recherches amérindiennes au Québec* 15, no. 3 (1985): 96–101.

Drichel, Simone. "Face to Face with the Other Other: Levinas versus the Postcolonial." *Levinas Studies* 7, no. 1 (2012): 21–42.

Durkalec, Agata, Tom Sheldon, and Trevor Bell. *Lake Melville: Avativut, Kanuittailinnivut (Our Environment Our Health)*. Scientific Report. Nain, NL: Nunatsiavut Government, 2016.

Ehrlich, Gretel. "Rotten Ice." *Harper's Magazine,* April 2015. https://harpers.org/archive/2015/04/rotten-ice/ (accessed 10 March 2019).

Eigenbrod, Renate. *Travelling Knowledges: Positioning the Im/migrant Reader of Aboriginal Literatures in Canada*. Winnipeg: University of Manitoba Press, 2005.

Engel, Jordan. "Decolonial Mapmaking | Reclaiming Indigenous Places and Knowledge." *Langscape Magazine* 4, no. 2 (2017). https://medium.com/langscape-magazine/decolonial-mapmaking-reclaiming-indigenous-places-and-knowledge-4779b7f8b81c (accessed 14 June 2021).

Environment and Natural Resources Canada. "Mercury: Fish Consumption Advisories." https://www.canada.ca/en/environment-climate-change/services/pollutants/mercury-environment/health-concerns/fish-consumption-advisories.html#NF (accessed 11 November 2021).

Examined Life. Directed by Astra Taylor. Sphinx Productions and NFB, 2008.

Face Vocal Band. "The Parting Glass." YouTube, 28 April 2018. https://www.youtube.com/watch?v=2Sql9X4H0VY (accessed 8 April 2020).

Fédération québécoise du canot et du kayak. *Guide des parcours canotables du Québec, Tome II*. Saint-Constant, QC: Éditions Broquet, 2001.

Ferguson, Wendell. "Lyrics." *I Pick Therefore I Jam*. http://www.wendellferguson.com/pg1_frm.html (accessed 9 September 2020).

———. "Rocks and Trees." 11 December 2013. https://www.youtube.com/watch?v=kKwFUS-pQObc (accessed 5 August 2020).

Filippi, Bénédicte. "Kamanitushinanut—L'Esprit Innu." *Ici Côte-Nord*, Radio Canada, 21 June 2019. https://ici.radio-canada.ca/nouvelle/1188381/langue-innue-esprit-innu.

First Peoples' Cultural Council. "Orthographies." 5 August 2020. http://www.fpcc.ca/language/toolkit/Orthographies.aspx (accessed 25 April 2021).

Fontaine, Naomi. *Kuessipan/À Toi.* Montreal: Mémoire d'Encrier, 2011.

———. *Shuni.* Montreal: Mémoire d'Encrier, 2019.

Fontaine, Natasha Kanapé. "Ma parole rouge sang." In "Francophonie en Amérique: Entre rêve et réalité." *Relations* 778 (May–June 2015): 24–25. https://id.erudit.org/iderudit/77928ac (accessed 19 June 2020).

———. "Petit cahier d'un voyage au loin du pays natal." *Le Devoir*, 22 June 2015. https://www.ledevoir.com/opinion/idees/443360/petit-cahier-d-un-voyage-au-loin-du-pays-natal (accessed 20 December 2019).

———. "Pour que nous puissions VIVRE." 8 April 2016. https://www.youtube.com/watch?v=_PYdBW5fGhk (accessed 25 June 2020).

———. "Tetepiskat." *Générations 150*. NFB/ONF, n.d. http://bit.ly/2rosBFF (accessed 6 August 2020).

Fortier, Jean-François. "L'Île René-Levasseur, oeil du Québec ou de Nitassinan? Une lecture sociologique des enjeux contemporains de la gouvernance territoriale autochtone." *Aspects sociologiques* 15, no. 1 (2008): 93–116.

Freire, Paulo. *Pedagogy of the Oppressed*. Translated by Myra Bergman Ramos. New York: Herder and Herder, 1970.

Gal, Susan. "Visions and Revisions of Minority Languages: Standardization and Its Dilemmas." In *Standardizing Minority Languages: Competing Ideologies of Authority and Authenticity in the Global Periphery*, edited by Pia Lane, James Costa and Haley De Korne, 222–42. New York: Routledge, 2018.

Garimara, Doris Pilkington. *Follow the Rabbit-Proof Fence*. Brisbane: University of Queensland Press, 1996.

Gaudry, Adam. "Maps." Forewords to *The Indigenous Peoples' Atlas of Canada*. Canadian Geographic, 2021. https://indigenouspeoplesatlasofcanada.ca/forewords/maps/ (accessed 10 March 2020).

Geopoetics. "What Is Geopoetics?" n.d. http://geopoetics.org (accessed 7 May 2020).

Gill, Marie-Andrée. "*Eukuan nin matshi-manitu innushkueu. Je suis une maudite sauvagesse* d'An Antane Kapesh." *Nuit blanche* 156, Fall 2019, 10–11.

Global Forest Watch, Peru. https://gfw.global/3bQaYBY (accessed 25 April 2021).

Gouvernement du Québec. "Réserve écologique Louis-Babel." http://www.mddep.gouv.qc.ca/biodiversite/reserves/louis_babel/res_27.htm (accessed 5 April 2020).

Government of Canada. "Canadian Geographical Names Database." Natural Resources Canada. https://www.nrcan.gc.ca/earth-sciences/geography/querying-canadian-geographical-names-database/canadian-geographical-names-database/19870 (accessed 23 January 2022).

———. "Guidelines for the Merit Review of Indigenous Research." Social Sciences and Humanities Research Council. https://www.sshrc-crsh.gc.ca/funding-financement/merit_review-evaluation_du_merite/guidelines_research-lignes_directrices_recherche-eng.aspx (accessed 7 November 2019).

———. "Language and Culture." *Delivering on Truth and Reconciliation Calls to Action*. 2019. https://www.rcaanc-cirnac.gc.ca/eng/1524494530110/1557511412801 (accessed 11 November 2021).

———. "Rivière Georges." Canadian Geographical Names Database. http://www4.rncan.gc.ca/search-place-names/unique/d2a5dcfabe1711d892e2080020a0f4c9 (accessed 20 August 2020).

———. "TCPS-2: CORE," Module 1. Panel on Research Ethics. https://tcps2core.ca/ (accessed 23 March 2017).

———. "Valerie Henitiuk: SSHRC Postdoctoral Prize." Social Sciences and Humanities Research Council. 14 February 2014. http://www.sshrc-crsh.gc.ca/results-resultats/prizes-prix/2005/postdoctoral_henitiuk-eng.aspx (accessed 30 July 2020).

———. "Wilderness Area Declaration Regulations." National Parks of Canada. 2017. https://laws-lois.justice.gc.ca/eng/regulations/SOR-2000-387/page-1.html (accessed 25 January 2022).

Government of Northwest Territories. "GNWT Introduces Changes to the Vital Statistics Act." News release, 28 July 2017. https://www.gov.nt.ca/newsroom/news/news-release-gnwt-introduces-changes-vital-statistics-act (accessed 3 December 2019).

Grace, Sherrill. *Canada and the Idea of North*. Montreal and Kingston: McGill-Queen's University Press, 2001.

Grant, Taryn. "Siding with First Nation, N.S. Judge Overturns Alton Gas Approval." CBC News, 24 March 2020. https://www.cbc.ca/news/canada/nova-scotia/alton-gas-nova-scotia-supreme-court-appeal-decision-1.5508130 (accessed 5 June 2020).

Grenoble, Lenore A., and Lindsay J. Whaley. *Saving Languages: An Introduction to Language Revitalization*. Cambridge: Cambridge University Press, 2006.

Grossman, Edith. *Why Translation Matters*. New Haven, CT: Yale University Press, 2010.

Guardians of Eternity: Confronting Giant Mine's Toxic Legacy. Directed by France Benoit. Sheba Films, 2015. http://www.guardiansofeternity.ca.

Hammond, Cynthia. "The Gathering of Earth: 101 Mountains." *Journal of Religion and Culture* 10 (1999): 93–114.

Hanrahan, Maura. "Good and Bad Indians: Romanticizing the Beothuk and Denigrating the Mi'kmaq." In *Tracing Ochre: Changing Perspectives on the Beothuk,* edited by Fiona Polack, 33–53. Toronto: University of Toronto Press, 2018.

Haque, Eve. *Multiculturalism within a Bilingual Framework: Language, Race, and Belonging in Canada*. Toronto: University of Toronto Press, 2012.

Harley, Brian. *The New Nature of Maps: Essays in the History of Cartography*. Baltimore: Johns Hopkins University Press, 2001.

Harper, Douglas. "Talking about Pictures: A Case for Photo Elicitation." *Visual Studies* 17, no. 1 (2002): 13–26.

Harper, Stephen. "The Call of the North." Address by the Prime Minister Stephen Harper in Yellowknife, NWT, 16 August 2006. https://www.canada.ca/en/news/archive/2006/08/call-north-address-prime-minister-stephen-harper.html (accessed 9 September 2020).

Harron, Janet. "Landmark Achievement: Hundreds of Innu Place Names for Southern and Central Labrador Awarded Legal Status." *Gazette*, 22 March 2017. https://gazette.mun.ca/research/land-mark-achievement/ (accessed 12 April 2017).

Heeney, Alex. "'In the Innu language, every word is an image': Kim O'Bomsawin on *Call Me Human*." *Seventh Row*, 9 March 2021. https://seventh-row.com/2021/03/09/kim-obomsawin-call-me-hu-man/ (accessed 22 March 2021).

Heim, Michael Henry. "To Foreignize or Not to Foreignize: From a Translator's Notebook." In *In Translation: Honouring Sheila Fischman,* edited by Sherry Simon, 83–91. Montreal: McGill-Queen's University Press, 2013.

Henitiuk, Valerie. "Going to Bed with Waley: How Murasaki Shikibu Does and Does Not Become World Literature." *Comparative Literature Studies* 45, no. 1 (2008): 40–61.

———. "'My tongue, my own thing': Reading *Sanaaq*." *TTR: Traduction, terminologie, rédaction* 29, no. 2 (2018): 13–41.

———. "Of Breathing Holes and Contact Zones: Inuit-Canadian Writer Markoosie in and through Translation." *Target: International Journal of Translation Studies* 29, no. 1 (2017): 39–63.

———. "The Single, Shared Text? Translation and World Literature." *World Literature Today* 86, no. 1 (2012): 30–34.

———. *Worlding Sei Shônagon: The Pillow Book in Translation*. Ottawa: University of Ottawa Press, 2012.

Henzi, Sarah. "Littératures autochtones et traduction." News/Nouvelles. *Canadian Literature: A Quarterly of Criticism and Review*, 12 September 2017. http://canlit.ca/litteratures-autochtones-et-traduction/ (accessed 1 August 2020).

Highway, Tomson. *A Tale of Monstrous Extravagance: Imagining Multilingualism*. Edmonton: University of Alberta Press, 2015.

———. "The Time Tomson Highway Went to *Mameek* and Survived to Tell the Tale." In *Across Cultures, Across Borders: Canadian Aboriginal and Native American Literatures*, edited by Paul de Pasquale, Renate Eigenbrod, and Emma LaRoque, 45–56. Peterborough, ON: Broadview Press, 2010.

Hiller, James, and Leslie Harris. "Newfoundland and Labrador." *Encyclopædia Britannica*, 7 February 2019. https://www.britannica.com/place/Newfoundland-and-Labrador (accessed 26 April 2019).

Hine, Dougald. "Notes from Underground #7: I Only Have One Prediction for You." *Bella Caledonia*, 9 January 2020. https://bellacaledonia.org.uk/?p=80060 (accessed 10 January 2020).

Hinton, Leanne, and Ken Hale, eds. *The Green Book of Language Revitalization in Practice*. San Diego: Academic Press, 2001.

Hirsch, Marianne. *Family Frames: Photography, Narrative, and Postmemory*. Cambridge, MA: Harvard University Press, 1997.

Homer-Dixon, Thomas. "We Need a Forest of Tongues." *Globe and Mail*, 3 July 2001. http://www.homerdixon.com/2001/07/03/we-need-a-forest-of-tongues/ (accessed 2 November 2017).

Honk If You Want Me Off the Road. Directed by Elizabeth Yeoman and Sharon Roseman. 2016. https://vimeo.com/196130980.

Howlett, Karen. "Ontario Settles Long-Running Land-Claims Dispute." *Globe and Mail*, 14 December 2009. https://www.theglobeandmail.com/news/national/ontario-settles-long-running-land-claims-dispute/article1205926/ (accessed 5 June 2020).

Hunters and Bombers. Directed by Hugh Brody and Nigel Markham. NFB/ONF, 1991. DVD.

Huston, Nancy. *Âmes et corps—Textes choisis 1981–2003*. Montreal et Paris: Leméac/Actes Sud, 2004.

I, Nuligak: An Inuvialuit History of First Contact. Directed by Peter Raymont and Patrick Reed. White Pine Pictures, 2005.

Incident at Restigouche. Directed by Alanis Obamsawin. NFB/ONF, 1984. DVD.

Indigenous Mapping Workshop. Inuvik, NWT, 2019. https://mk0indigenousmakdcov.kinstacdn.com/wp-content/uploads/2019/10/IMW_Invuik_2019_Agenda_Online_07OCT2019.pdf (accessed 10 May 2020).

Indigenous Mapping Workshop. Perth, Australia, 2020. https://www.imwaustralia.com (accessed 10 May 2020).

Indigenous Voices Awards. http://thepeopleandthetext.ca/21June2021 (accessed 6 November 2021).

Innu Nation. "Innu Place Names Website a Worldwide First." November 2008. https://www.innu.ca/images/stories/nreleaseinnuplaceswebsitefinal211108.pdf (accessed 20 August 2020).

Innu Nation and Sheshatshiu Innu First Nation. *Pepamuteiati Nitassinat: As We Walk across Our Land*. 2008. https://www.innuplaces.ca (accessed 20 August 2020).

International Energy Agency (IEA). *Sustainable Recovery Tracker*. Paris: IEA, 2021. https://www.iea.org/reports/sustainable-recovery-tracker (accessed 21 January 2022).

Isuma TV. "Costume Interview." n.d. http://www.isuma.tv/atanarjuat/costume-interview (accessed 8 January 2020).

———. "Zacharias Kunuk Interview." 25 May 2010. http://www.isuma.tv/atanarjuat/zacharias-kunuk-fast-runner-interview?og_last=5135 (accessed 8 January 2020).

Jacobsen, Rowan. "A Wave of Plastic." *Orion Magazine*, Summer 2020. https://orionmagazine.org/article/a-wave-of-plastic/?mc_cid=4b67c48485&mc_eid=61577dc77e (accessed 3 July 2020).

Jay-Rayon, Laurence. Review of *Literature in Translation: Teaching Issues and Reading Practices*, by Carol Maier and Françoise Massardier-Kenney, dirs. (2010). *Meta: Journal des traducteurs / Translators' Journal* 58, no. 1 (2013): 256–59.

Je m'appelle humain. Directed by Kim O'Bomsawin. Terre Innue, 2020.

Jean, Noelle Didier. "Listuguj Remembers the 1981 Salmon Raids." *Campbellton Tribune*, 11 June 2015.

Jenson, Jane. "Commissioning Ideas: Representation and Royal Commissions." In *How Ottawa Spends 1994–95: Making Change,* edited by Susan D. Phillips, 39–69. Ottawa: Carleton University Press, 1994.

Johnson, Jon. "Pathways to the Eighth Fire: Indigenous Knowledge and Storytelling in Toronto." PhD diss., York University, 2015.

Johnson, Rhiannon. "Inuk Director's New Film Shows One Day in the Life of Noah Piugattuk That Changed Everything." CBC News, 12 September 2019. https://www.cbc.ca/news/indigenous/one-day-life-noah-piugattuk-film-1.5280887 (accessed 13 January 2020).

Jollie, Edward. Preface. *Edward Jollie Reminisces 1841–1865*. https://sites.google.com/site/marapito/jolliepreface (accessed 11 May 2020).

Jonah, Anne Marie Lane. "Reconciling Chignecto: The Many Stories of Siknikt." *Acadiensis*, 16 July 2019. https://acadiensis.wordpress.com/2019/07/16/reconciling-chignecto-the-many-stories-of-siknikt/#_ednref10 (accessed 5 May 2020).

Journey of Nishiyuu. http://nishiyuujourney.ca (accessed 8 March 2020).

Just Watch Me. Directed by Catherine Annau. NFB/ONF, 1999.

Justice, Daniel Heath. *Why Indigenous Literatures Matter.* Waterloo, ON: Wilfrid Laurier University Press, 2018.

Kamboureli, Smaro. "Beyond Understanding Canada: Belatedness and Canadian Literary Studies. In *Beyond "Understanding Canada": Transnational Perspectives on Canadian Literature*, edited by Melissa Tanti, Jeremy Haynes, Daniel Coleman, and Lorraine York, 3–21. Edmonton: University of Alberta Press, 2017.

Kapesh, An Antane. *Eukuan nin matshi-manitu innushkueu: I am a damn savage/Tanite nene etutamin nitassi? What Have You Done to My Country?* English translation and afterword by Sarah Henzi. Waterloo, ON: Wilfrid Laurier University Press, 2020.

———. *Eukuan nin matshi-manitu innushkueu. Je suis une maudite sauvagesse*. Edited and with a preface by Naomi Fontaine. French translation by José Mailhot. Montreal: Mémoire d'encrier, 2019.

———. *Eukuan nin matshi-manitu innushkueu. Je suis une maudite sauvagesse*. French translation by José Mailhot. Montreal: Leméac, 1976.

Kashtin. *Kashtin*. Trans Canada, 1989. CD.

Keeling, Arn, and John Sandlos. "Ghost Towns and Zombie Mines: The Historical Dimensions of Mine Abandonment, Reclamation and Redevelopment in the Canadian North." In *Ice Blink:*

Navigating Northern Environmental History, edited by Stephen Bocking and Brad Martin, 377–420. Calgary: University of Calgary Press, 2017.

———. *Toxic Legacies Project*. http://www.toxiclegacies.com (accessed 9 September 2020).

Kimmerer, Robin. *Braiding Sweetgrass: Indigenous Wisdom, Scientific Knowledge and the Teachings of Plants*. Minneapolis: Milkweed Editions, 2013.

———. "Speaking of Nature." *Orion Magazine,* March/April 2017. https://orionmagazine.org/article/speaking-of-nature/ (accessed 28 February 2020).

King, Betty Nygaard, and Edith Fowke. "The Blackfly Song." In *The Canadian Encyclopedia*, 11 August 2006. https://www.thecanadianencyclopedia.ca/en/article/the-black-fly-song-emc (accessed 16 November 2021).

King, Hayden. "'I regret it': Hayden King on Writing Ryerson University's Territorial Acknowledgement." *Unreserved*, CBC Radio, 20 January 2019. https://www.cbc.ca/radio/unreserved/redrawing-the-lines-1.4973363/i-regret-it-hayden-king-on-writing-ryerson-university-s-territorial-acknowledgement-1.4973371 (accessed 16 March 2020).

King, Thomas. "Godzilla vs. Post-Colonial." In *New Contexts of Canadian Criticism*, edited by Ajay Heble, Donna Palmateer Pennee, and J.R. (Tim) Struthers, 241–48. Peterborough, ON: Broadview Press, 1997.

———. *The Truth about Stories: A Native Narrative.* Toronto: House of Anansi Press, 2003.

Klein, Naomi. "Dancing the World into Being: A Conversation with Idle No More's Leanne Simpson." *Yes! Solutions Journalism*, 16 March 2013. https://www.yesmagazine.org/social-justice/2013/03/06/dancing-the-world-into-being-a-conversation-with-idle-no-more-leanne-simpson/ (accessed 13 January 2020).

Klein-Lataud, Christine. "Les voix parallèles de Nancy Huston." *TTR: Traduction, terminologie, rédaction* 9, no. 1 (1996): 211–31.

Kolbert, Elizabeth. "Greenland Is Melting." *New Yorker*, 17 October 2016. https://www.newyorker.com/magazine/2016/10/24/greenland-is-melting (accessed 30 March 2020).

———. "How to Write about a Vanishing World." *The Best American Essays,* edited by Rebecca Solnit, 124–30. Boston and New York: Houghton Mifflin Harcourt, 2019.

Krause, Kea. "What's Left Behind." *Believer* 113, 1 October 2015. https://believermag.com/whats-left-behind/ (accessed 4 April 2020).

Kusugak, Michael. "Nunannguaq." Forewords to *The Indigenous Peoples' Atlas of Canada.* Canadian Geographic, 2021. https://indigenouspeoplesatlasofcanada.ca/forewords/nunannguaq/.

Lacasse, Jean-Paul. *Les Innus et le Territoire.* Sillery: Septentrion, 2003.

Lacombe, Michèle. "Leanne Betasamosake Simpson's Decolonial Aesthetics: 'Leaks'/Leaks, Storytelling, Community, and Collaboration." *Canadian Literature* 230/231 (Autumn 2016): 45–63.

———. "'Pimuteuat/Ils marchent/They Walk': A Few Observations on Indigenous Poetry and Poetics in French." In *Indigenous Poetics in Canada*, edited by Neal McLeod, 159–82. Waterloo, ON: Wilfrid Laurier University Press, 2014.

Lacombe, Michèle, Heather Macfarlane, and Jennifer Andrews. "Indigeneity in Dialogue: Indigenous Literary Expression across Linguistic Divides—L'autochtonie en dialogue: L'expression littéraire autochtone au-delà des barrières linguistiques." Introduction to *Studies in Canadian Literature/Études en littérature canadienne* 35, no. 2 (2010): 5–12.

Lalonde, Catherine. "Joséphine Bacon, poétesse innue–'Quand les anciens s'en vont, ce sont des bibliothèques nationales qui se perdent.'" *Le Devoir*, 12 June 2010. https://www.ledevoir.com/

culture/290684/josephine-bacon-poetesse-innue-quand-les-anciens-s-en-vont-ce-sont-des-biblio-theques-nationales-qui-se-perdent (accessed 21 January 2021).

Lane, Pia, James Costa, and Haley De Korne, eds. *Standardizing Minority Languages: Competing Ideologies of Authority and Authenticity in the Global Periphery*. New York and London: Routledge, 2017.

Laub, Dori. "Truth and Testimony: The Process and the Struggle." *American Imago* 48 (1991): 75–91.

Laughland, Oliver. "Everlyn Sampi: Pain, Pride and the Trail of the Rabbit-Proof Fence." *Guardian*, 18 June 2013. https://www.theguardian.com/film/2013/jun/18/rabbit-proof-fence-everlyn-sampi (accessed 10 October 2019).

Lawrence, Bonita. "Unrecognized Peoples and Concepts of Extinction." In *Tracing Ochre: Changing Perspectives on the Beothuk,* edited by Fiona Polack, 297–320. Toronto: University of Toronto Press, 2018.

Le Clézio, Jean-Marie G. "Quel avenir pour la Romaine? Poétesse innue contre multinationale." *Le Monde*, 1 July 2009. https://www.lemonde.fr/idees/article/2009/07/01/quel-avenir-pour-la-romaine-par-jean-marie-g-le-clezio_1213943_3232.html (accessed 2 April 2021).

Legat, Allice. *Walking the Land, Feeding the Fire: Knowledge and Stewardship among the Tłı̨chǫ Dene.* Tucson: University of Arizona Press, 2012.

Leisman, Gerry, Ahmed A. Moustafa, and Tal Shafir. "Thinking, Walking, Talking: Integratory Motor and Cognitive Brain Function." *Frontiers in Public Health* 4, no. 94 (2016): 1–19. https://www.ncbi.nlm.nih.gov/pmc/articles/PMC4879139/ (accessed 18 May 2020).

Lelièvre, Michelle. *Unsettling Mobility: Mediating Mi'kmaw Sovereignty in Post-Contact Nova Scotia.* Tucson: University of Arizona Press, 2017.

Le Texier, Thibault. *Histoire d'un mensonge: Enquête sur l'expérience de Stanford*. Paris: La Découverte, 2018.

Lewis, Roger J. "What Is a Truck House?" *Stop Alton Gas*. https://stopaltongas.wordpress.com/whyoppose/treaties/ (accessed 8 June 2020).

Lewis, Walter. "On Leaving Only Footprints . . . An Interview with Marlene Creates." *Walter's Wanderings: Walking, Photography, Landskip and Knowledge*, 29 September 2014. https://walter-lewisblog.wordpress.com/2014/09/29/on-leaving-only-footprints/ (accessed 17 April 2020).

Li, Qing. "Effets des forêts et des bains de forêt (shinrin-yoku) sur la santé humaine: une revue de la littérature." *Santé Publique* (13 May 2019): 135–43.

———. "Effect of Forest Bathing Trips on Human Immune Function." *Environmental Health and Preventive Medicine* 15, no. 1, (2010): 9–17.

Longrigg, Clare. "Money and Maps: Is This How to Save the Amazon's 400bn Trees?" *The Guardian*, 6 November 2019. https://www.theguardian.com/world/2019/nov/06/local-tribe-save-amazon-indigenous-peruvians (accessed 29 April 2020).

Luka, Mary Elizabeth. "Walking Matters: A Peripatetic Re-thinking of Energy Culture." In *Energy Culture: Art and Theory on Oil and Beyond,* edited by Imre Szeman and Jeff Diamanti, 61–75. Morgantown: West Virginia University Press, 2019.

Lund, Katrín. "Landscapes and Narratives: Compositions and the Walking Body." *Landscape Research* 37, no. 2 (2012): 225–37.

Lutz, Hartmut, ed. and trans. *The Diary of Abraham Ulrikab: Text and Context*. Foreword and cover art by Alootook Ipellie. Ottawa, ON: University of Ottawa Press, 2005.

Macfarlane, Robert. *Landmarks*. London and New York: Penguin Random House, 2016.

Magrane, Eric, Linda Russo, Sarah de Leeuw, and Craig Santos Perez, eds. *Geopoetics in Practice.* Abingdon, UK and New York, NY: Routledge, 2020.

Maier, Carol, and Françoise Massardier-Kenney, eds. *Literature in Translation: Teaching Issues and Reading Practices.* Kent, OH: Kent State University Press, 2010.

Mailhot, José, Marguerite MacKenzie et al. *Aimun Mashinaikan Innu-English Dictionary.* Sheshatshiu NL: Mamu Tshishkutamashutau, 2013.

Mailhot, José. *The People of Sheshatshit.* Translated by Axel Harvey. St. John's, NL: ISER Books, 1997/2001.

Maracle, Lee. "Indigenous Poetry and the Oral." In *Indigenous Poetics in Canada*, edited by Neal McLeod, 305–10. Waterloo, ON: Wilfrid Laurier University Press, 2014.

Martin, Keavy. "Arctic Solitude: Mitiarjuk Nappaaluk's *Sanaaq* and the Politics of Translation in Inuit Literature." *Studies in Canadian Literature/Études en littérature candienne* 35, no. 2 (2010): 13–29.

Massardier-Kenney, Françoise, Brian James Baer, and Maria Tymoczko, eds. *Translators Writing, Writing Translators.* Kent, OH: Kent State University Press, 2016.

McCall, Sophie. *First Person Plural: Aboriginal Storytelling and the Ethics of Collaborative Authorship.* Vancouver: UBC Press, 2011.

McKay, Don. "Great Flint Singing." In *Open Wide a Wilderness: Canadian Nature Poems*, edited by Nancy Holmes, 1–32. Waterloo, ON: Wilfrid Laurier University Press, 2009.

———. "Local Wilderness." *Fiddlehead* 169 (1991): 5–6.

Mercer, Juanita. "Innovation Award–Winning SmartICE 'Great Thing to Have in Nain.'" *Telegram*, 22 May 2019.

Mercredi, Duncan. "Achimo." In *Indigenous Poetics in Canada*, edited by Neal McLeod, 17–22. Waterloo, ON: Wilfrid Laurier University Press, 2014.

Merrill, Christopher. "Stephanos Stephanides on Memory Fiction." *Origins: The International Writing Program Podcast*, 15 August 2017. University of Iowa. https://soundcloud.com/user-54821448/stephanos-stephanides-on-memory-fiction (accessed 1 February 2019).

Mika, Carl, Vanessa Andreotti, Garrick Cooper, Cash Ahenakew, and Denise Silva. "The Ontological Differences between Wording and Worlding the World." *Language, Discourse and Society* 8, no. 1 (June 2020): 17–32.

Mi'kmaq Resistance: Defend the Sacred. sub.Media. https://vimeo.com/246159254 (accessed 10 June 2020).

Milewski, Terry. "Changing O Canada: Is God Next?" CBC News, 11 June 2016. https://www.cbc.ca/news/politics/o-canada-god-lyrics-1.3626325 (accessed 10 August 2020).

Milroy, James. "Language Ideologies and the Consequences of Standardization." *Journal of Sociolinguistics* 5, no. 4 (2001): 530–55.

Milroy, James, and Lesley Milroy. *Authority in Language: Investigating Standard English.* 3rd ed. London: Routledge, 1999.

Moore, Jason W. *Anthropocene or Capitalocene? Nature, History, and the Crisis of Capitalism.* Oakland, CA: PM Press, 2016.

Moyes, Lianne. "From One Colonial Language to Another: Translating Natasha Kanapé Fontaine's 'Mes lames de tannage.'" *TranscUlturAl* 10, no. 1 (2018): 64–82.

Mullin, Malone. "Still Waiting for N.L.'s Famous Iceberg Season? Don't Hold Your Breath, Scientists Say." CBC News, 26 May 2021. https://www.cbc.ca/news/canada/newfoundland-labrador/sluggish-iceberg-season-nl-1.6034212 (accessed 19 January 2022).

The Mushuau Innu: Surviving Canada. Directed by Ed Martin. Best Boy Productions, 2004.

Myers, Joe, and Rosamund Hutt. "This Visualization Shows You 24 Hours of Global Air Traffic—In Just 4 Seconds." *World Economic Forum*, 12 July 2016. https://www.weforum.org/agenda/2016/07/this-visualization-shows-you-24-hours-of-global-air-traffic-in-just-4-seconds/ (accessed 30 March 2020).

Nahanni, Phoebe. "The Mapping Project." In *Dene Nation: The Colony Within*, edited by Mel Watkins, 21–129. Toronto: University of Toronto Press, 1977.

NASA Jet Propulsion Laboratory. "Greenland's Rapid Melt Will Mean More Flooding." California Institute of Technology, 10 December 2019. https://www.jpl.nasa.gov/news/news.php?feature=7556 (accessed 31 March 2020).

Nassar, Aya. "Geopoetics: Storytelling Against Mastery." *Dialogues in Human Geography* 11, no. 1 (2021): 27–30.

NationTalk. "NTI: Inuktut Writing Prize Launched." *NationTalk*, 9 July 2020. http://nationtalk.ca/story/nti-inuktut-writing-prize-launched (accessed 10 July 2020).

Nehamas, Alexander. *Only a Promise of Happiness: The Place of Beauty in a World of Art.* Princeton, NJ: Princeton University Press, 2010.

Nelson, Sarah. Petition to King George III, 1789. Archived at the National Library of Australia, Bib ID 2910771.

Neuhaus, Mareike. *The Decolonizing Poetics of Indigenous Literatures*. Regina, SK: University of Regina Press, 2015.

Nin e tepueian—Mon cri. Directed by Santiago Bertolini. Studio Via Le Monde, 2019.

NoiseCat, Julian Brave. "Armageddon in Our Bones, Utopia in Our Souls." Forewords to *Indigenous Peoples' Atlas of Canada*. Canadian Geographic, 2021. https://indigenouspeoplesatlasofcanada.ca/forewords/armageddon-in-our-bones-utopia-in-our-souls/ (accessed 12 May 2020).

Nolette, Nicole. *Jouer la traduction: Théâtre et hétérolinguisme au Canada francophone*. Ottawa: Presses de l'Université d'Ottawa, 2015.

———. "Partial Translation, Affect and Reception: The Case of *Atanarjuat: The Fast Runner*." *Inquire: Journal of Comparative Literature* 2, no. 1 (2012): n.pag. http://inquire.streetmag.org/articles/53 (accessed 22 June 2020).

Nuligak (Bob Cockney). *I Nuligak*. Edited and translated by Maurice Metayer. Illustrated by Ekootak. Markham, ON: Simon and Schuster, 1971.

Norman, Jerry. *Chinese*. Cambridge: Cambridge University Press, 1988.

O'Gorman, Melanie, and Manish Pandey. "Cultivating the Arctic's Most Valuable Resource: An Analysis of the Barriers to High School Completion among Youth in Nunavut (Report)." 23 September 2015.

———. "Explaining Low High School Attainment in Northern Aboriginal Communities: An Analysis of the Aboriginal Peoples' Surveys." *Canadian Public Policy/Analyse de Politiques* 41, no. 4 (December 2015): 297–308.

O'Mara, Shane. *In Praise of Walking: A New Scientific Exploration.* London: The Bodley Head, 2019.

O'Neill, Maggie, and Ismail Einashe. "Walking Borders, Risk and Belonging." *Journal of Public Pedagogies* 4 (2019): 31–50.

O'Neill, Maggie, and Brian Roberts. *Walking Methods: Research on the Move*. London: Routledge, 2019.

Oppezzo, Marily, and Daniel L. Schwartz. "Give Your Ideas Some Legs: The Positive Effect of Walking on Creative Thinking." *Journal of Experimental Psychology: Learning, Memory, and Cognition* 40, no. 4 (2014): 1142–52.

Parks Canada. "Akami-Uapishk[U]-KakKasuak-Mealy Mountains National Park Reserve Park Management." 28 March 2018. https://www.pc.gc.ca/en/pn-np/nl/mealy/info/index (accessed 5 April 2020).

Parry, Evalyn. "To Live in the Age of Melting: Northwest Passage." 2014. https://evalynparry.bandcamp.com/track/to-live-in-the-age-of-melting-northwest-passage (accessed 17 March 2019).

Pastore, Ralph. "The Beothuks." *Museum Notes*, Fall 1991. The Rooms, St. John's NL. https://www.therooms.ca/the-beothuks (accessed 12 November 2017).

Patrick, Donna, Kumiko Murasugi, and Jeela Palluq-Cloutier. "Standardization of Inuit Languages in Canada." In *Standardizing Minority Languages: Competing Ideologies of Authority and Authenticity in the Global Periphery*, edited by Pia Lane, James Costa, and Haley De Korne, 135–53. New York and London: Routledge, 2018.

Patsauq, Markoosie. *Hunter with Harpoon*. Translated by Valerie Henitiuk and Marc-Antoine Mahieu. Montreal and Kingston: McGill-Queen's University Press, 2020.

Paul, Daniel N. *We Were Not the Savages: First Nations History*. http://www.danielnpaul.com/Map-Mi%27kmaqTerritory.html (accessed 25 April 2020).

Pedri-Spade, Celeste. "'But They Were Never Only the Master's Tools': The Use of Photography in De-Colonial Praxis." *AlterNative* 13, no. 2 (2017): 106–13.

———. "Waasaabikizo: Our Pictures Are Good Medicine." *Decolonization: Indigeneity, Education and Society* 5, no. 1 (2016): 45–70.

Penashue, Elizabeth. "Innu Games." *Them Days: Stories of Early Labrador* 32, no. 3 (2008): 8–12.

———. "Like the Gates of Heaven." In *It's Like The Legend*, edited by Nympha Byrne and Camille Fouillard, 157–75. Charlottetown PEI: Gynergy Books, 2000.

———. "Miam ka auieiat: It's Like a Circle." In *Despite This Loss: Essays on Loss, Memory and Identity in Newfoundland and Labrador*, edited by Ursula Kelly and Elizabeth Yeoman, 246–53. St. John's, NL: ISER, 2010.

———. *Nitinikiau Innusi: I Keep the Land Alive*. Winnipeg: University of Manitoba Press, 2019.

———. "A Winter in Hospital." *Them Days: Stories of Early Labrador* 32, no. 1 (2008): 10–14.

Penashue, Elizabeth, and Rose Gregoire. "Nitassinan: Our Land, Our Struggle." *PEACE Magazine* (Aug–Sept. 1989): 14.

Penashue, Elizabeth, and Elizabeth Yeoman. "The Ones That Were Abused: Thinking about the Beothuk through Translation." In *Tracing Ochre: Changing Perspectives on the Beothuk,* edited by Fiona Polack, 75–93. Toronto: University of Toronto Press, 2018.

Petitpas, Bis. "L'influence du livre *Je suis une maudite sauvagesse* d'An Antane Kapesh." *Bonjour la côte*, Radio Canada, 14 August 2019. https://ici.radio-canada.ca/premiere/emissions/bonjour-la-cote/segments/entrevue/128296/livre-sauvagesse-an-antane-kapesh (accessed 22 March 2021).

Petrilli, Susan, and Augusto Ponzio. "Translation as Listening and Encounter in the Other in Migration and Globalization Processes Today." *TTR: Traduction, terminologie, rédaction* 19, no. 2 (2006): 191–223.

———. "Translation, Encounter among Peoples and Global Semiotics." Paper presented at the 11th World Congress of the International Association for Semiotic Studies, Nanjing, China, 5–9 October 2012. http://www.augustoponzio.com/files/petrilli---ponzio-translation-final.pdf (accessed 26 April 2021).

Pietropaolo, Paolo. *Ode to the Salish Sea*. 2009. https://www.constellationsaudio.com/sounds/salish-sea (accessed 22 May 2020).

Premat, Christophe. "The Survivance in the Literature of the First Nations in Canada." *Baltic Journal of English Language, Literature and Culture* 9 (2019): 75–92.

Proescholdt, Kevin. "What's Wrong with Monitoring Volcanoes in Wilderness?" *Counterpunch*, 9 October 2018. https://www.counterpunch.org/2018/10/09/whats-wrong-with-monitoring-volcanoes-in-wilderness/ (accessed 4 April 2020).

Quintavalle, Rufo. "Politics and People Fuelling Amazon Rainforest Fires." *Canada's National Observer*, 17 September 2019. http://tinyurl.com/y5fjap7k (accessed 19 March 2020).

Rabbit-Proof Fence. Directed by Philip Noyce. HanWay Films, 2002.

Rawat, Rajiv. "NWT Orthography Backgrounder." Prince of Wales Northern Heritage Centre. https://www.pwnhc.ca/orthography-tools/ (accessed 1 December 2019).

Recollet, Karyn, and Jon Johnson. "'Why Do You Need to Know That?' Slipstream Movements and Mapping 'Otherwise' in Tkaronto." *Journal of Public Pedagogies* (2019): 177–90.

Reder, Deanna. "Book Review of Tomson Highway's *From Oral to Written*." *The People and the Text*, 29 April 2018. http://thepeopleandthetext.ca/29April2018 (accessed 2 November 2021).

Rees, Tobias. "Introduction: Today, What Is Anthropology?" In *Designs for an Anthropology of the Contemporary,* edited by Paul Rabinow, George Marcus, James Faubion, and Tobias Rees, 1–12. Durham, NC: Duke University Press, 2008.

Regroupement Petapan. "Innu Assi." 2014. http://petapan.ca/page/innu-assi (accessed 13 June 2020).

Rich, Nathaniel. "The Invisible Catastrophe." *New York Times Magazine*, 31 March 2016. https://www.nytimes.com/2016/04/03/magazine/the-invisible-catastrophe.html (accessed 30 March 2020).

Roy, Wendy. "Visualizing Labrador: Maps, Photographs, and Geographical Naming in Mina Hubbard's *A Woman's Way through Unknown Labrador*." *Studies in Canadian Literature/Études en littérature Canadienne* 29, no. 1 (2004): 13–34.

Rubenstein, Dan. "The Walking Cure." *Walrus*, October 2013, 32–39.

Ruers, Jamie. "The Uncanny." *Museum Blog*, 18 September 2019. London: Freud Museum. https://www.freud.org.uk/2019/09/18/the-uncanny/ (accessed 15 June 2020).

Sacks, Oliver. *On the Move: A Life*. Toronto: Vintage Canada, 2015.

Sahtú Renewable Resources Board. "Dene Mapping." https://www.srrb.nt.ca/index.php?option=com_content&view=article&id=137&Itemid=833 (accessed 5 June 2020).

Said, Edward. *Culture and Imperialism*. New York: Vintage Books, 1993.

Saladin d'Anglure, Bernard. Foreword to *Sanaaq*, by Mitiarjuk Nappaaluk, vii–xviii. Translated by Peter Frost. Winnipeg: University of Manitoba Press and Avataq Cultural Institute, 2014.

Samson, Colin, and James Wilson. *Canada's Tibet: The Killing of the Innu.* London: Survival International, 1999.

Samian. *Face à la musique.* Disques 7ième Ciel, 2010. CD.

Sandeen, Eric. "The Family of Man in Guatemala." *Visual Studies* 30, no. 2 (2015): 123–30.

Sartwell, Crispin. "Beauty." In *Stanford Encyclopedia of Philosophy*, Winter 2017 edition, edited by Edward N. Zalta. https://plato.stanford.edu/archives/win2017/entries/beauty/ (accessed 25 April 2021).

Scranton, Roy. *We're Doomed. Now What? Essays on War and Climate Change.* New York: Soho Press, 2018.

Senior, Nancy. "Whose Song, Whose Land? Translation and Appropriation in *Plainsong/Cantique des Plaines.*" *Meta: Journal des traducteurs/Translators' Journal* 46, no. 4 (Dec 2001): 675–86.

Sherwood, Harriet. "Getting Back to Nature: How Forest Bathing Can Make Us Feel Better." *The Guardian,* 8 June 2019. https://www.theguardian.com/environment/2019/jun/08/forest-bathing-japanese-practice-in-west-wellbeing (accessed 10 November 2021).

Sider, Gerald M. *Skin for Skin: Death and Life for Inuit and Innu.* Durham, NC: Duke University Press, 2014.

Simon, Roger, Sharon Rosenberg, and Claudia Eppert. *Between Hope and Despair: Pedagogy and the Remembrance of Historical Trauma.* Lanham, MD: Rowman and Littlefield, 2000.

Simon, Sherry, ed. *Changing the Terms: Translating in the Postcolonial Era.* Ottawa: University of Ottawa Press, 2000.

Sinclair, Niigaanwewidam James. "The Power of Dirty Waters: Indigenous Poetics." In *Indigenous Poetics in Canada*, edited by Neal McLeod, 203–15. Waterloo, ON: Wilfrid Laurier University Press, 2014.

Sioui Durand, Guy. "Maurizio Gatti: Être écrivain amérindien au Québec. Indianité et création littéraire." *Recherches sociographiques* 48, no. 2 (2007): 183–86.

Skutnabb-Kangas, Tove, and Robert Phillipson. "A Human Rights Perspective on Language Ecology." In *Ecology of Language*, edited by Angela Creese, Peter Martin, and Nancy Hornberger, 3–14. Vol. 9 of *Encyclopedia of Language and Education*, 2nd ed., New York: Springer, 2008.

Smith, Linda Tuhiwai. *Decolonizing Methodologies: Research and Indigenous Peoples.* London: Zed Books, 1999.

Smith, Trudi. "Repeat Photography as a Method in Visual Anthropology." *Visual Anthropology Review* 20 (2007): 179–200.

Somerville, Margaret, with Leanne Tobin and Jacinta Tobin. "Walking Contemporary Indigenous Songlines as Public Pedagogies of Country." *Journal of Public Pedagogies* 4 (2019): 13–27.

Song, Chorong, Harumi Ikei, Bum-Jin Park, Juyoung Lee, Takahide Kagawa, and Yoshifumi Miyazaki. "Psychological Benefits of Walking through Forest Areas." *International Journal of Environmental Research and Public Health* 15, no. 12 (December 2018). https://www.researchgate.net/publication/329546285_Psychological_Benefits_of_Walking_through_Forest_Areas (accessed 18 May 2020).

Spivak, Gayatri Chakravorty. "Can the Subaltern Speak?" In *Marxism and the Interpretation of Culture*, edited by Cary Nelson and Lawrence Grossberg, 271–313. Chicago: University of Illinois Press, 1988.

———. *A Critique of Postcolonial Reason.* Cambridge, MA: Harvard University Press, 1999.

———. *In Other Worlds*. New York and London: Routledge, 1998.

———. "Supplementing Marxism." In *Whither Marxism? Global Crises in International Perspective*, edited by Bernd Magnus and Stephen Cullenberg, 109–19. London: Routledge, 1995.

Springgay, Stephanie, and Sarah E. Truman. *Walking Methodologies in a More-Than-Human World: WalkingLab*. Abingdon and New York: Routledge, 2018.

———. "Walking in/as Publics: Editors Introduction." *Journal of Public Pedagogies* (2019): 1–12. http://www.publicpedagogies.org/wp-content/uploads/2019/11/01-Springgay.pdf (accessed 27 May 2020).

St-Amand, Isabelle. "Discours critiques pour l'étude de la littérature autochtone dans l'espace francophone du Québec." *Studies in Canadian Literature/Études en littérature canadienne* 35, no. 2 (2010): 30–52.

Statistics Canada. "Census in Brief: The Aboriginal Languages of First Nations People, Métis and Inuit." 25 October 2017. https://www12.statcan.gc.ca/census-recensement/2016/as-sa/98-200-x/2016022/98-200-x2016022-eng.cfm (accessed 18 December 2019).

Stewart, Kathleen. *Ordinary Affects*. Durham, NC: Duke University Press, 2007.

Sugars, Cynthia. *Canadian Gothic: Literature, History and the Spectre of Self-Invention*. Cardiff: University of Wales Press, 2014.

Sundberg, Juanita. "Decolonizing Posthumanist Geographies." *Cultural Geographies* 21, no. 1 (2014): 33–47.

Tanner, Adrian. "Innu (Montagnais-Naskapi)." Last edited 18 May 2021. *Canadian Encyclopedia*, 2010. https://www.thecanadianencyclopedia.ca/en/article/innu-montagnais-naskapi (accessed 21 February 2020).

There's Something in the Water. Directed by Elliot Page and Ian Daniel. 2 Weeks Notice, 2019.

Thornton, Kat. "Rumi for the New-Age Soul: Coleman Barks and the Problems of Popular Translations." Ajam Media Collective, 9 March 2015. https://ajammc.com/2015/03/09/rumi-for-the-new-age-soul/ (accessed 19 February 2020).

Thorpe, Jocelyn. *Temagami's Tangled Wild: Race, Gender, and the Making of Canadian Nature*. Vancouver: UBC Press, 2012.

Tisseyre, Charles Alexndre. "Innu Nikamu: Sur les traces d'un pionnier." Acceuil/Arts, Radio Canada, 28 July 2014. https://ici.radio-canada.ca/nouvelle/677833/innu-nikamu-origines-chanson-innue-philippe-mckenzie (accessed 22 January 2021).

Todd, Sharon. "Listening as Attending to the 'Echo of the Otherwise': On Suffering, Justice, and Education." *Philosophy of Education Yearbook* (2002): 405–12.

Toomey, Patrick. "The NSA Continues to Violate Americans' Internet Privacy Rights." *ACLU*, 22 August 2018. https://www.aclu.org/blog/national-security/privacy-and-surveillance/nsa-continues-violate-americans-internet-privacy (accessed 29 November 2019).

Toronto Symphony Orchestra. "Our Shared Mosaic, 2017." https://canadamosaic.tso.ca/anthem/ (accessed 10 August 2020).

Tourisme Côte-Nord. "Manicouagan-Uapishka Biosphere Reserve." https://tourismecote-nord.com/en/discover-our-region/portrait-of-the-cote-nord-region/manicouagan-uapishka-biosphere-reserve/ (accessed 25 January 2020).

Tourisme Québec. "Abitibi-Témiscamingue." https://www.quebecoriginal.com/en-ca/where-to-go/regions-cities/abitibi-temiscamingue (accessed 20 January 2020).

———. "Manicouagan." https://www.quebecoriginal.com/en-ca/where-to-go/regions-cities/manicouagan (accessed 30 January 2020).

Tremonti, Anna Maria. "Anthropocene Project Highlights the Apocalyptic Beauty of Humans' Effect on the Planet." Interview with Jennifer Baichwal, Edward Burtynsky, and Nicholas de Pencier. *The Current*, CBC Radio, 26 September 2018. https://www.cbc.ca/radio/thecurrent/the-current-for-september-26-2018-1.4838781/anthropocene-project-highlights-the-apocalyptic-beauty-of-humans-effect-on-the-planet-1.4838811 (accessed 25 April 2021).

Triolo, Nicholas. "Why David Quammen Is Not Surprised." *Orion Magazine*, web exclusive, 17 March 2020. https://orionmagazine.org/2020/03/why-david-quammen-is-not-surprised/ (accessed 3 April 2020).

Trusler, Wendy, and Carol Devine. "Cleaning a Continent." *Journal of Wild Culture*, 17 August 2015. https://wildculture.com/article/cleaning-continent/1402 (accessed 10 March 2019).

Truth and Reconciliation Commission of Canada*: Calls to Action*. Winnipeg: Truth and Reconciliation Commission of Canada, 2015. http://trc.ca/assets/pdf/Calls_to_Action_English2.pdf (accessed 16 November 2019).

———. *Canada's Residential Schools: Reconciliation*. Vol. 6, Final Report of the Truth and Reconciliation Commission of Canada. Montreal and Kingston: McGill-Queen's University Press, 2015. http://publications.gc.ca/site/eng/9.807830/publication.html (accessed 1 March 2021).

———. *What We Have Learned: Principles of Truth and Reconciliation*. Truth and Reconciliation Commission of Canada, 2015. http://publications.gc.ca/collections/collection_2015/trc/IR4-6-2015-eng.pdf (accessed 17 March 2021).

Tsing, Anna Lowenhaupt, Andrew S. Mathews, and Nils Bubandt. "Patchy Anthropocene: Landscape Structure, Multispecies History, and the Retooling of Anthropology: An Introduction to Supplement 20." Supplement, *Current Anthropology* 60, no. S20 (2019): S186–97. https://www.journals.uchicago.edu/doi/full/10.1086/703391 (accessed 19 May 2020).

Tuck, Eve. "Breaking Up with Deleuze: Desire and Valuing the Irreconcilable." *International Journal of Qualitative Studies in Education* 23, no. 5 (2010): 635–50.

———. "Research on Our Own Terms." Plenary address at the Labrador Research Forum, Labrador Institute, Happy Valley-Goose Bay, 1 May 2019.

———. "Suspending Damage: A Letter to Communities." *Harvard Educational Review* 79, no. 3 (Fall 2009): 409–28.

Tuck, Eve, and K. Wayne Yang, "Decolonization Is not a Metaphor." *Decolonization: Indigeneity, Education and Society* 1, no. 1 (2012): 1–40.

———. "R-Words: Refusing Research." In *Humanizing Research: Decolonizing Qualitative Inquiry with Youth and Communities,* edited by Django Paris and Maisha T. Winn, 223–47. Thousand Oakes, CA: Sage Publications, 2014.

Tuck, Eve, K. Wayne Yang, and Rubén Gaztambide-Fernández. "Citation Practices Challenge." *Critical Ethnic Studies* (April 2015). http://www.criticalethnicstudiesjournal.org/citation-practices (accessed 30 April 2020).

Tuglavina, Sophie. "My Own Cultural and Language Experiences." In *Despite This Loss: Essays on Loss, Memory and Identity in Newfoundland and Labrador*, edited by Ursula Kelly and Elizabeth Yeoman, 157–75. St. John's, NL: ISER, 2010.

Tunney, Catherine. "More Than a Million Canadian Citizens and Permanent Residents Returned Home Last Week." CBC News, 23 March 2020. https://www.cbc.ca/news/politics/three-flight-peru-champagne-1.5506506 (accessed 25 March 2020).

Tymoczko, Maria. "Translation and Political Engagement: Activism, Social Change and the Role of Translation in Geopolitical Shifts. *The Translator* 6, no. 1 (2000): 23–47.

———. "Translation: Ethics, Ideology, Action." *Massachusetts Review* 47, no. 3 (Fall 2006): 442–61.

———. "Translation, Ideology and Creativity." *Linguistica Antverpiensia New Series: Themes in Translation Studies* 2 (2003): 27–45.

Tymoczko, Maria, Brian James Baer, and Françoise Massardier-Kenney. Introduction to *Translators Writing, Writing Translators*, edited by Françoise Massardier-Kenney, Brian James Baer, and Maria Tymoczko, 1–18. Kent, OH: Kent State University Press, 2016.

Tytelman, Carolina. "Place and Forest Co-management in Nitassinan/Labrador." PhD diss., St. John's, NL: Memorial University of Newfoundland, 2016.

Van den Hoonaard, Will. C., and Ann Hamilton. *The Ethics Rupture: Exploring Alternatives to Formal Research-Ethics Review*. Toronto: University of Toronto Press, 2016.

Vansintjan, Aaron. "The Anthropocene Debate: Why Is Such a Useful Concept Starting to Fall Apart?" *Uneven Earth*, 16 June 2015. http://unevenearth.org/2015/06/the-anthropocene-debate/ (accessed 10 January 2020).

Van Wyck, Peter C. *The Highway of the Atom*. Montreal and Kingston: McGill-Queen's University Press, 2010.

Vaudrin-Charette, Julie. "Reading Silenced Narratives." *in education* 21, no. 2 (2015): 150–70. https://ineducation.ca/ineducation/article/view/223/811 (accessed 29 June 2020).

Venuti, Lawrence. *The Translator's Invisibility: A History of Translation*. London and New York: Routledge, 2008.

Villeneuve, Jean-Francois. "La colère d'An Antane Kapesh, toujours aussi pertinente 43 ans plus tard." *Espaces autochtones*, 9 August 2019. https://ici.radio-canada.ca/espaces-autochtones/1251743/an-antane-kapesh-innu-litterature-essai (accessed 20 July 2020).

Vizenor, Gerald. "Aesthetics of Survivance: Literary Theory and Practice." In *Survivance: Narratives of Native Presence*, edited by Gerald Vizenor, 1–23. Lincoln: University of Nebraska Press, 2008.

———. *Manifest Manners: Narratives on Postindian Survivance*. Lincoln: University of Nebraska Press, 1999.

Voosen, Paul. "The Arctic is Warming Four Times as Fast as the Rest of the World: An Important Climactic Indicator Has Been Misreported by a Factor of Two." *Science*, 14 December 2021. https://www.science.org/content/article/arctic-warming-four-times-faster-rest-world (accessed 20 January 2022).

Vowel, Chelsea. "Giving My Children Cree Names Is a Powerful Act of Reclamation." Indigenous/Opinion, CBC News, 4 November 2018. https://www.cbc.ca/news/indigenous/opinion-cree-names-reclamation-chelsea-vowel-1.4887604 (accessed 8 July 2020).

Wabanaki Water Walk (fundraiser). Facebook page. https://www.facebook.com/donate/331929450831292/ (accessed 1 June 2020).

Wadden, Marie. *Nitassinan: The Innu Struggle to Reclaim Their Homeland*. Toronto: Douglas and McIntyre, 1991.

Walking Lab and Public Pedagogies Institute, eds. *Journal of Public Pedagogies* (2019). http://www.publicpedagogies.org/journal/ (accessed 27 May 2020).

Weeks, Maya. "Blue Capitalism." *Guts*, 31 May 2017. http://gutsmagazine.ca/blue-capitalism/ (accessed 1 March 2019).

Whitaker, Robin. Review of *The Ethics Rupture: Exploring Alternatives to Formal Research-Ethics Review*, by Will C. van den Hoonaard and Ann Hamilton, eds. *CAUT Bulletin Archives 1996–2016*, December 2016. https://bulletin-archives.caut.ca/bulletin/articles/2016/12/book-review-the-ethics-rupture-exploring-alternatives-to-formal-research-ethics-review (accessed 13 November 2017).

Whitlock, Gillian. "In the Second Person: Narrative Transactions in Stolen Generations Testimony." *Biography* 24, no. 1 (2001): 197–214.

Willemsen, Jeroen, and Kristoffer Friis Bøegh. "Linguists Need Preservation of Languages to Study Human Language." *ScienceNordic*, 25 February 2019. https://phys.org/news/2019-02-linguists-languages-human-language.html (accessed 9 July 2020).

Williams, Raymond. *Marxism and Literature.* London and New York: Oxford University Press, 1977.

Window Horses. Written and animated by Ann Marie Fleming. Stickgirl Productions, Sandra Oh and NFB, 2016.

Windtalkers. Directed by John Woo. Metro Goldwyn Meyer, 2002.

Woolard, Kathryn. "Language and Identity Choice in Catalonia: The Interplay of Contrasting Ideologies of Linguistic Authority." In *Lengua, Nación e Identidad: La regulación del plurilingüismo en España y América Latina*, edited by Kirsten Süselbeck, Ulrike Mühlschlegel, and Peter Masson, 303–23. Madrid and Frankfurt am Main: Iberoamericana Vervuert, 2008.

Wyatt, Kyle Carsten. "What Do You Call 101 Hidden Islands in Quebec? Literature-Inspired Naming of Land in the Remote Caniapiscau Reservoir Has Caused Controversy." *Atlas Obscura*, 28 August 2017. https://www.atlasobscura.com/articles/caniapiscau-reservoir-island-names (accessed 9 May 2020).

Yeoman, Elizabeth. "The Least Possible Baggage: About Walking." *Ideas*, CBC Radio, 2004.

———. "The Meaning of Meaning: Affective Engagement and Dialogue in a Second Language." *Canadian Modern Language Review/La revue canadienne des langues vivantes* 52, no. 4 (1996): 596–611.

———. "Sam's Café: A Case Study of Computer Conferencing as a Medium for Collective Journal Writing." *Canadian Journal of Educational Communication* 24, no. 3 (1995): 209–27.

Young, Holly. "The Digital Language Divide: How Does the Language You Speak Shape Your Experience of the Internet?" *The Guardian*. http://labs.theguardian.com/digital-language-divide/ (accessed 18 December 2019).

Index

C

D

N